WS
104
SUT

Child and Adolescent Behaviour Problems

D0414797

CHILD AND ADOLESCENT BEHAVIOUR PROBLEMS

A Multidisciplinary Approach to
Assessment and Intervention

Carole Sutton Phd

BPS BOOKS THE BRITISH PSYCHOLOGICAL SOCIETY

First published in 2000 by BPS Books (The British Psychological Society),
St Andrews House, 48 Princess Road East, Leicester, LE1 7DR, UK.

© 2000, Carole Sutton
Transferred to Digital print 2003

All rights reserved. No part of this publication may be reproduced or
transmitted, in any form or by any means, without permission.

This book is sold subject to the condition that it shall not, by way of trade or
otherwise, be lent, resold, hired out, or otherwise circulated without the
publisher's prior consent in any form of binding or cover other than that in
which it is published and without a similar condition including this
condition imposed on the subsequent purchaser.

A catalogue record for this book is available from the British Library.

ISBN 1 85433 321 6

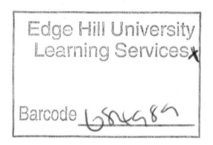

Edge Hill University
Learning Services

Barcode

Typeset by Book Production Services

Printed and bound in Great Britain by
Marston Lindsay Ross International Ltd,
Oxfordshire

Whilst every effort has been made to ensure the accuracy of the contents of
this publication, the publishers and authors expressly disclaim responsibility
in law for negligence or any cause of action whatsoever.

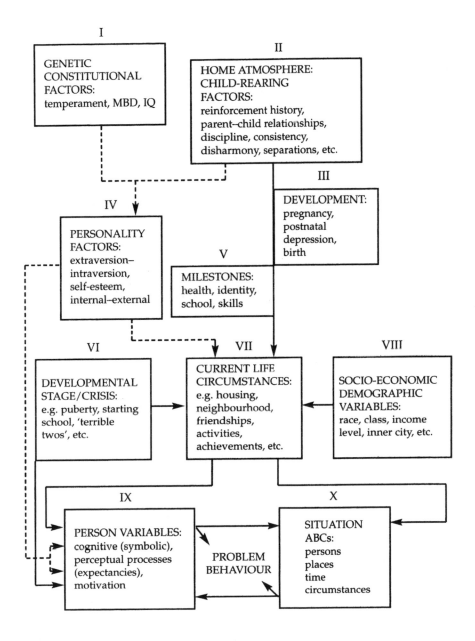

I

GENETIC
CONSTITUTIONAL
FACTORS:
temperament, MBD, IQ

II

HOME ATMOSPHERE:
CHILD-REARING
FACTORS:
reinforcement history,
parent–child relationships,
discipline, consistency,
disharmony, separations, etc.

III

DEVELOPMENT:
pregnancy,
postnatal
depression,
birth

IV

PERSONALITY
FACTORS:
extraversion–
intraversion,
self-esteem,
internal–external

V

MILESTONES:
health, identity,
school, skills

VI

DEVELOPMENTAL
STAGE/CRISIS:
e.g. puberty, starting
school, 'terrible
twos', etc.

VII

CURRENT LIFE
CIRCUMSTANCES:
e.g. housing,
neighbourhood,
friendships,
activities,
achievements, etc.

VIII

SOCIO-ECONOMIC
DEMOGRAPHIC
VARIABLES:
race, class, income
level, inner city, etc.

IX

PERSON VARIABLES:
cognitive (symbolic),
perceptual processes
(expectancies),
motivation

PROBLEM
BEHAVIOUR

X

SITUATION
ABCs:
persons
places
time
circumstances

Frontispiece: The 10 factor clinical formulation [Herbert, 1981], adapted from
Clarke (1977). The dotted line represents indirect, predisposing contributory
factors.

To Professor Dorota Iwaniec

In appreciation of her support and encouragement
and of the scholarship she has brought
to the field of social work practice.

Contents

List of tables and figures

Acknowledgements

I should like to record my gratitude to Simon Claridge who sent me details of the paper concerning Circle of Friends; to John Moore for commenting on parts of the text; to Cate Boulton, Jane Askew, Joan Cunnington and Sharon Gregory for taking the work forward so enthusiastically; to Alison Reeve and Audrey Dunning, who gave practical and moral support; to Joe Dawson who helped me make sense out of confusion; to Roy Kirk who answered my queries on educational matters; to Judith Stevenson who tracked down elusive references; to Jean Macqueen for her swift and efficient compiling of the index, and to Professor Martin Herbert, without whom the book would never have been written.

Crown copyright material is reproduced with the permission of the Controller of Her Majesty's Stationery Office.

Introduction

The evidence that many children's emotional and behavioural difficulties have their origins in the earliest years of their lives continues to accumulate. International research in psychology, psychiatry, genetics, neurology and in other disciplines test ever-more-sophisticated hypotheses in an attempt not only to distinguish the key variables in the tapestry of factors which contribute to a child's distress, but also to identify interventions and treatments to relieve that distress. Thus, by systematic and painstaking research some of the various contributions of 'nature' and 'nurture' to children's difficulties are being pinpointed and their complex interactions explored, while the impact and effectiveness of different helping strategies of intervention are being systematically evaluated. It will be one of the key themes of this book that we must focus as early as possible, and through the cooperation of as many disciplines as possible, on the *prevention* of children's emotional and behavioural difficulties: to assume that children will grow out of them, when the evidence is to the contrary, is sheer folly.

Many researchers have attempted to tease out the interacting contributions of 'nature' and 'nurture' to the temperament and behaviour of the developing child. Studies concerning the contribution of 'nature' include the extremely important work of Thomas and Chess (1977), who studied the temperaments of infants as they matured through childhood, adolescence and adulthood; they were able to claim, on the basis of the consistency of certain patterns of responses and behaviour which they identified, that human beings inherit some fundamental temperamental dispositions: for example, a tendency to restlessness by contrast with placidity, and a tendency to respond calmly or with distress to changes in familiar routines. Similarly, it is now increasingly accepted from studies of twins and other sibling relationships that Attention Deficit/Hyperactivity Disorder (ADHD) has a genetic component (Barkley, 1995). This does not mean that such characteristics are immutable: rather, they are predispositions towards styles of interactions and behaviour which environmental factors may still influence. Other large bodies of studies have addressed the impact of 'nurture' or, broadly, the impact of a range of environmental factors upon children's development. For example, a major body of work by Cooper and Murray (1997, 1998) has explored the impact of episodes of postnatal depression on the mother herself, on her interactions with her young infant and child and, in due course, on the children concerned.

This research shows that maternal depression exerts its influence upon children's cognitive and behavioural development as late as their fifth years. These studies will be examined in some detail in later chapters.

It is often very difficult indeed to tease apart the contributory factors. For example, the longitudinal studies of Olweus (1979) are of particular importance. Olweus concluded from his work, spanning, in some cases, periods of twenty years, that there was a substantial degree of stability in the area of children's aggression and that 'marked individual differences in habitual aggression level manifest themselves early in life, certainly by the age of 3'. Now, is this stability innately underpinned? or has it already been learned in the hurly-burly of play with other children? or has it been actively taught by a parent concerned that his son should be able to stand up for himself? In any case, even if tendencies to aggressive behaviour are innate, this does not mean that such individual tendencies cannot be moderated. It does suggest, however, that *early intervention* to moderate habitual aggression is essential – to prevent such patterns from becoming entrenched.

Other researchers have attempted to identify those treatments or interventions which have produced beneficial outcomes for children and young people with emotional and behavioural difficulties. There is, as we shall see, a high percentage of troubled children in our communities. Clearly, it is a matter of the greatest importance that thoroughly tested and retested means of helping them should be taught to caregivers, both family members and professionals. Yet, at the present time, knowledge about such tried and tested means for helping children is to be found primarily in journals and in a few textbooks; see Webster-Stratton and Herbert (1994) and Sutton (1999). But at least a start has been made in this respect. A body of well-trained practitioners, familiar with the finer points of theory which successful interventions require, is almost totally lacking.

Further, as I found when researching for this book, a research literature providing a multidisciplinary perspective on children's difficulties scarcely exists. Thus, it is rarely possible for practitioners – psychologists, teachers, social workers, health visitors and psychiatrists – to work together *from a common research base* to help children, confident not only in each other's professionalism but also in each other's knowledge of key theoretical concepts. This book is intended as a contribution to that multidisciplinary pool of knowledge and skill.

The starting points for this book

This book starts from a number of premises:

1 That a veritable tapestry of variables contributes to children's emo-

tional and behavioural difficulties. These are shown in the frontispiece (Herbert, 1987).

2 That at least some indicators of subsequent difficulties, particularly habitual aggressiveness, are often discernible in the earliest years of a child's life (Olweus, 1979).

3 That supportive interventions to help these children and their parents should therefore be made available in these earliest years.

4 That parents should be enabled to say what forms of help they need and that, within the limits of what is known from research to be helpful and within the limits of available resources, they should be helped to participate in the delivery of those forms of help.

5 That because children's difficulties manifest themselves in the home, at the nursery, in school and in the clinic, the help made available should be multidisciplinary and coordinated.

6 That the effects of help offered should be systematically appraised so that:

   a) parents are able to report how far they found the services offered helpful, and

   b) the cost-effectiveness of the services can be evaluated.

Another way of describing a multivariate model of children's difficulties is to say that children, themselves systems, belong to many different systems: family, educational, social and cultural. Hence, many differing influences are brought to bear on the child as he or she matures and enters these different systems. When children have difficulties, organizations within the various systems to which the child belongs attempt to help them. Health organizations develop services to support young families via health visitors, speech therapists and dieticians; educational systems provide educational welfare officers and school counsellors; and social organizations provide social services, either on a statutory or a non-statutory ('voluntary') basis. *It is exceedingly difficult to coordinate services across so many different systems, each composed of different individuals with his or her own personal history, beliefs about the origins of children's difficulties and how they should be dealt with.* Accordingly, this book will insist that it is essential that the well-being of children is the focus of an integrated approach.

The structure of the book and the chapters

The book falls into four parts: Part I begins with a chapter presenting data dealing with children's emotional and behavioural difficulties available from British national surveys, and addresses the seriousness of the situation which confronts researchers, policy-makers and practitioners. It also considers what is known of the origins of some children's difficulties. Chapter 2 considers central government plans for helping troubled children, as set out in major policy documents for health, education and social services, taking into account the vital contribution of the voluntary sector and the importance of the voices of parents themselves. It also examines the challenges of working together in an integrated way.

Part II also contains two chapters, each addressing a body of relevant theoretical material. Chapter 3 sets out the body of psychological concepts known as cognitive-behavioural theory which, when used by practitioners in the context of a supportive and empathic relationship with family members, has been repeatedly shown by research to provide practitioners with an invaluable repertoire of knowledge and skills. Indeed, there is abundant evidence that when practitioners develop a warm, empathic and respectful therapeutic alliance with family members and can help *them* to employ principles and concepts drawn from cognitive-behavioural theory, they have been able to help 'thousands of children with a wide variety of problems'. (Gordon and Davidson, 1981.) Chapter 4 addresses the challenges of engaging and working with families, many of which are deeply deprived and disadvantaged themselves. It also explores the stages which parents are likely to pass through as they make progress, only to lapse and lose heart. Here the onus falls upon the practitioner to recognize the probability of lapse occurring, to offer anticipatory guidance and to act to remotivate the family members to make yet another start.

Part III introduces the ASPIRE process, a mnemonic for the stages of working with children and their families: Assessment, Planning, Implementing the plan, Review and Evaluation. Chapter 5 is devoted to assessment in a multidisciplinary context; chapter 6 deals with the three subsequent stages of the process.

Part IV comprises five chapters, one each dealing with multidisciplinary practice in the fields of infancy, the toddler and pre-school child, the primary school child, the secondary school child and, finally, young people who offend against the law. Each one considers specific research pertinent to the field and then offers suggestions about multidisciplinary practice therein. The book ends with a brief summary and discussion of some ways forward, together with a number of relevant appendices.

While the structure of the chapters in the first three parts varies, that of the chapters in Part IV is the same. Each one opens with a brief examination of what is known from research about factors predisposing to the development of emotional and behavioural difficulties in children. It continues with a consideration of findings concerning helpful approaches in supporting families. It goes on to illustrate the use of the ASPIRE process as a way of structuring work with families, and it concludes with typical examples of multidisciplinary work with those concerned.

PART I

THE CHALLENGES OF HELPING CHILDREN IN A MULTIDISCIPLINARY CONTEXT

Children's emotional and behavioural difficulties: nature, prevalence and origins

A huge amount of research by practitioners from many disciplines – geneticists, dieticians, psychologists, psychiatrists, sociologists and many others – has sought to clarify the nature, extent and origins of children's emotional and behavioural difficulties. While some of the major contributory variables which researchers have teased out are represented in the frontispiece (Herbert, 1987), it is likely that yet other important factors will be identified. This chapter will explore some of the emerging evidence under the following headings: first, the needs of children; second, the nature and prevalence of their difficulties; and, third, factors contributing to children becoming troubled.

The needs of children

It is extremely encouraging to see increased consensus among researchers, theorists and practitioners about children's most fundamental needs for emotional health and overall well-being. Kellmer-Pringle (1974) was among the earliest to formulate these needs in a coherent way, and her formulation has received much support; it has been further organized and simplified by Cooper (1985) (see Table 1.1).

Children do not move smoothly through these stages: they move jerkily, irregularly and may move forwards and backwards over the course of time. In respect of *safety*, for example, they may move forward and backwards within the same day or indeed within the same hour. The issue of safety and security is a seriously neglected one in my view (Sutton, 1991). While Anna Freud (1946/47) wrote illuminatingly about defence mechanisms, denial, projection and other matters, more fundamental issues such as our acute sensitivity to personal challenge or threat as conveyed by a turn of phrase, *or even a word*, have been seriously neglected by students of human nature. For our preoccupation with safety and security has a *biological and physiological basis*; we are predisposed to be alert to threat, both physical and psychological. Some children have had so little safety in their lives, having suf-

---

Table 1.1: The needs of children (Cooper, 1985)

Basic physical care
Which includes warmth, shelter, adequate food and rest, grooming (hygiene) and protection from danger.

Affection
Which includes physical contact, holding, stroking, cuddling and kissing, comforting, admiration, delight, tenderness, patience, time, making allowances for annoying behaviour, general companionship and approval.

Security
Which involves continuity of care, the expectation of continuing in the stable family unit, a predictable environment, consistent patterns of care and daily routine, simple rules and consistent controls and a harmonious family group.

Stimulation of innate potential
By praise, by encouraging curiosity and exploratory behaviour, by developing skills through responsiveness to questions and to play, by promoting educational opportunities.

Guidance and control
To teach adequate social behaviour which includes discipline within the child's understanding and capacity, and which requires patience and a model for the child to copy, for example, in honesty and concern and kindness for others.

Responsibility
For small things at first such as self care, tidying playthings, or taking dishes to the kitchen, and gradually elaborating the decision-making the child has to learn in order to function adequately, gaining experience through mistakes as well as successes, and receiving praise and encouragement to strive and do better.

Independence
To make their own decisions, first about small things but increasingly about the various aspects of life within the confines of the family and society's codes. Parents use fine judgement in encouraging independence, and in letting the child see and feel the outcome of his or her own poor judgement and mistakes, but within the compass of the child's capacity. Protection is needed, but over-protection is as bad as too early responsibility and independence.

---

fered physical, sexual or emotional abuse, or endured repeated changes of caregiver, that they are perpetually coping with a fundamental insecurity, and are unable to develop the close emotional relationships which underpin and are underpinned by a sense of safety. Their threshold for perceived threat is therefore likely to be extremely low and they may react swiftly with aggression to such perceptions. Other children will have been traumatized by natural disaster or war; they, too, are likely to be unable to develop trusting relationships, but may remain hypervigilant and suspicious.

So, according to their inherited temperaments and the circumstances of their environments, children learn to cope with the demands of life. If they are fortunate, they learn to cope by going to adults for comfort and reassurance; if they are unfortunate, they learn to cope by withdrawing or by redirecting their distress and frustration against adults or other children. If the latter, it is vital that adults are confident enough to set clear, firm limits to a troubled child's behaviour to protect other children from his or her frustration or distress.

The nature and prevalence of children's difficulties

Better reporting and coordination of data are leading to the availability of more accurate information on the nature of children's difficulties and the numbers of children experiencing them. I shall consider first Rutter's (1987) categorization of children's emotional and behavioural difficulties, then several sources of information about prevalence: this will include data from the Department of Health in Britain.

Table 1.2 shows a helpful categorization of children's emotional and behavioural difficulties. This is a simplified version of material drawn

Table 1.2: Variables differentiating diagnostic categories of children's disorders (Rutter, 1987, key added)

Diagnostic group	Age of onset	Sex	Reading difficulties	Family discord	Response to treatment
Emotional disorder (Anxieties, phobias obsessions, depressions)	Any	=	—	—	++++
Conduct disorder (Aggressiveness, disruptiveness, tantrums)	Any	M	++	+	+
Hyperactivity	<5 years	M	+++	+	+
Autism	<2.5 years	M	+++	—	+
Developmental decay	Infancy	M	+++	—	++

Key:
—   No association
+   Positive association
++   Fairly positive association
+++   Considerably positive association

from international publications such as the *Diagnostic and Statistical Manual of Mental Disorders* (4th edition) *(DSM-IV)* (American Psychiatric Association, 1994) and *ICD-10: International Classification of Mental and Behavioural Disorders* (World Health Organization, 1992). It also shows other key data, such as the typical age of onset of the difficulties, gender breakdown and other characteristics associated with the disorder.

Table 1.3 shows the prevalence of specific child and adolescent mental health *problems* – common difficulties recognized as typically of brief duration and not requiring any formal professional intervention. 1.4 shows the prevalence of specific child and adolescent mental health *disorders* among 10-year-old children in 1995. Where two figures are given, these reflect different prevalences in different localities. For emotional disorders, for example, the first figure of 4.5 per cent reflects prevalence in a rural area, while the second, 9.9 per cent, reflects that in an inner London borough. The prevalence of these disorders is deeply worrying. The figures suggest that nearly one in twenty 10-year-olds in rural settings and nearly one in ten of those in inner-urban settings meet international criteria for such emotional disorders as dis-

---

Table 1.3: Prevalence of specific child and adolescent mental health problems (Department of Health, 1995b)

Nocturnal enuresis	8 % of 7-year-old children 1 % of 14-year-old children
Sleep difficulties	13 % of London 3-year-olds have persistent difficulty settling at night 14 % of London 3-year-olds wake persistently during the night
Feeding difficulties in children	12–14 % among preschool children
Abdominal pain without organic cause	10 % in 5–10-year-olds
Severe tantrums	5 % of 3-year-olds in an urban community
Simple phobias	2.3–9.2 % of children
Educational difficulty	Specific reading retardation: 3.9 % (Isle of Wight) 9.9 % (London) of 10-year-olds General reading backwardness: 8.3 % (Isle of Wight) 19 % (London) of 10-year-olds

abling anxiety, fears and phobias. The figures for children with conduct disorders are even higher, and give particular cause for concern. The evidence suggests (Rutter, 1987) that while the prognosis for children with emotional difficulties is fairly good – that is, their difficulties tend to diminish – this is not the case for children with conduct disorders, such as aggressiveness, disruptiveness and destructiveness; many of them enter the path to offending. Central government departments are right to provide funding and introduce strategies to enable support and specific services to be offered to families of very young children, as this is where so many of the difficulties are known to begin.

Factors contributing to children becoming troubled

Studies of troubled children are becoming increasingly sophisticated, taking into account more and more variables from the tapestry of factors which affect each child. For example, in a review of studies on aggressive behaviour disorders in children, Greenberg *et al.* (1993) grouped the developmental factors contributing to these disorders into four clusters – which may be seen as drawn from the same pool of variables as those shown by Herbert (1981) in the frontispiece:

1 Family stressors
2 The nature of discipline given to the children
3 Child characteristics, including temperament or neurobiological factors
4 Attachment relationships

Each of these groupings will be considered in turn.

Family stressors

It is well established that children growing up in families already coping with social disadvantage are more likely than advantaged children to experience behavioural and emotional difficulties. Indeed, some commentators would say that social disadvantage *of itself* is sufficient to precipitate problems in bringing up children. However, this is unlikely to be the whole story, for not all children in socially disadvantaged families experience difficulties, and, of course, many advantaged families *do* experience such difficulties. Since social disadvantage may include isolation, lack of support from family members, low levels of education and poor housing, these stressors are obviously likely to lead to difficulty in establishing routines, in working

Table 1.4: Prevalence of specific child and adolescent mental health disorders (Department of Health, 1995b)

Emotional disorders with onset in childhood	4.5–9.9 % of 10-year-olds 25–33 % among clinic attenders
Major depression	0.5–2.5 % among children 2–8 % among adolescents
Conduct disorders	6.2–10.8 % among 10-year-olds 35–50 % among clinic attenders
Tic disorders	1–13 % of boys and 1–11 % of girls
Obsessive compulsive disorder	1.9 % of adolescents
Hyperkinetic disorder	1.7 % of primary school boys 1 in 200 in the whole population suffer severe hyperkinetic disorders. Up to 17 % at least suffer some hyperkinetic disorders.
Encopresis (faecal soiling)	2.3 % of boys and 0.7 % of girls aged 7–8 years 1.3 % of boys and 0.3 % of girls aged 11–12 years
Anorexia nervosa	0.5–1 % of 12–19-year-olds 8–11 times more common in girls
Bulimia nervosa	1 % of adolescent girls and young women
Attempted suicide	2–4 % of adolescents
Suicide	7.6 per 100,000 15–19-year-olds
Substance misuse: **Alcohol**	79 % of 13-year-olds have drunk alcohol, with 29 % usually drinking once a week
Solvents and illegal drugs	16 % of 16-year-olds involved in regular use
Minor tranquilisers	Very few involved in regular consumption
Cannabis	3–5 % of 11–16-year-olds have used it 17 % in older teenagers
Heroin and cocaine	Less than 1 %
Hallucinogens	Increase reported

Table 1.5: Family Adversity Index (Rutter and Quinton, 1977)

Father unskilled worker
Overcrowding: at least four children or more than one person per room
Persisting marital discord or one-parent family situation
Maternal depression or neurosis
Delinquency in the father
Institutional care of the child exceeding one week in duration

out household rules and in practising consistency in parenting. Rutter's Family Adversity Index (Rutter and Quinton, 1977) has been of considerable importance in showing the link between family stressors and disorder in the child. (See Table 1.5.)

Blanz *et al.* (1991) describe the usefulness of the Index as follows:

> The presence of each item is scored as 1 point and the total number counted. Thus the adversity score amounts to a maximum of 6. From this cumulated score, it was possible to show that the risk of psychiatric disorder rises regularly with each increase in adversity score, irrespective of the particular items involved... The presence or absence of a particular item did not make any difference.

Indeed, a German study of 300 children by these researchers (Blanz *et al.*, 1991), showed that scores on Rutter's Family Adversity Index recorded when a child was aged 8 were associated with serious behaviour problems when the child was 13. It was found in particular that early-onset disorders (ones which began when the child was around 8 or younger, as distinct from those which began in adolescence) were associated with chronic family adversity. In both age groups, 8 and 13, conduct disorders were closely associated with chronic family adversity.

There is evidence for a poorer prognosis for children born to younger mothers, particularly teenage mothers who are not supported by a partner or family. Farrington (1995a), in a review of studies of the outcomes for the children born to these young mothers, reported:

> In western industrialized countries, at least, early child-bearing – or teenage pregnancy – predicts many undesirable outcomes for the children, including low school attainment, anti-social school behaviour, substance abuse and early sexual intercourse. The children of teenage mothers are also more likely to become delinquents.

Farrington goes on to note, however, that 'the presence of the biological father mitigated many of these adverse factors and generally had a protective effect'.

The nature of discipline offered to children

As Figure 1.1 shows (Maccoby and Martin, 1983), harsh and rejecting styles of parenting have consistently been associated with aggressive patterns of behaviour among children. As I have written elsewhere (Sutton, 1995):

> The figure shows two major dimensions of parenting style: warmth (love)–hostility (rejection) and restrictiveness–permissiveness. The italicized words show styles intermediate between these polarities and characteristic behaviours of parents towards their children. The words within the four quadrants show the characteristic responses of their children

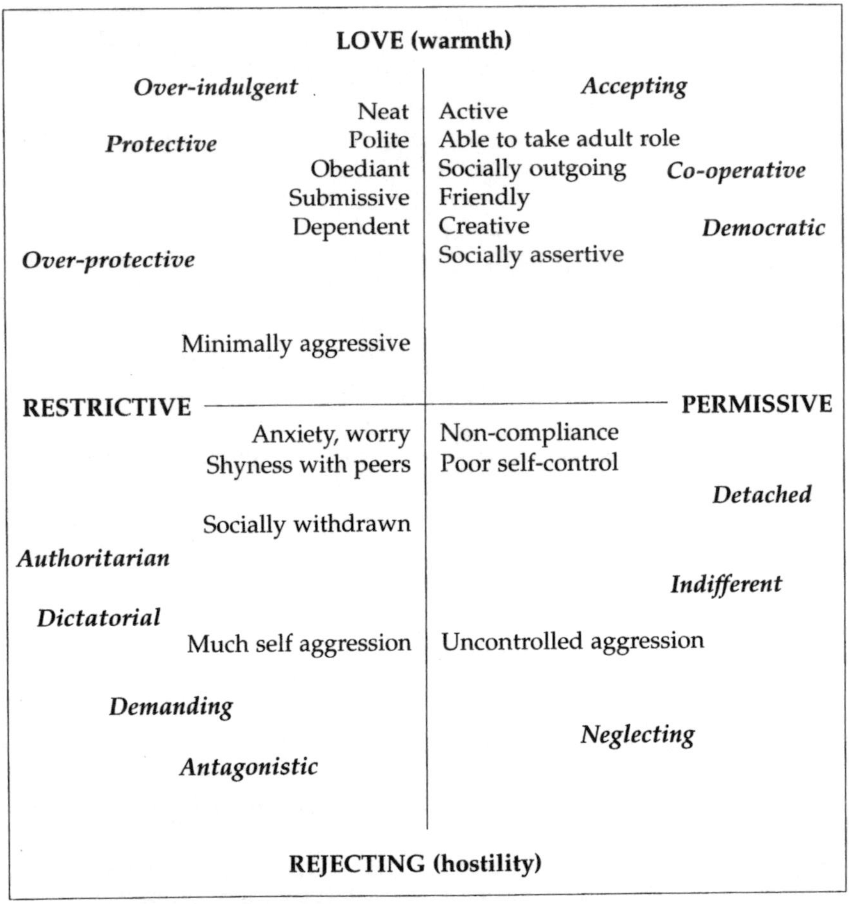

Figure 1.1: Patterns of parenting, and of children's behavioural responses (Maccoby and Martin, 1983) In P. Mussen (Ed.) *Handbook of Child Psychology, Vol 4. Socialization: Personality and Social Development.* New York. John Wiley and Sons Limited. Reproduced with permission.

The figure shows, for example, how a child who has few limits set for his or her behaviour and receives little affection is likely to have limited self-control and may use aggression to get his or her own way. Such children, especially if they have aggressive role models at home, tend to become anti-social.

Similarly, it is known that withdrawing approval from a child, for instance by warning that certain behaviour will result in him or her not being loved, causes much anxiety. It may lead to compliance, but also to submissiveness and dependency. Indifference and neglect also erode a child's sense of security.

Children also learn by imitation of and identification with their parents or those who care for them. Huesman *et al.* (1984), in a longitudinal study, showed that patterns of parenting experienced by children when they were aged 8 were reproduced by these same children when they were aged 30 and parents themselves. Unfortunately, parents who experienced long years of harshness as children and who then practise these harsh and aggressive styles on their own children often find the idea of change unacceptable: intervention is *exceedingly* difficult. The styles have been 'over-learned' across many years and sometimes across many generations; they seldom give place to what may be seen by some parents as 'weak' approaches to child-rearing. When I am training health visitors, social workers and other staff caring for children, I am often asked how to help families who, when encouraged to adopt a more nurturing and positive style towards their children, say that this is 'soft', 'cissy' or 'middle class'. It is seen as 'counter-culture'. Parents object, 'Life's hard; he's got to learn to look after number one'. This is, of course, true up to a point, but when a child is *actively taught* to threaten other children, to fight, to bully and to be disruptive, these strategies become counter-productive. I shall consider this issue further in Chapter 8.

Leach (1999) contributed an important review of the evidence concerning the effects of smacking. She examined the evidence from three 'landmark American studies' (Gunnoe and Mariner, 1997; Strauss *et al.*, 1997; and Brezina, 1998), all concerned with what is cause and what is effect in the physical punishment of children. She summarized the studies' conclusions as follows:

In three studies children were scored on an index of anti-social behaviour derived from established scales of childhood behaviour problems at 'Time one', and the amount of physical punishment... they experienced was measured. *Two years later ('Time two') the anti-social behaviour index was repeated. Results in all three studies showed that the more physical punishment a child was subjected to at the first measurement point, the greater the likelihood that his or her level of anti-social behaviour would have increased by the second.* (My italics)

Such evidence greatly strengthens the case against physical punishment of children. An extremely large and important longitudinal Canadian study of patterns of parenting has shown the impact of different styles of bringing up children. This study, reported by Greenfield (1998), found that 'parenting style, much more than income, determines both children's behaviour and their academic success in school'. This study involved 23,000 families; parenting style was divided into four types, from 'positive interaction', in which parents laughed and played games with their children, via intermediate types through to 'hostile interaction', in which parents administered much punishment, told their children they were bad and showed much anger towards them. This study is important because it shows that not only do children who experience hostile parenting show highly increased levels of serious behaviour difficulties, *but that they also suffer delays in motor and speech development* and in the capacity to display confident social behaviour.

Children whose parents treat them in this hostile way, using frequent physical punishment, are likely to experience a number of effects. (See Table 1.6.)

Child characteristics including temperament and neurobiological factors

Features of the child him- or herself are, of course, strongly represented in the list of variables contributing to misbehaviour. Studies by Thomas and Chess (1977), for example, have confirmed what many parents have long known: that despite being born of the same mother and father, siblings come into the world with different personality characteristics.

Table 1.6: Probable effects of physical punishment

---

1 The children experience the fear of being frequently attacked, either physically or emotionally, or both.
2 In some, this induces high states of anxiety and insecurity, which may lead to tendencies to withdraw.
3 In others, who may have parents who act as models of aggressive behaviour, it may lead to tendencies to imitate patterns of shouting, hitting and assaulting others.
4 In yet others, the pain and humiliation may lead to intense anger and a determination to inflict the same assaults upon the punisher or upon others.
5 While the processes of becoming attached are likely still to operate in such circumstances, the children are likely to be insecurely attached to parents who beat them.

From their longitudinal studies they have identified children with three personality types: 'easy', 'difficult' and 'slow to warm up'. 'Easy' children are adaptable and easy to manage. Early in life they take up regular patterns of sleeping and waking, and seem generally responsive and contented. 'Difficult' children are less adaptable: it is more difficult to get them into a routine of sleeping and feeding regularly, and they seem more irritable in their responses to new situations and people. 'Slow to warm up' children fall between the previous two groups; it takes time to settle them into a routine, but once they have settled they are fairly easy to manage.

There is now firm evidence of the negative impact of smoking during pregnancy on infants and that smoking during pregnancy is strongly associated with foetal and infant mortality. This is a particularly worrying finding in the light of evidence of an increase in the number of young women who are *taking up smoking*, and in the light of the findings by many researchers that many young mothers do so to help them cope with the stresses of parenting.

A child characteristic now broadly accepted as being at least partly organic in origin is attention deficit/hyperactivity disorder (ADHD). Children with this difficulty, which as Table 1.4 shows, affects no less than 1.7 per cent of boys of primary school age, leads to patterns of behaviour characterized by impulsivity, disruptiveness and low attention span. The aetiology of this disorder is complex and there is still disagreement among paediatricians, psychologists and other specialists both about diagnosis and, once diagnosis is made, the best way of dealing with it. Whatever the areas of disagreement, it is still of great importance that there should be a coordinated response to the child coping with ADHD.

Impaired-attachment relationships

The concept of 'attachment' needs clarification. The term was introduced by Bowlby (1969) who used it to refer not to the totality of the infant–parent relationship but to the cluster of behavioural and emotional sequences shown by infants towards their main caregivers in situations of stress. These behavioural and emotional sequences 'have as a goal the reduction of arousal and reinstatement of a sense of security, usually best achieved in infancy by close physical contact with a familiar caregiver' (Lyons-Ruth, 1996).

There have been several attempts to identify various types of attachment among infants and young children. Much research into attachment has used the 'Strange Situation' (Ainsworth *et al.*, 1978) as a way of teasing out and distinguishing levels of attachment in 1-year-old children. This involves observing an infant in a situation in which the mother is present at first, but then is briefly absent, leaving her bag on a seat as an indication that she will return. A person unknown to the child then gently attempts to engage the child in play, before the mother returns. Next, the mother leaves again and the stranger returns; finally the mother returns and stays. Ainsworth *et al.* (1978) were particularly interested in the behaviour of the children at this final reunion, and classified them in three main categories, now termed 'secure', 'avoidant' and 'ambivalent' (Lyons-Ruth, 1996). For example, Table 1.7 shows the characteristic behaviours said to be shown by securely attached children Herbert (1991).

More recently, however, van IJzendoorn (1995) has undertaken a meta-analysis of attachment studies and has confirmed a fourth category, which was named 'disorganized' by Main and Solomon in 1990. Infants in this category are considered to show confused behaviours when reunited with their mothers or main caregivers, and do not fall smoothly into any of the three previously identified categories. Links have been made by researchers (for example, Lyons-Ruth, 1996) between the form of attachment demonstrated by the baby and the sensitivity of the care which the baby has experienced. It is claimed that mothers of infants who are securely attached are more responsive to their infants' needs, pick up more accurately the cues being offered by the baby and interact with them with sensitive timing. The mothers of infants who are less securely attached are often considered to have experienced less sensitive mothering (see, for example, Belsky and Rovine, 1988). While research continues, for example, into whether the observed differences are linked more to innate differences within children or to the relationship with the caregiver (e.g. Bretherton, 1985), it appears that many investigators are persuaded of the association

---

Table 1.7: Indicators of secure attachment (Herbert, 1991)

Secure attachments (infant to parent) may be indexed by the baby's:

- Interest and attentiveness when with the parent (looking, gazing, listening)
- Relaxation and/or calmness when in the company of the parent.
- Dependency behaviours directed at the parent, for example, holding, seeking closeness; when older, seeking comfort and help.
- Evident preference for the parent to others.
- Curiosity and exploration, using the parent as a 'base'.
- Pleasure, enthusiasm, joy, (e.g. smiling, vocalizing) in the presence of the parent.
- Protest, displeasure, concern when separated from the parent; comforted when he or she returns.

Note. By four months of age it is possible to observe each of these behaviours in a series of free exchanges between parent and baby. By the middle of their first year most normal children begin to show attachments to significant people in their environment. From then on young children are much more vulnerable to separation from loved ones.

between caregiver sensitivity and responsiveness and the pattern of attachment displayed by the child. For example, Lyons-Ruth (1996) reported the association found between avoidant patterns of attachment (where the infant does not protest when briefly separated from the mother) and the behaviour of the mother towards her child:

> ... when the caregiver returns, infants in this group displace attention away from her entrance, fail to greet her and initially move away if she approaches them. Numerous laboratories have documented relations between infant avoidance and mothers' suppressed anger, lack of tenderness in touching and holding, insensitive intrusiveness and rejection of attachment behavior.

Because of the convergence of opinion among researchers on the great importance of these early years, much sophisticated research has focused on them. There has been much interest in whether children showing these avoidant or disorganized patterns of attachment subsequently go on to display unruly patterns of behaviour later in childhood. There is some evidence that they do (Erickson *et al.*, 1985), especially in families which are already seen as high risk; less vulnerable families do not show this association as clearly.

Lyons-Ruth (1996) reported:

> Several studies now document a relation between disorganized attachment patterns and childhood aggression. Lyons-Ruth, Alpern and Repacholi (1993)... found that three measures predicted deviant levels of hostile aggression towards peers in kindergarten: infant security of attachment, serious maternal psychosocial problems, and maternal hostile–intrusive behavior toward the infant at home. Preschoolers with highly hostile behavior were six times more likely to have been classified as disorganized in their attachment relationships in infancy than to have been classified as secure.

The necessity for a critique

It will be apparent to readers that these claims are highly controversial. It seems that there are echoes here of 'mother blaming' – reviving memories of the insistence by Bowlby (1953) that mothers must be constant companions of their children until they are 5 years old if the children are not to be irreparably damaged. A critique is essential.

First, in view of the studies by Thomas and Chess (1977) which emphasize that babies have individual temperaments which tend to persist, we surely do not yet understand the whole story. This view is strengthened by the research of Crockenberg (1981) who investigated the effects on babies of two interacting variables: the infant's temperament and the level of support available to the mother. She studied a group of forty mothers and their infants during the first year of the children's lives. She found that insecure attachment was likely to occur only when the mother had an irritable baby *and also* perceived that she had low social support from family and friends. Clearly, we have not yet teased out all the variables contributing to the overall tapestry.

However, it seems likely that researchers in attachment would respond that they are *not* attempting to attribute blame to these mothers: their task as researchers is to record behaviour and development and to make interpretations of it. Indeed Lyons-Ruth (1996) specifically notes the impact of psychosocial difficulties experienced by the mothers of babies with disorganized patterns of attachment, and she cites maternal depression, adolescent parenthood and multi-problem family status as risk conditions.

In essence, then, these researchers claim then that some children get off to a difficult start because of temperamental characteristics which they bring into the world with them; because of the stressors which attend their earliest months and years; and because their mothers or caregivers are unable to provide the sensitive care needed for optimum attachment relationships to develop. These factors cannot easily be changed by members of the helping professions.

Some things, however, can be done. Postnatal depression has been the subject of extensive research, both because of its impact upon the mothers themselves and because of the associated effects on the newborn infant and other children in the family. Cooper and Murray (1998) have carried out their research not with a narrow focus upon attachment on the part of the infants concerned, but from a broader perspective which starts with the experiences of the mothers. Because postnatal depression is a research field which can be translated into preventive work on a multidisciplinary basis, and because this preventive work is already being undertaken, it will be examined more fully in Chapter 7.

Summary points

❐ Children have fundamental needs for basic physical care, warmth, shelter, food and rest, and protection from danger. They also need affection, physical contact, holding, cuddling, delight, tenderness, approval and companionship. They need continuity and consistency of care, if possible in a stable family unit, among people who give them encouragement and praise and who stimulate their innate potential. They need guidance and discipline within their child's understanding, together with models of behaviour which they can follow. They need to assume responsibility for small tasks such as tidying playthings and kindness to other children, and, as they grow, they need gradually increasing independence to make their own decisions, all in the context of the child's understanding and capacity.

☐ A high percentage of children experience emotional disorders or problems, and a separate high percentage display behavioural problems; in inner-urban areas these percentages are almost double those found in rural areas.

☐ Early onset of serious behaviour difficulties, that is, before the child is 8, is associated with *family adversity*, as indicated by the father being an unskilled worker, overcrowding, persisting marital discord, maternal depression, criminality in the father and care of the child in an institution for more than one week.

☐ Several studies show that a harsh style of parenting, associated with criticism, much fault-finding, punishment and telling children that they are bad, leads not only to conduct problems at home and in school, but also to delayed development of motor and social skills and to slowness in gaining language skills.

☐ Studies show that the more physical punishment a child is subjected to, the more antisocial behaviour he or she is subsequently likely to display.

2

Multidisciplinary practice: the context and challenges of working together

It is increasingly recognized that a multifactorial model of causality is essential for understanding and helping children with emotional and behavioural difficulties; this is illustrated by the frontispiece to this book (Herbert, 1981). Yet it is this very multiplicity of factors which challenges planners and practitioners when trying to develop services for troubled children. How can we get to grips with so large and unmanageable a set of systems?

This chapter will focus first upon law and social policy as they affect children and young people with emotional and behavioural difficulties. It will then examine some of the difficulties experienced by professionals in working together. The third part will look at some ways of facilitating practitioners' work together, as well as ways of easing inter-group tensions and enhancing individuals' knowledge, skills and motivation.

The statutory and social policy context to improving services

The statutory framework for the task of improving services for children and young people in Britain is the Children Act 1989. This gives local authorities a general duty to:

Section 17 (a) Safeguard and promote the welfare of children within their area who are in need and

Section 17 (b) So far as is consistent with that duty, promote the upbringing of such children by their families, by providing a range and level of services appropriate to those children's needs.

For the purposes of the Act, a child is taken to be in need if:

- he/she is unlikely to achieve or maintain, or have the opportunity of achieving or maintaining, a reasonable standard of health or development without the provision of such services by a local authority,
- his/her health or development is likely to be significantly impaired, or further impaired without the provision for him of such services, or
- he/she is disabled.

It is the responsibility of the Social Services Committee and the Director of Social Services to assess local needs and priorities and to develop the provision of services accordingly.

Since the Children Act became law in 1989, a sheaf of publications has been published to supplement it. In particular, there have been a number of crucial publications urging improvements in services offered to children and their families in three specific areas: health, social services and education. Also, there have been calls for substantial efforts to provide more *coordinated* services for children and their families. We shall briefly consider some of the main publications insofar as they relate to children with emotional and behavioural difficulties, and to multiagency/multidisciplinary working (see Table 2.1).

Table 2.1: Government publications referred to in Chapter 2

Audit Commission (1994), *Seen But Not Heard: Co-ordinating Community Child Health and Social Service for Children in Need.* London, HMSO.

Children Act 1989. London, HMSO.

Department of Health (1991), *Working Together under the Children Act 1989: A Guide to Arrangements for Inter-Agency Cooperation for the Protection of Children from Abuse.* London, HMSO.

Department of Health (1995a), *Child Protection: Messages from Research.* London, HMSO.

Department of Health (1995b), Social Services Inspectorate and Department for Education. *A Handbook on Child and Adolescent Mental Health.* London, HMSO.

Department of Health (1998a), *The Quality Protects Programme: Transforming Children's Lives.* Department of Health.

Department of Health (1998b), *Partnership in Action. (New Opportunities for Joint Working between Health and Social Services.) A Discussion Document.* London, HMSO.

Department of Health (1999), *Modernising Health and Social Services: National Priorities Guidance 1999/2000–2001/2.* Department of Health.

National Health Service/Hospital Advisory Service (1995), *Child and Adolescent Mental Health Services: Together We Stand.* London, HMSO.

The Stationery Office (1999), *Working Together to Safeguard Children. A Guide to Inter-Agency Working to Safeguard and Promote the Welfare of Children.* Norwich, HMSO.

Services for troubled children within a framework of national priorities

The larger agenda in terms of *national* priorities for health and social services is set out in *Modernising Health and Social Services: National Priorities Guidance 1999/2000–2001/2*. This is published as an action paper with a clear agenda (Department of Health, 1999). The welfare of children and young people with emotional and behavioural difficulties falls under two main headings: 'Social services lead' and 'Shared lead'.

The full table is included as Table 2.2 to show support for children and young people in the context of other demands on, and priorities within, health and social services. As educational policy also affects the welfare of children and young people, we shall consider some material from documents dealing with this arena too. Let us consider some of the issues that arise from Table 2.2.

Services for troubled children as 'social services lead' priorities

These priorities have direct relevance for children with emotional and behavioural difficulties, many of whom live in children's homes. We shall examine the measures in turn under the two designated priorities for social services: children's welfare and inter-agency working.

Children's welfare

The action paper confirms that:

> A large number of children are socially excluded or at risk of social exclusion. Many of them are children in need within the meaning of the Children Act 1989; and about 55,000 of them are looked after by local authorities at any one time. All these children are at great risk of neglect, harm or for other reasons have very poor life chances and often very poor health in later life... the Government has now

Table 2.2: National priorities for modernizing health and social services (Department of Health, 1998)

Social Services Lead	Shared Lead	NHS Lead
Children's welfare	Cutting health inequalities	Waiting lists/times
Inter-agency working	Mental health	Primary care
Regulation	Promoting independence	Coronary heart disease
		Cancer

launched *Quality Protects*, a comprehensive three-year programme to improve the quality of services for children who require the active support of social services.

(Department of Health, 1999, p. 12)

Quality Protects is designed to improve the management of children's services. The main elements include:

Clear objectives for improvement set out in the Action Plan concerning:
- reducing the number of children looked after who have three or more placements a year, many of whom are likely to be children with emotional and behavioural difficulties
- improving the educational attainment of troubled children
- their need for a full health assessment and
- the level of employment which in due course they should be able to attain.

(Department of Health, 1999, p. 12)

Inter-agency working

This priority focuses upon the necessity of improving:

the extent and quality of co-operative work between different public agencies with responsibilities to support looked-after children, children in need and other children at risk of exclusion.

Modernising Health and Social Services, p. 7

Three specific programmes have been introduced to help authorities to achieve these improvements:

(i) *Youth Offending Teams*: Multiagency teams, composed of practitioners from the police and probation service, education, health and social services, working to help young people avoid becoming more deeply entrenched in patterns of offending.

ii) *Crime Reduction Strategy*: This will include early interventions to prevent the development of criminality and antisocial behaviour.

iii) *Sure Start Partnerships*: These will be developed between key agencies, particularly health and social services, to further developmental and preventive work with children at risk and their families. The large sums of money made available are intended to enable local and health authorities to develop their preventive and developmental work with children most at risk, and with their families.

(Department of Health, 1998b, p. 13)

Coordinating services for children in need

In 1994 the Audit Commission published *Seen But Not Heard: Co-ordinating Community Child Health and Social Services for Children in Need*. This report reaffirms that support for children and their families is provided by primary and community health services, local authorities and voluntary bodies. Full details are included here (Table 2.3) because they set the context for services for children with emotional and behavioural difficulties.

Figure 2.1, from the same report, shows clearly that health and social services have overlapping responsibilities for the provision of services for children in need. Such overlap, bringing with it room for uncertainty about who carries ultimate responsibility, necessitates extremely close collaboration between those who must provide services.

A summary of the recommendations made by the Audit Commission in *Seen But Not Heard* is included in this book as Appendix 2.1. However, note now that the recommendations particularly relevant to the working of multidisciplinary teams include:

* Recognition at the top of the organization of the importance of the strategy, and a corporate approach to its development.

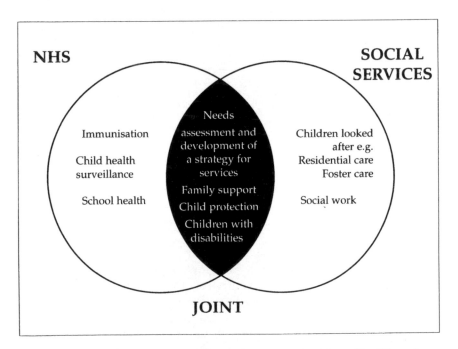

Figure 2.1. Overlapping responsibilities for service provision of health and social services (Audit Commission, 1989).

Table 2.3: Specific requirements of the Audit Commission report *Seen But Not Heard: Co-ordinating Community Child Health and Social Services for Children in Need* (1994)

1   Traditionally, health services have provided universal services, while social services have provided a more specialized service. In future, community health agencies will need to *focus* more of their resources; that is, provide services to a *narrower* band of families with children. Local authorities, by contrast, will need to broaden their remit, that is, provide services to a *broader* band of families with children.

2   To fulfil the requirements of the Children Act 1989, community health and social services agencies will have to:
     a)   Focus on the needs of children and families and provide services which meet specific objectives.
     b)   Check outcomes to verify effectiveness of services.
     c)   Work jointly to provide an integrated range of services and work in partnership with parents.
     To translate these areas into action requires initiatives at every level: thus,

3   *Central government* should promote more inter-agency coordination by raising the status of *children's services plans* which should be joint and mandatory.

4   *Health, social services and education authorities* need to formulate these plans jointly.
     They should contain:
     –   joint assessment of needs;
     –   agreements on the needs to be addressed;
     –   the extent of the needs;
     –   their relative priorities.
     The areas to be addressed by these children's services plans include:
     –   family support, with each agency's role addressed and including jointly funded initiatives;
     –   child protection arrangements, ensuring that each agency's role is clear;
     –   children with disabilities, providing a higher profile for them;
     –   looked after children, ensuring access to education, health care and support on leaving care.
     There also needs to be action *within* each of these main agencies: thus,

5   *Health commissioners* should start to shape and direct health services for children more effectively, with a focus upon:
     –   determining needs, which should be assessed and prioritized for action;
     –   establishing surveillance programmes according to national guidelines;
     –   targeting services to families with identified needs;
     –   evaluating outcomes;
     –   commissioning child health clinics selectively to avoid duplication;
     –   local projects, often in conjunction with voluntary and private groups, should be promoted and evaluated;

Table 2.3: (continued)

- – the school health service's purpose should be defined more precisely;
- – information requirements should be identified, which allow the effectiveness of services to be monitored.

6 *Providers of children's community health services* must be able to:
- – target agreed needs, using information from practitioners;
- – evaluate services effectively;
- – improve information systems;
- – review how best to deploy staff – by patch, GP practice or a mixture...

7 *Social services departments* must become more proactive rather than reactive, paying particular attention to Part III section 17 of the Children Act 1989 which covers authorities' responsibilities to children in need. They should:
- – identify where children in need are living and allocate services accordingly;
- – review existing services, their costs and effectiveness in relation to needs, releasing resources for redeployment wherever possible;
- – review social work practice and organization, focusing on
  - – effective workload management and supervision
  - – time management
  - – referral procedures and specializations
  - – the implementation of a needs-led rather than service-driven approach;
- – encourage the growth of proactive support services;
- – improve information systems in order to be able to link needs, services and outcomes in a demonstrable way;
- – develop clear, timetabled plans to implement strategies.

- • Parents are partners and should also be involved.
- • Agencies must act together jointly to produce strategy and operational agreements. Joint equipment budgets and shared respite care are a good beginning.

Services for troubled children as 'shared lead' priorities: child and adolescent mental health

This area is of the greatest importance for the well-being of children with emotional and behavioural difficulties. Although many people feel that it is not appropriate that services for troubled children are located within the mental health services, the movement to normalize mental health care, to emphasize the promotion of health (rather than focus upon illness) and to make services routinely accessible to all, means that this location is likely to remain.

The action plan set out in *Modernising Health and Social Services* states that a key objective of organizations with 'shared lead' responsibilities is to:

Improve provision of appropriate, high quality care and treatment for children and young people by building up locally based child and adolescent mental health services (CAMHS).

This plan endorses the major review *Child and Adolescent Mental Health Services: Together We Stand* (1995), which was published by the Hospital Advisory Service after an extensive enquiry into the availability of support services for children and young people with mental health problems, including emotional and behavioural difficulties. This review has had considerable impact. Its investigation of the commissioning and management of provision for children and young people revealed struggling services overwhelmed with referrals, and a fragmented and uncoordinated patchwork of provision. Central government has made substantial funds available to help implement its proposals.

The publication offers a strategic approach to commissioning and delivering a comprehensive child and adolescent mental health service (see Figure 2.2). It recommends four tiers of provision of services, each staffed by practitioners with distinctive skills and resources to offer to children, young people and their families. Figures 2.3 and 2.4 show examples of the processes which authorities commissioning services for children and young people may usefully move through.

Some of the key points made here include (Department of Health, 1999, p. 74):

- Clear identification of, and agreement on, each agency's primary responsibilities and which services should be provided through cooperative arrangements.
- Recognition of the legitimate roles and responsibilities of children and young people, their parents, guardians and carers, and encouragement of their contribution to service planning and evaluation.

Figure 2.5 illustrates the intended hierarchy, or 'inverted cone' of provision, incorporating services from education, health, social services and the voluntary sector. Clearly, such a model brings into close contact people with *very different* training, orientation and professional status. When practitioners are required to 'work together' these differences can cause major difficulties; they are discussed below.

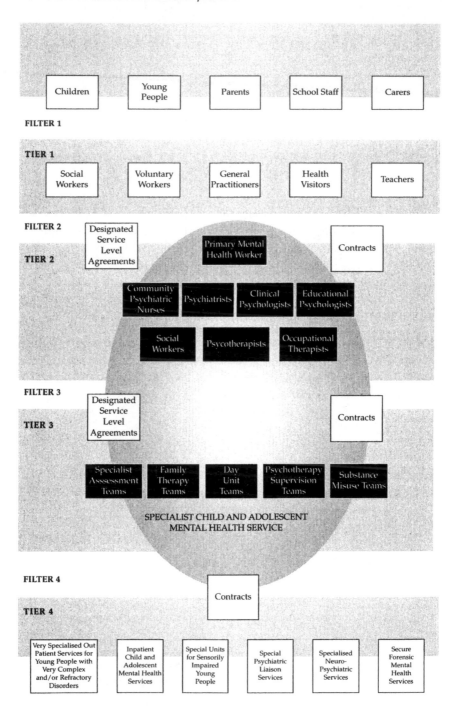

Figure 2.2. A strategic approach to commissioning and delivering a comprehensive child and adolescent mental health services (NHS Advisory Service, 1995, p. 63).

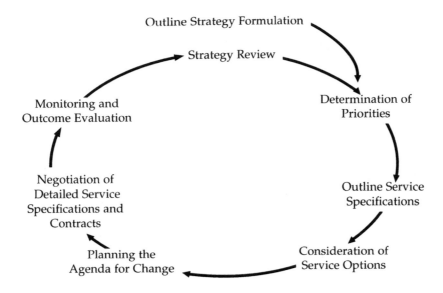

Figure 2.3. An idealized approach to commissioning mental health services (NHS Advisory Service, 1995, p. 72).

The skills of mental health services professionals

Together We Stand (1995) includes a helpful statement about the skills of professionals in mental health services which is particularly applicable to multidisciplinary methods of working:

> The range of professions which undertake work with children and adolescents who have mental health problems and disorders bring different skills to the multi-disciplinary pool, which should be consolidated by each worker's individual training, interests and experience. It is important to stress that few skills can be the sole prerogative of one discipline. In a mature service, the key worker for each client/patient should be chosen because his or her skills or experience are appropriate to the needs of the client/patient. The criterion for selection should not be the worker's discipline of origin. Irrespective of which tier of service is involved, there are some basic attributes which all members of a multi-disciplinary service or team should possess and these include:
>
> - Empathetic interviewing and counselling skills.
> - A working knowledge of child development.
> - Up-to-date working knowledge of child and family problems and disorders.

- Understanding of the particular impact of major events on children's lives, e.g. abuse, bereavement, etc.
- An awareness of how the professional's own life experiences informs their approach to others.
- Familiarity with manifestations of serious or potentially serious psychiatric disorders.

Further skills required by those who work at Tiers 2, 3 and 4 include:

- Special interview techniques suitable for eliciting information from all age groups, e.g., play therapy skills.
- A knowledge of family, group and systems dynamics and how these affect individuals in them.
- Sufficient knowledge and ability to apply appropriate psychologically-based therapies and psychiatric treatments.

(p. 95)

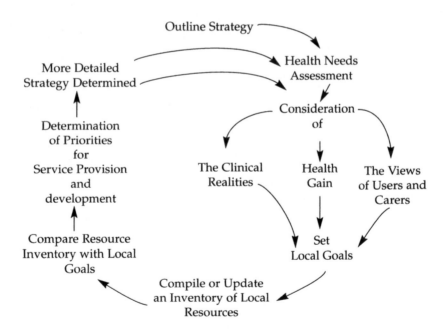

Figure 2.4. Determination of priorities (NHS Advisory Service, 1995) (p. 72).

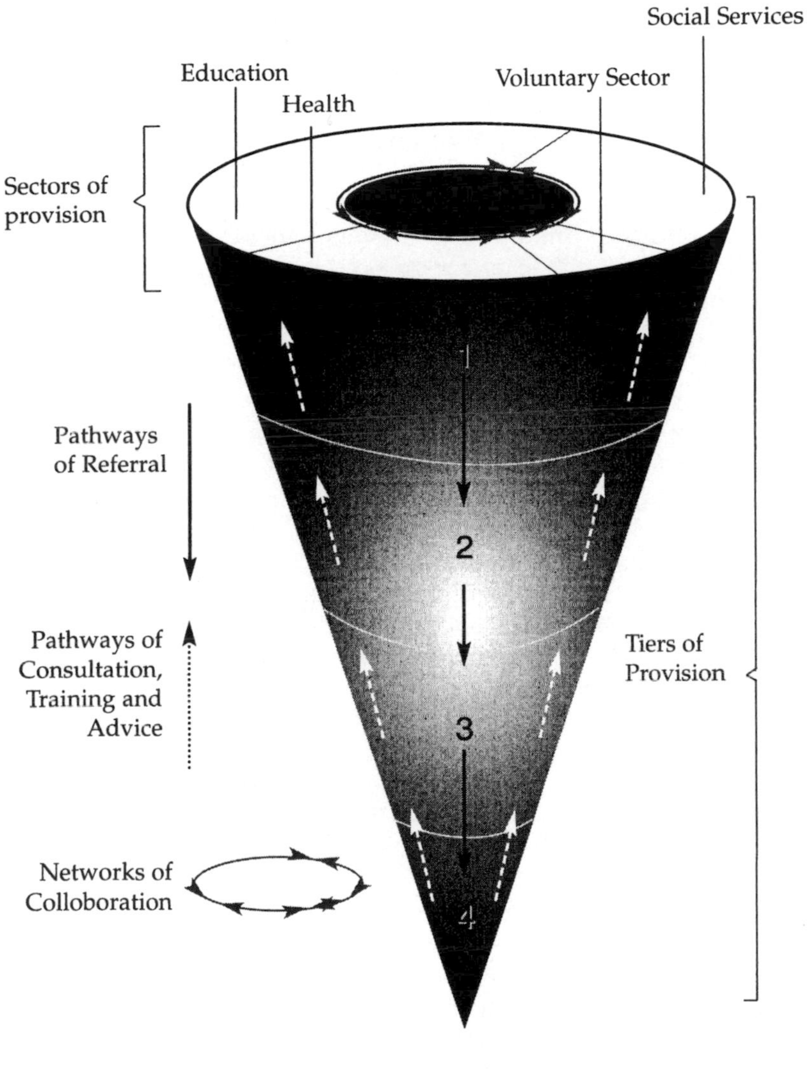

Figure 2.5. The inverted cone of provision (NHS Advisory Service, 1995).

sues of children's special educational needs

The 1981 Education Act clarified the concepts of special educational provision and special educational need [SEN], aimed at a minority of children. These children are not defined by their disability, but are deemed to have needs that require resources or support additional to the normal provisions in a school, such as extra teaching time, welfare support or special equipment.

The Advisory Centre for Education, ACE, noted in 1994:

> Changes to the law on special education mean that from September 1994, all Local Education Authorities and schools will be required to have regard to a Code of Practice when managing their special needs provision. (p. 1)

It continued:

> Once a child has been identified as having special educational needs, parents, and/or the school can ask to have him/her formally assessed by the LEA [Local Education Authority], with a view to having a Statement of SEN drawn up. A range of different disciplines contribute to the assessment – education, psychological, medical, social. Parents are also involved. The Statement sets out a description of the child's special needs and the provision – that additional support – that is to be made to meet those needs… It is a legally binding document.

This code duly came into effect, and all schools were required to appoint a member of staff to act as Special Educational Needs Coordinator (often called 'Senco') to ensure that procedures were in place to meet children's needs. The code established three school-based stages and two LEA stages for identifying, making provision for, and monitoring special educational needs. The five stages are summarized in Table 2.4.

A major issue is whether children with emotional and behavioural difficulties fall within the meaning of the term 'special educational needs'. Many, including myself, would argue that they do, and that those Local Educational Authorities pleading shortage of resources as a justification for avoiding this commitment are being extremely short-sighted. These children need preventive support as early in life as possible; their needs are likely to intensify, not diminish, unless they are given help at an early age.

Table 2.4: The five stages for identifying, making provision for, and monitoring a child's educational needs (Advisory Centre for Education, 1994)

i) Class or subject teachers identify a child's SEN and, consulting the school's SEN coordinator, gather information and take initial action through making, monitoring and reviewing an individual education plan for the child.
ii) The school's SEN coordinator takes lead responsibility for managing the child's special educational provision, working with the child's teachers.
iii) Teachers and the SEN coordinator are supported by specialists from outside the school.
iv) The LEA considers the need for a statutory assessment and, if appropriate, makes a multidisciplinary assessment.
v) The LEA considers the need for a Statement of SEN and, if appropriate, makes a Statement and arranges, monitors and reviews provision.

The emergence of similar structures of service provision

It is encouraging to see that in all the many and varied reports and codes cited in this chapter, there are consistently similar recommendations concerning service provision for children in need. The recommendations about the *structures* of such services are summarized in Table 2.5.

These common structures are more than a simple hierarchy, however; they are essentially a series of closely interlinked systems. The members of the systems are likely to constitute a multidisciplinary team which, as indicated in Figure 2.5, will be located at all or most levels, and contain members who can deal with many troubled children's needs – even those which have multifactorial causation: (see frontispiece).

Table 2.5: Broad common structures and procedures advocated in reports

Level 1 Because of the emphasis upon prevention and self-support, help should be made available locally and as soon as possible. For example, children should be helped within their schools by teachers, school nurses and school counsellors. At home, they and their families can be supported by voluntary visitors, or those with some introductory sequences of training.
Level 2 Referral to primary care services: e.g. GP, health visitors, social workers.
Level 3 Referral to secondary care services: e.g. educational or clinical psychologists, speech therapists, foster parents and others.
Level 4 Referral to specialist services: special units, treatment centres.

Difficulties in working together

Practitioners in the fields of child protection and child support know that there is great concern that professions and agencies should cooperate in the task of helping children and their families. A sheaf of government and other publications continues to urge upon practitioners the necessity for collaboration culminating in *Working Together to Safeguard Children* (Department of Health/Home Office/Department for Education and Employment, 1999).

The number and frequency of these publications highlights what is common knowledge: that agencies have repeatedly experienced difficulties in cooperating, sharing information and developing collaborative plans of action for children and their families. These difficulties have sometimes led to the deaths of children. What is not common knowledge is how difficult it is to achieve collaborative practice. *Many of the enquiries into tragedies in the field of child protection have concluded that they were due to failures of liaison among professionals.* Some of the main difficulties arise from the following:

The composition of teams

Multidisciplinary teams have existed for many years. Child Development Units, typically staffed by a paediatrician, an educational psychologist, a nutritionist and other professionals are often found within hospital settings. Many health authorities also have groups known as Child Guidance or Child and Family Consultation teams, which tend to have long waiting lists and to be overwhelmed with referrals. There is a serious shortage of multidisciplinary teams to undertake preventive work when children are still young because of an urgent need for more and better trained workers at Tier 1 of the hierarchy (Sutton, 1999). Some authorities, such as Leicester, Leicestershire and Rutland Health Trust in the UK, are working to train experienced specialist practitioners such as nursery nurses to extend their role to encompass preventive work at this level.

The composition of existing teams varies, of course. Family consultation teams are often headed by a psychiatrist or a psychotherapist, but in others a clinical psychologist may have overall responsibility. Other team members may include social workers, play therapists and psychologists with specific professional qualifications. Many practitioners are, however, inadequately trained in working as part of a multi-agency team. They do not know the areas of specialist knowledge and skill in the repertoire of each fellow-practitioner. The teams often have extremely limited administrative support and are overwhelmed with referrals. Moreover, the team-members are subject to recognized psychological processes which can undermine the task of effectively working together.

Inter-group processes

In inviting and expecting groups of people to collaborate, we need to be aware of and take account of group processes and dynamics, as these apply both *within* and *between* groups. The terms 'in-group' and 'out-group' convey the tendency of groups to polarize when views differ. Each group or sub-group develops a distinct identity based on one or more dimensions, such as a belief system, a profession, a form of training or a particular focus of concern. Each group thus constitutes an 'in-group', which distinguishes itself from one or more 'out-groups' who follow a different creed (or theory), have a different identity or a different training. Such group identities are likely to become more intense if the groups are in competition for the same resources. So the relationship is reciprocal: each group is an 'in-group' to itself, and sees others, whom it categorizes as 'different', as the 'out-group(s)'. There are all too many examples: Catholics and Protestants, capitalists and communists, conservatives and socialists, even field social workers and residential social workers.

In view of the importance of this phenomenon, and the suffering and miseries which it can cause, it has been the focus of much research. From their extensive studies Tajfel and Turner (1979) concluded:

> The mere perception of belonging to two distinct groups ... is sufficient to trigger inter-group discrimination favouring the in-group. In other words, the mere awareness of the presence of an out-group is sufficient to provoke inter-group competitive or discriminatory responses on the part of the in-group,

Other writers in this field, for example, Stoner (1978) have identified characteristic developments when groups begin to polarize. These are shown in Table 2.6.

In the light of the realization that the tendency to form groups with a shared identity, such as 'psychiatrist', 'psychologist', 'field social worker' etc., is a common human quality, and yet one which can be appallingly destructive, the tensions which sometimes arise between practitioners may be more readily understood. Consider some of the factors which militate against harmonious group relationships within a multidisciplinary team (see Table 2.7).

Strategies to facilitate working together

In exploring how to promote successful collaborative working, we shall consider first the development of joint strategies among planners and policy-makers at the highest level; next the development of similar structures of service provision; third, joint training; fourth,

---

Table 2.6: Typical developments when groups polarize (Stoner, 1978)

1	*A rise in internal cohesion*	Group members tend to set aside former disagreements and to close ranks in the face of a real or perceived threat from another group.
2	*The rise of leaders*	As inter-group conflict increases, those people who are more aggressive, able or articulate are given power by the group in the expectation that they will lead the group to 'victory'.
3	*Distortion of perception*	Group members' perception of their own in-group, and of the out-group, become distorted. Each in-group tends to regard the skill and characteristics of their group as superior to those of the out-group.
4	*Rise of negative stereotypes*	As each group belittles the other's ideas, the differences between the groups are seen as greater than they actually are, while the differences within each group are seen as fewer than they actually are.
5	*Selection of strong representatives*	Each group selects representatives who, it believes, will not capitulate under pressure from the other side. Each group tends to view its own leaders positively and the opposing leaders negatively.
6	*Development of blind-spots*	Strong identification with the in-group develops, and this tends to obscure clear thinking and the resolution of differences.

---

matters of guidance on procedures; fifth, ways of dealing with inter-group difficulties; and finally, issues of knowledge, skill and motivation of personnel. Each issue overlaps with the others, of course.

The development of joint strategies at the highest level

The authors of the Health Advisory Service review *Together We Stand*, who examined the commissioning and management of child and adolescent mental health services, spoke for many similar groups when they emphasized:

> ... the interactional processes of cooperation and collaboration involved, which apply in all elements and at all levels of service and include,

- Joint commissioning across agencies.
- The ownership and sharing of strategy and agenda for action by the chairs of agencies and their chief executive officers.
- Collaboration at every level of service management and delivery within and across agencies.
- ... Close working relationships between practitioners of a wide variety of disciplines.

(Department of Health/Hospital Advisory Service (1995), p. 12)

Table 2.7: Factors militating against harmonious relationships within and between agencies

---

Within an agency
1 Status differences between various groups: psychiatry, psychology both clinical and educational, occupational therapy, social work, health visiting and so on.
2 Differences of salary, numbers of days' holiday and overall working conditions associated with those status differences.
3 Differences of length and depth of training of differing professional groups.
4 Differences of theoretical orientation of differing professional groups: for while all might claim to take a 'child-centred' approach, some practitioners might have been trained in psychodynamic and psychoanalytic approaches, others in cognitive or cognitive-behavioural approaches and yet others might claim to take an 'integrative' approach.

Between agencies
1 Competition for scarce resources from funding bodies: health trusts, departments of social service.
2 Competition for a voice in influencing future developments of services.
3 Competition to 'build empires', to extend the size of one's team or the reach of one's influence.
4 Competition for public attention and recognition.

Active collaboration among the leaders of agencies and their officers at the most senior levels is an essential precondition of significant collaboration further down the hierarchies. The structures of our various authorities, statutory and voluntary, are still heavily influenced by their history, they are unwieldy to administer and, like huge ships, slow to respond to calls for changes of direction. At the very least, their captains should be steering towards common objectives and following a charted course which will result in them reaching the same destination together.

The discussion document *Partnership in Action* (1998) claims that it will

remove barriers to joint working by introducing powers... to enable...

Pooled budgets – health (Health Authorities or Primary Care Trusts) and social services to bring their resources together into a joint budget accessible to both those who commission and those who provide services...

Lead Commissioners – one authority (Health Authority, Primary Care Trust or Social Services Authority) to transfer funds and delegate functions to the other to take responsibility for commissioning botrh health and social care...

Integrated Provision – an NHS Trust or Primary Care Trust (that provides as well as commissions services) to provide social care services beyond the level possible under current powers...

The concept of 'shared responsibility' is further echoed in the major publication *Working Together to Safeguard Children. A Guide to Inter-Agency Working to Safeguard and Promote the Welfare of Children* (Department of Health/Home Office/Department for Education and Employment, 1999). It calls for an integrated approach to promoting children's welfare and recognises that:

- Constructive relationships between individual workers need to be supported by a strong lead from elected or appointed authority members, and the commitment of chief officers.
- At the strategic level, agencies and professionals need to work in partnership with each other and with service users, to plan comprehensive and coordinated children's services.

This deep, permanent collaboration is likely to require pooled budgeting. As services are provided by an ever-widening range of practitioners from increasingly different backgrounds, so the battles which have raged in the fields of adult care concerning who will pay for what must be avoided by a policy of deliberate blurring of boundaries. Although there may be battles about this concept, they must be fought, and must be won by those who have the vision and courage to put the good of the nation's children before the claims of people with vested interests in the status quo.

Joint training

If people are to work together effectively, the more training experiences they share the better. As research on ways of helping children with emotional and behavioural difficulties progresses, so it is likely that there will emerge a common body of *evidence-based* knowledge. In these circumstances, multidisciplinary modules are needed to augment programmes of unidisciplinary training for each of the professions involved.

The publication *Working Together to Safeguard Children* makes explicit recommendations about inter-agency training of practitioners in child protection. Because of the direct parallels between child-protection work and work with children with emotional and behavioural difficulties, and, indeed, because some of these children may be in need of protection under the Children Act 1989, the following passage is instructive:

> Inter-agency training should complement the training available to staff in single-agency or professional settings. It can be a highly effective way of promoting a common and shared understanding of the respective roles and responsibilities of different professionals and can contribute to effective working relationships.
>
> Training should create an ethos which values working collaboratively with other professionals, respects diversity (including culture, race and disability), is child-centred, promotes partnership with children and families and recognises families strengths in responding to the needs of their children.
>
> Inter-agency training should focus on the way in which those engaged in child welfare work with others to meet the needs of children. This training should complement the training available to staff in single-agency settings.
>
> *(Department of Health/Home Office/Department for Education and Employment, 1999, p. 97)*

It seems likely that the trend towards training people across, as well as within, disciplines will continue, especially in respect of preventive services for children with emotional and behavioural difficulties. Cooperation among practitioners and a common language of concepts at this level may make the difference between a child staying in a nursery or primary school and being excluded from it.

The necessity for published policy and procedures to guide practice

Despite the difficulties of working together, some agencies, particularly health and social services, have made great progress towards successful collaborative practice, notably in the field of the care of children in need of protection. In Britain this responsibility falls primarily upon social workers, but other agencies have key supportive roles.

Learning from the experience of the social work profession

Partly as a consequence of severe formal criticisms published in reports into a number of very serious incidents in which children died at the hands of parents, step-parents or relatives, departments of social services have hammered out procedures which other practitioners can now emulate. So we turn now to a research study which highlights specific features of inter-agency practice which can inform and improve the working practices of practitioners helping children with emotional and behavioural difficulties.

Horwath and Calder (1998) sought to find out how many local authorities had provided their social workers with key documents to inform and guide practice when working with other agencies to protect children on the Child Protection Register. They insist on the usefulness of having such documentation, citing the work of Hallett (1995) who, in the same field of child protection:

> found that [documents on] procedural guidance not only helped staff to structure and organize their work but assisted in containing anxiety. They were also vehicles for clarifying professional roles and resolving inter-agency differences. Without a framework it is difficult to establish a common understanding of what is expected of those who should be working together implementing the child protection plan.

Horwath and Calder approached 117 local authorities in Britain to gather data about the extent to which they had prepared three written documents to guide social work practitioners: concerning policy, concerning procedures, and concerning practice guidance. Although they found variable levels of policy and procedural guidance among the local authorities they did find many instances of excellent practice. The key features below were identified:

The development of a 'core group'
The core group is, as the name suggests, a group of workers who are most central to the welfare of a given child, who may or may not have had his or her name entered upon the Child Protection Register. For a young child, the core group might consist of the key social worker, the health visitor, the head or manager of the day nursery at which the child spends three mornings a week, and the Home Start worker who visits the family at home weekly. This group takes primary responsibility for the welfare of the child and is necessarily the most knowledgeable about the changing circumstances of a focus-child's life. It is this group which monitors changes in the life of the family as they may affect the well-being of the focus-child – for example, a further instance of domestic violence committed by the child's father upon the mother.

The writing of a child-protection/care plan and agreement

The 1991 publication *Working Together*, focusing on the needs of children who are victims of child abuse, spelled out the need for a plan of action common to both members of the core group of professionals seeking to help the child *and* other participating agencies:

5.17.1   A written plan will need to be constructed with the involvement of the carers/parents and in the light of each agency's statutory duties and will identify the contributions which each will make [to] the child, to the other family members and the abuser.

5.17.2   Once the plan has been agreed it will be the responsibility of individual agencies to implement the parts of the plan relating to them and to communicate with the key worker and others as necessary. The key worker will have the responsibility for pulling together and coordinating the contributions of the various agencies.

5.17.3   The production of the protection plan must include consideration of the wishes of the child and parents, local resources, the suitability of specialist facilities, their availability for addressing the particular needs of the child and his or her family. Special attention will need to be given to ensuring the services provided under the plan are coordinated, structured and ethically and culturally appropriate for the child and the family, with built-in mechanisms for programme review and crisis management.

5.17.4   Children and parents should be given clear information about the purposes and nature of any intervention together with a copy of the plan. Every effort should be made to ensure that they have a clear understanding of the objectives of the plan, that they accept it and are willing to work to it

(Department of Health, 1991, p. 32)

The plan is, or should be, distinct from the agreement (see Table 2.8). The child-protection plan is the written statement compiled by the participants at a case conference indicating how the child is to be safeguarded and by whom. Horwath and Calder (1998) write:

A good plan is described as one which has aims, together with strategies for achieving those aims that acknowledge the risks and consider what may go wrong.

By contrast,

> the written agreement is usually perceived as the contract that is made with the family regarding the implementation of the plan.

Having two separate documents may be superfluous in respect of children with emotional and behavioural difficulties, but the two may be brought together in a coordinated package, as illustrated in Appendix 6.3.

Table 2.8: Components of a package of intervention (Horwath and Calder, 1998)

---

1 *The care plan*
   Establishes an overall aim
   Identifies specific objectives
   Sets out strategies for achieving the objectives
   Names a key worker for a given period of time

2 *The written agreement*
   Clarifies the contribution of each of the participants to achieving the objectives of the care plan
   States means of reviewing and revising a care plan, if needed

---

The appointment of a key worker

The notion of appointing a key worker as a primary point of contact for each child and/or family is seen as essential not only by area child protection review committees but also by the authors of *Together We Stand*, referred to above. This person acts as coordinator of services and resources for the family and holds the main case record. This practice is already in place for many children with disabilities: it should be extended to children with emotional and behavioural difficulties.

Horwath and Calder recommend 'areas for consideration' when such practice guidance is being developed. While some of these are peculiar to child-protection investigations, others appear to have much to offer when two or more agencies are collaborating, and are accordingly included as Appendix 2.2.

In summary...

A number of strategies have attracted some measure of practice research support:

1 Each child or young person should have a named key worker who is responsible for coordinating the child's services and treatment.
2 Each child or young person, as soon as the period of initial assess-

ment is completed and the period of planning is embarked upon, should have a Support Plan.

3 Copies of this plan should be available to all the agencies who have contact with the young person, so that coordinated services may be provided.

Ways of dealing with inter-group difficulties

It is increasingly recognized that the patterns of behaviour shown in Table 2.6 are a response to *perceived threat*. If a threat is detected (whether real or merely perceived), people become preoccupied with safety; they seek others who, they believe, will have the same concerns as themselves: they look for security in numbers. If the threat is seen to persist, for instance if it appears that the out-group's working circumstances will be improved at the expense of the in-group (perhaps they are to be given lower caseloads), then inter-group hostility tends to intensify.

As I have written elsewhere (Sutton, 1994), the evidence on the resolution of conflict suggests four conclusions. First, bringing people together does not of itself reduce conflict; studies show that it is just as likely to intensify. Second, negotiation about issues of, say, access to resources, does not reliably reduce conflict; unless the terms upon which representatives can negotiate have been established beforehand, it is often the case that those they represent reject the settlement so carefully arrived at. Third, bringing groups together to work towards goals which they all want but which they cannot achieve separately does reduce inter-group conflict. Finally, both real-world and experimental evidence suggests that open and consistent efforts at conciliation can make for better (less conflict-ridden) inter-group relations.

Issues of knowledge, skill and motivation of personnel

What else does research offer to help us facilitate working together within multidisciplinary teams? According to Hunter (1999) there are three key questions:

1 Do all those required to collaborate know what they have to do?
2 Do they have the knowledge, skills and resources to collaborate?
3 Do they want to collaborate?

Let us address these questions in the context of multidisciplinary practice:

Do those required to collaborate know what they have to do?

When agencies as diverse as health, education, social services and voluntary agencies come together, and encounter parents or representatives of the child whom the collaboration is intended to serve, it is inevitable that there will be major misunderstandings between them. At the very least, there are likely to be discrepancies in experience and expectations of management structure (such as whether it should be strongly hierarchical or relatively flat), levels in the hierarchy at which decisions are made, and financial management. This is so, even when the agencies exist under statute to serve the needs of vulnerable members of the population – in this case, vulnerable young people. These misunderstandings are all the more probable when agencies have differing boundaries and this confusion is not resolved.

Here, therefore, are some questions which the chairs of the various agencies and their senior executives might pose when, as the authors of *Seen But Not Heard* require, these officers come together at the most senior level to identify need, to plan strategies for meeting those needs, to prioritize and so on:

a) Is there a statement of aims and objectives common to, or at least acknowledged by, all the participating agencies?
b) Is it clear what are the statutory roles and responsibilities which fall to each of the collaborating agencies: for example, which aspects of the assessment of a child's needs must be carried out by an educational psychologist?
c) Is it clear which decisions and responsibilities fall to a given agency but also which are to be taken at Joint Strategy Committee level?
d) Is it clear what the task of collaboration requires of practitioners? For example,
   do they know precisely their roles and responsibilities:
   • within their own agency?
   • in respect of collaboration with other agencies?
e) Do practitioners know the procedures for decision-making:
   • within their own agency?
   • in respect of collaboration with other agencies?
f) Do they know the procedures for decision-making regarding financial outlay:
   • within their own agency?
   • in respect of collaboration with other agencies?

Do they have the requisite knowledge, skills and resources?

At the present time, when administrative structures are changing, and statutory responsibilities are being clarified, all within the context of a revolution in information technology, it is highly unlikely that practitioners do have the requisite resources and abilities to contribut fully efficiently to helping troubled children.

Consider the *knowledge base*: research concerning children and young people is pouring out in the journals so fast that it is difficult to keep up with it. Yet practitioners have few opportunities, once they have left their academic institutions, to keep up to date with current research. Indeed, some have scarcely been introduced to the concepts of research and evidence-based practice in their institutions. In a recent survey, social work students claimed to have been introduced to no less than 80 theories in the course of their professional training programmes (Marsh and Tresiliotis, 1996). How will they know which ones to use in discourse and collaboration with other practitioners? Certainly, parents are unlikely to know of such theories, and may be actively sceptical of the very concept.

In respect of *skills*, the same concerns obtain. If social workers do not have an adequate knowledge base they cannot possibly practise the skills which are based upon that knowledge. For example, in the case of a seriously aggressive child they need the know-how to help families collect frequencies of a child's specific aggressive behaviours – such as the number of times a little girl hits her sister, or the number of times a child interrupts his parents' sleep – before they can make an adequate cognitive-behavioural intervention.

In respect of *resources*, there are major problems. Central government in Britain is making considerable efforts to allocate resources to preventive approaches, but there are shortages of appropriately trained staff to carry out this strategy, shortages of computers and people competent and confident to use them, and shortages of personnel to evaluate the services which are offered. Moreover, from the parents' point of view, there is a perpetual shortage of the resource that many of them really want, namely affordable day care.

Do practitioners want to collaborate?

There is little *evidence* available to answer this question. Many people recognize the desirability of closer collaboration than is the norm at present, but there are perceived costs as well as perceived benefits in change. For some, the prospect of closer collaboration may mean loss of power; for others it may mean an opportunity to develop desirable new skills. For practitioners with substantial power the answer may be 'Yes, but on my terms'; that is, retaining the authority that comes with the senior position in their teams, strongly influencing appointments and directing the division and distribution of work. However, other practitioners may recognize the limitations of their own training and perspectives and be perfectly ready to participate in multidisciplinary teams to learn from the knowledge and experience of other members.

Clearly, personality factors are of great importance here. Some people with dominant personalities find it almost impossible to play a junior role in multidisciplinary teams and are forever upsetting other team-members because they neglect to consult them or appear to seek power for its own sake. Such people may be appreciated in their agency because they play a vital role gaining resources in competition with other agencies. However, they may have a negative impact in their own teams because of their own dominance aspirations.

A further problem is that of access to information. Confidentiality is clearly extremely important, but if the aim is to develop multidisciplinary practice to help families with troubled children, practitioners must address the issue and agree an effective policy on whether and how information concerning those families may be disseminated – *always, of course, with the family's agreement*. Consider the following example: a 5-year-old has a serious behaviour difficulty and, in the belief that their child is hyperactive and needs medication, the parents visit their general practitioner. Though they may agree that other health service professionals, such as the health visitor, should be informed of the diagnosis, they may be extremely reluctant for the child's school to be told, despite the fact that sharing the outcome of the medical consultation may be in the child's best interests. Yet that right to confidentiality must be scrupulously observed if faith in the helping services is to be maintained.

In conclusion, we see how difficult is the task of working together. Yet work together we must, if the interests of troubled children and young people are to be served. In my many discussions of these problems with practitioners I have encountered ample goodwill. Since we are now beginning to see that the leadership for collaboration must come from the highest levels, that clear structures and written procedures must be in place to guide practice, and that there is the beginnings of a research base for interdisciplinary practice, we may feel a measure of optimism for the future.

Summary points

☐ The statutory framework for the task of improving services for children and young people is the Children Act 1989.

☐ Services for troubled children are a lead responsibility of the social services departments. Health and social services share responsibility for some overlapping areas, such as family support.

☐ Children with emotional and behavioural difficulties may be seen as falling within the remit of all three of the main statutory agencies, health, education and social services, as well as within that of the voluntary sector. A major initiative to respond to their needs and those of their families, however, has been located within the child and adolescent mental health services, CAMHS.

❐ It is intended that there shall be four main tiers of provision of services to support children:
   i)   prevention and self-support;
   ii) referral to primary care services;
   iii) referral to secondary care services; and
   iv) referral to specialist services, such as special units.

❐ Practitioners are frequently urged to 'work together'. This is not as easy as it sounds.

PART II

THEORY AND PRACTICE

3

Key theoretical concepts

The human situation is infinitely complex. Social scientists have developed many ways of conceptualizing and coming to grips with this complexity, but here I shall briefly consider just two: the first is of human beings as part of 'systems'; the second is of a range of 'perspectives' on human beings.

Human beings as parts of 'systems'

A system has two main features: it is an assembly of parts or components connected together in an organized way; and, a change in one part of a system is likely to lead to consequences, 'knock-on effects' in another part. So, climatic change or a policy alteration in the economy in one part of the world is likely to have effects, some expected, some not, elsewhere. Human beings are themselves 'systems', assemblies of closely integrated networks in which breathing, digesting food, circulating blood, reproduction and the other highly organized and integrated webs of activity together compose a living person. All the smaller systems contribute to the smooth functioning of the larger system, the body; a significant change in one part, such as the effect of flu on the respiratory system, is likely to affect the functioning of others – the circulatory and digestive systems – and the larger system too. Yet we are not only assemblies of systems; we also exist *within* systems: the family system, the education system, the political system and so on. We are affected *by* others in those systems, such as our relatives and teachers, and we ourselves also affect other systems, for example, other families and other organizations like schools and hospitals. We are all intimately connected in networks of relationships: no-one is an island.

As I have written elsewhere (Sutton, 1994):

Human beings then are inextricably linked with other human beings, since our deepest needs can only be met by other people. We are, however, also very different from one another. So we have this tension: human beings are at one and the same time both intimately bound up with each other and yet highly individual.

A range of perspectives on the human being

As another way of coping with complexity, disciplines such as psychology have taken a number of *perspectives* on human beings as systems. The ideal, of course, is a 'holistic' approach, in which each person is perceived in his or her entirety, encompassing the physical body, development and learning, human experience, creativity, potential and so forth. However, to keep things manageable, five main perspectives on the human being, often called 'models', have been developed. (See Table 3.1.)

I shall briefly consider these perspectives, each of which overlaps and interacts with the others, before focusing more fully on the behavioural and cognitive perspectives, as research has found that these approaches are particularly valuable in understanding and helping troubled children.

The biological perspective

This focuses upon human beings as biological systems, who come into the world with, in some respects, genetically determined or predisposed characteristics. Genes, interacting with environmental influences, govern the processes of growth and maturation and make a contribution to some of our psychological characteristics; they determine our biological sex and physical characteristics such as our eye, skin and hair colouring; and they are implicated in some aspects of our health and mental health, such as sickle-cell anaemia and schizophrenia.

Table 3.1: Five perspectives on the human being

The biological perspective:
  focuses on the person as a biological phenomenon.
The psychodynamic/emotional perspective:
  focuses on feelings, conscious and unconscious, and associated patterns of interaction.
The behavioural and social learning perspective:
  focuses on learning in a social context.
The cognitive perspective:
  focuses on individual perceptions, thoughts, beliefs and judgements.
The humanistic perspective:
  focuses on human potential for growth and development.

The study of how innate factors affect development is a very complex field indeed. It is extremely difficult to tease apart the respective contributions of inheritance and the impact of the 'environment' in its broadest sense: upbringing, culture, particular-life events. Carefully designed studies such as those of Tellegen and colleagues (1988) sought to distinguish various contributions to human development and how they interacted by tracing 44 pairs of identical twins who had been separated in infancy. When these twins were subsequently brought together at an average age of 34 years, they showed major similarities on measures of sociability, intelligence and emotional stability or instability. These findings, together with the results of other rigorously designed studies, suggest that we inherit about 50 per cent of our potential for these characteristics.

An area of theory with huge implications for practice, but which seems to me to have been much neglected in psychology textbooks, is the human response to threat. Because this response is physiologically underpinned it is appropriate to look at it from a biological perspective, but as it also has cognitive and behavioural connotations it can only be fully appreciated by consideration from all perspectives. In essence, it is now known that if we experience or perceive a threat (which may not be an actual threat) our brains and bodies secrete hormones, notably epinephrine (adrenalin) and norepinephrine (noradrenalin) into the bloodstream. This prepares the body for a number of possible responses, all of which are likely to help survival under threat. These are shown in Table 3.2.

As practitioners, we are wise to remain ever-aware of the instant availability of this 'fight–flight' response. However gentle our criti-

Table 3.2: Physiological and psychological responses to threat

Response	Physiologically underpinned	Psychologically underpinned
Aggressive	*Fight* Copes with threat by resisting it with aggression	*Contesting* Copes with threat by arguing or disputing
Submissive	*Flight* Copes with threat by running away	*Conceding* Copes with threat by giving in or giving way
Non-responsive	*Freeze* Copes with threat by remaining immobile	*Clamming up* Copes with threat by keeping silent

cism, however moderate our remonstration, it is almost inevitable that this will be perceived as a threat. According to the circumstances of our encounter, and the temperament and the learned patterns of response of the person concerned, he or she will either retaliate or submit. We need to be aware of this phenomenon, and to tailor our choice of setting for interviews, our words and our body language accordingly.

The psychodynamic and emotional perspective

Throughout the twentieth century, bodies of theoretical ideas have been tested and explored for their usefulness in dealing with problems of mental health, human relationships and personal difficulties such as substance and alcohol abuse. More than once, it has seemed that a body of concepts had been brought together that threw new light on how to resolve a great host of difficulties, only for it to be found later that while some insight had been provided, and some help given, for a few problems, many remained untouched.

This was the case, for example, with Freudian theory. As a result of his researches with troubled people in Vienna in the early 1900s, Freud found that he could heal or markedly improve a number of disorders which had psychological origins, such as hysterical paralysis or blindness. He also found that he could bring great emotional relief to patients by allowing or enabling them to talk about any feeling or distress without comment or criticism – in what we would now call a totally non-judgemental manner. Because many of the areas of difficulty seemed to be associated with the intense emotions of childhood, and sometimes directly with sexual feelings and conflicts, Freud developed a theory of psychosexual stages of life. Freud's stages are: the oral stage, corresponding to the first year of life; the anal stage, corresponding to the second and third years, when children are toilet-trained; the oedipal or electra stage, corresponding to the fourth and fifth years; the latency period, corresponding roughly to the primary school years; and finally puberty and adulthood, when sexual development flowers into maturity. Major difficulties in progressing smoothly through these stages could, Freud claimed, lead to fixations at a given stage; these might lead, for example, to particular patterns of behaviour, such as obsessions and ritualistic sequences, constantly being enacted. While there has been intense interest in these ideas, extensive and rigorous research has not found universal evidence of their validity.

Freud has other claims to fame however (see Atkinson and colleagues, 1990): first, he devised the method of 'free association'; that is, saying whatever comes into our minds in an uncensored way, as a method of gaining insight into otherwise inaccessible mental processes; second, he showed that much of our behaviour is a compromise between our wishes and our fears and anxieties; and, third, he demonstrated that much of our behaviour is influenced by processes which are non-conscious.

Our feelings, then, are of crucial importance. However, I have space to consider them only briefly here. When we are trying to support families or individuals, it will usually be helpful to allow or enable them to release powerful feelings in a non-judgemental and supportive environment. Sometimes, it is only after the release of such feelings that one can make progress in developing a constructive intervention. As I have written elsewhere (Sutton, 1999):

> Whatever their formal role, for all social workers [or other practitioners] there will be times when they need simply to *listen* – a key feature of helpful therapeutic intervention. Women who have been raped, beaten or emotionally abused; people who have been bereaved in grievous circumstances; people who have had their trust in others shattered, but have never had the opportunity to talk of, let alone express the feelings associated with, these experiences, may find in a trusting and supportive counselling relationship an opportunity for the release of powerful emotions.

This has certainly been my experience when working with the parents of troubled children and young people. Sometimes it was only after an opportunity of releasing pent-up emotion, unexpressed over years, had been provided in a calm and non-critical setting that it was possible to move on with them to make a shared assessment of the difficulties which the family was experiencing.

The behavioural perspective

Behaviourism

In reaction to the claims of Freud and his followers that they had established a scientific basis for the study of human development, there arose a number of challengers. Many were concerned to place the study of human experience upon as firm an empirical foundation as the physical sciences. J.B. Watson (1930), for example, in an attempt to found psychology on information that could be collected, tested and verified, proposed *behaviour* as a phenomenon which could be observed, measured and recorded by observers. Building upon the work of Pavlov, he was able to demonstrate that a great deal of learning takes place via a process which came to be known as 'conditioning'. This usage was coined because it refers to the learning of a behaviour *on condition that* it is associated with another event. Two main forms of conditioning have been distinguished: classical conditioning and operant conditioning.

Classical conditioning is the learning of a behaviour because it is asso-ciated in time with a specific stimulus with which it was not formerly associated. An example of this is a child who is given a painful injec-tion by someone in a white coat, and who subsequently screams in fear when he or she encounters someone else in a white coat – say, at the cheese counter in the supermarket. The white coat, formerly a neutral object, has become associated with pain and thus provokes the fear response in the child.

Operant conditioning is the learning of a behaviour which *operates upon* or affects the environment. In essence, if a behaviour is followed by an outcome or response which is pleasurable or rewarding to the person or animal concerned, the behaviour is likely to be repeated: if it is followed by an outcome which is not pleasurable, the behaviour is less likely to be repeated. If, for example, a shy student contributes in class and is acknowledged constructively by the tutor, that person is likely to contribute again; if the contribution is ridiculed, he or she is less likely to contribute again. The application of this body of theory will be examined in greater detail on page 130.

The cognitive perspective

This perspective takes account of the evidence that human beings are not merely driven by unconscious forces or reactions to environmental stimuli. Rather, we are thinking, reasoning beings who form opinions, make judgements, consider alternatives, plan strategies and are cre-ative in our efforts to make sense of the experience of being alive. According to this perspective, human beings gather and process infor-mation and act on their view of this information. You are using your cognitive faculties, for example, as you appraise and criticize the ideas I am putting forward in this book.

Jean Piaget (1896–1980), the renowned cognitive child psychologist, monitored the growth of children's cognitive capacities as they passed through various stages of development. Cognitive capacity appears to correspond with stages of brain development, shown, for example, by the fact that the stages of cognitive development follow a predictable sequence in all children, although some children will pass through them more swiftly than others. There is no space here to consider the detail of Piaget's work, but it is important that health visitors and social workers are familiar with the concepts he developed so that they can understand the limitations of young children's capacities to grasp ideas – for example, *the notion that human beings really do see the world and things that happen in it differently*. People attend to different things, they perceive different things and they put different interpretations upon what they perceive; perceiving reality, as I have indicated else-where, is akin to 'seeing pictures in the fire'.

Further, children also make judgements about events which, because of their immaturity and inexperience, or the ways in which they may have been told to interpret events, may be inaccurate and in some instances completely wrong. A child whose parent, in a moment of exasperation, says, 'You are a bad/horrible/wicked child' may carry this belief into adulthood; another may witness sexual intercourse and believe that the people concerned are fighting and someone is being hurt; while a third, who has been abused, may have been threatened that if she tells she will fall ill or be 'sent away'. Young children are trapped in their perceptions and interpretations.

So too with their parents. The beliefs of parents about their children and the reasons for their difficult behaviours are extremely important. Some beliefs may be accurate: for example, that a family bereavement or the death of a pet has been very important in the onset of a child's anxiety, or that a child's difficult behaviour may have been learned from seeing his father's aggressive treatment of his mother. Some, however, may be mistaken or based on inaccurate knowledge: for example, that a child of only six months is deliberately soiling his nappy just as his mother is ready to go out, or that a 1-year-old was 'born evil'. Parents with such beliefs, or cognitions, need a great deal of support and gentle encouragement to explore the *evidence* for their beliefs, in the hope that they may then reconsider them.

The humanistic perspective

This view of humanity is concerned with positive and optimistic features of human experience. Two psychologists who redressed the tendency of researchers to focus on human pathology, and who reasserted a constructive view of people and their potential for growth and development, are Abraham Maslow (1908–1970) and Carl Rogers (1902–1987).

Maslow's hierarchy of human needs is familiar to many students. Rogers, his contemporary, believed that human beings demonstrate one basic 'tendency and striving – to actualize, maintain and enhance the experiencing organism'. He sought, therefore, to identify the circumstances and conditions which could enable a given individual to achieve their potential. Rogers, together with those who have subjected his theories to detailed investigation, such as Truax and Carkhuff (1967), identified several characteristics or features of counsellors or psychotherapists which seem reliably to contribute to helping those in distress:

Unconditional positive regard by the therapist or practitioner for the client.
An attitude of personal warmth towards him or her.

The capacity for empathy, so that the client feels deeply understood.
Congruence: being genuine, not playing a part.

These counsellor characteristics have emerged from repeated studies
as key components of helpful counselling and are cornerstones of 'per-
son-centred counselling'. This same sensitive regard for people in distress, and especially for troubled children, is, unquestionably, the
foundation-stone of cognitive-behavioural approaches. While our
efforts to help children and their families will usually go beyond counselling, they are to be underpinned by the same attitudes of respect
and concern for people in distress which have proved so beneficial
within counselling.

Key principles of behavioural/learning theory

It will be necessary to bear in mind all five of the above perspectives
when attempting to help people in distress. Of course, it is also important to keep in mind perspectives deriving from other disciplines, such
as sociology, which rightly highlight the impact on vulnerable people
of structural disadvantage: poverty, unemployment and poor housing.
However, in this section I shall explore a body of theory deriving from
the integration of behavioural and cognitive perspectives, since it is
this approach which numerous studies find to be helpful in supporting children and families in distress.

This body of theory takes as given that all learning occurs in a social
context and within social systems: family, educational, political, religious, cultural and others. Thus, a child learns skills and gains abilities
within the larger system of his or her relationships with parents and
other caregivers both in specific settings, such as at family meals, or
within the wider social environment, such as the school.

According to behavioural/social learning theory there are four
main ways of learning:

1 Learning by classical/respondent conditioning
2 Learning by operant conditioning
3 Learning by observing others
4 Learning by cognitive processes

Learning by classical/respondent conditioning

This is the process of learning a behaviour because it is associated in
time with a specific stimulus with which it was not formerly associated. Thus, the behaviour is learned *on condition that* it is so associated.
A good example is that of a child who moved into a children's home

and whose behaviour at bath-time became panic-stricken: it transpired that it was at bath-time that she had been sexually abused. Her panic was elicited by the setting of the bathroom and the sight of the bath of water, itself a neutral object. Associations with distressing objects or situations may terrify children, who may then be characterized as 'silly' or 'playing up' or 'attention seeking'. This may not be the case at all; social workers, and anyone who has the full-time care of children – childminders, residential social workers or foster-parents – need to understand how such *apparently* meaningless fears can in fact be founded in real terror by way of the processes of conditioning which have taken place.

Learning by operant conditioning

This is the process of learning a behaviour which operates upon or affects the environment. Some key factors which operate are:

Positive reinforcement/feedback (reward)

This is any response or event which has the effect of increasing the probability of re-occurrence of the behaviour which preceded it. These positive responses, or rewards, may be social – for example, thanks, praise, appreciation and attention – or tangible – pay packets, salaries, presents, prizes and so on. A child commended by her teacher for working hard and a worker promoted to a more senior position are both likely to continue to work hard – at least in the short term.

Rewards can be *extrinsic*, arising from without: *material* – such as salaries, presents, bonuses, or *social* – approval, thanks, appreciation, attention; or they can be *intrinsic*, arising from within: self-approval, sense of satisfaction, pride in oneself.

Negative reinforcement/feedback

This is, technically, any event which has the effect of increasing the probability of the behaviour which preceded it occurring again; in these circumstances, however, the reward component is the stopping of something unpleasant. For example, a mother may pick up her child when he cries because she is rewarded by the crying stopping. Hence, her picking-up of the child will become more frequent if the child stops crying each time she picks him up – though this may not be in line with her wishes or intentions. The term 'reinforcement' always refers to an increase in frequency or strength of a behaviour. In popular usage, however, 'negative reinforcement' is often, inaccurately, equated with penalty.

Penalty or sanction (punishment)

This is any event (response) which has the effect of decreasing the probability of the behaviour which preceded it occurring again. These penalties too can be social – criticism, blame or suspension – or tangible – smacks, beatings, fines or confiscations.

Researchers have discovered a number of key processes by which people learn or unlearn patterns of behaviour. These include:

Acquisition of a behaviour

New behaviours are often learned by one of two main processes. First, 'continuous reinforcement', as when a person learning a new skill such as driving is commended for each successful demonstration of a specific component skill, such as changing gear; or when a toddler being toilet trained is praised initially each time he or she simply sits on the potty. Second, 'intermittent reinforcement', or 'occasional reward' as when the learner-driver or toddler, having acquired the basics of the new skill, is commended only now and again for carrying it out effectively. This occasional reward often maintains a behaviour, or keeps it going, for very long periods. Consider the typical effect of even a very occasional win upon the lottery!

Effects of different timings of reward or penalty

Abundant evidence shows that if one is deliberately intending to reward or penalize a behaviour, the feedback or consequence should occur as soon as possible after that behaviour, and should be linked as explicitly as possible with that behaviour. So, children learning to read need *immediate and specific* approving feedback for their successes from the teacher, and children who are cheeky to their mothers need *immediate and specific* reprimands or sanctions – *not* 'Wait until your father gets home!'. It follows that for maximum deterrence offenders ideally receive *immediate and specific* sanctions for their offences – *not* court hearings delayed by many months.

Shaping a behaviour

This refers to the gradual moulding of a specified pattern of behaviour from a starting point towards a level of skill which has been identified beforehand. For example, a child who is taught to play the piano can be thought of as having had her piano playing skills 'shaped' by her teacher. Similarly, a child with ADHD can be thought of as having her ability to complete a jigsaw 'shaped' by carefully timed positive feedback by the teacher.

Generalization of a behaviour

It is well established that some behaviours (though by no means all) carry over from one setting into another. For example, childhood patterns of shyness, friendliness, dominance or submissiveness tend to carry over into adult life. A specific example of generalization is that of a little girl who had a balloon burst in her face, frightening her very much; she subsequently showed fearful behaviour not only at the sight of a balloon, but also at the sight of any round object, such as a football. Moreover, she could not go to other children's houses until it had been established that no balloons or balls would be within sight. Her original fear had generalized to other objects similar to the original frightening one and to other situations similar to the original one.

Desensitization

If a person, child or adult has become afraid of a certain situation, such as being away from home, then gradually increasing exposure to that frightening situation in the context of a calm and supportive relationship leads to their gradually becoming less sensitive to what has frightened them. The little child frightened by the bursting balloon was not hurried into playing with balloons again. Her wise mother began by looking with her at story books where first, for a week or two, balls and, later, balloons were included in the illustrations. After another week she arranged for small balls and uninflated balloons to be included in the play box at playgroup, but without anyone paying much attention to them. Then, over a month or two, slightly larger balls were introduced and so on. This process of desensitization was not rushed; a gradual approach is essential in such circumstances.

Extinction of a behaviour

Many behaviours, particularly newly acquired ones, die away if they are not rewarded in some way. For example, volunteers whose contributions are never appreciated tend to give up volunteering; teenagers who make an effort to help in the house but who receive no thanks tend to abandon their efforts; and parents newly guided by practitioners towards commending their children rather than criticizing them tend, unless there is regular encouragement, to slip back into former habits of being critical.

Learning by imitation/modelling

Bandura (1977) has highlighted the way in which children, and also adults, learn complex sequences of behaviour mainly by observing other people and imitating their actions and strategies. Sociologists have also highlighted the importance of imitation in their studies of the phenomenon of role modelling and the powerful influence that high-profile individuals can have over children and young people. Studies of the learning of gender roles and patterns, not only of anti- but also of pro-social behaviour, have had a profound influence on our understanding of this phenomenon (Mussen and Eisenberg-Berg, 1977).

Realizing the importance of modelling has helped me to understand why a parent struggling to manage her child with behaviour difficulties finds it much easier to imitate the actions of a firm and confident model, such as a family aide, than to follow instructions from an occasional visitor, such as a health visitor or social worker.

Learning by cognitive processes

Early research on learning was carried out from a primarily behavioural perspective, but, as is evident from the examples given above, cognitive processes are almost invariably involved.

Cognitive theory comprises a large body of concepts about how human beings take in and process information. It thus focuses on individual patterns of perception, thinking and reasoning, belief and judgement, and the influences which affect these cognitions.

The studies of Piaget on the developmental changes which occur as children mature have been extremely influential. Piaget focused on the interaction between the child's naturally maturing abilities and his or her experiences in the environment; he saw children as actively seeking information in order to make sense of the world. His stage theory of children's maturing understanding in terms of the sensorimotor, the preoperational, the concrete operational and the formal operational stages is well known. He also went on to examine how the development of moral reasoning corresponds with the child's developing cognitive understanding; this work was taken further by Kohlberg (1973), who extended Piaget's work with children to include adolescence and adulthood.

It is generally agreed that while all children and adults do pass sequentially through stages of cognitive and moral development, they do not all reach the 'higher' stages; progress will depend on a range of variables, including intelligence, socioeconomic factors and cultural influences. Moreover, cognitions are highly idiosyncratic; we do not all perceive an event, or attribute meaning to an event, in similar ways:

we make subjective interpretations, arrive at private conclusions and develop personal beliefs.

Practitioners working with families which have children with behaviour difficulties often find that parents have arrived at a belief about the origins of their child's problems. It can be extremely illuminating to help parents and family members express these beliefs. Those I have encountered include: 'It's bad blood... ', 'She [a 2-year-old] doesn't love me any more...', 'He is evil...','He's hyperactive ...' and 'It's his dad coming out in him...'. At this stage all I wish to do is to draw attention to the fact that parents have beliefs, about their children or themselves, which may actively block our attempts to help them to manage their children in more constructive and positive ways.

Convergence of two sets of concepts: cognitive-behavioural theory

During the middle decades of this century these two bodies of theory, that to do with learning and that to do with cognition, were on almost parallel tracks, with their proponents seldom encountering or influencing each other. Gradually, however, researchers such as Mischel (1973) brought the two bodies of theory and concepts closer together. This integrated form became known as 'social learning' theory.

Social learning theory acknowledged and emphasized the effects on learning of both environmental factors and individual cognitions. As the importance of cognitive factors has become increasingly recognized, so this integrated body of concepts has come to be called 'cognitive behavioural' theory. While each body of theory on its own yielded important ways of understanding people and helping them with their difficulties, the integrated cognitive-behavioural theory proved even more fruitful in terms of approaches and strategies. These are summarized below.

Approaches based primarily on cognitive theory

Cognitive psychologists such as Beck (1967, 1976) and Lazarus (1971) developed approaches which addressed people's self-defeating or unhelpful patterns of thinking and belief. Beck, working with people experiencing disabling depression and anxiety, was among the first to highlight the effect of the *thought processes* often typical of people with these disorders. He realized that they were in effect *rehearsing their difficulties*, rather than developing coping strategies for dealing with them. For example, one person might be repeatedly thinking, 'I'll never pass the driving test; I'm far too nervous', so plunging themselves into a vicious downward spiral of increasing anxiety and ineffectiveness. Another might be constantly reminding herself of a harsh comment made by a teacher many years before, in effect saying, 'You'll never amount to anything... You're far too lazy'. Such rehearsal of negative comments or beliefs can readily become self-fulfilling prophecies. So, the idea of directly addressing a person's patterns of thinking is immediately relevant to addressing the cognitions of parents about their children.

In a number of important books Beck (1967, 1976) and his collaborators (Beck *et al.*, 1979) set out principles which took account of the effects of learning theory, but went beyond them by helping distressed and troubled people to become aware of their own thought patterns and examine their foundations, validity and effects. In anxious people, for example, they highlighted the cognitive characteristics shown in Table 3.3.

Formulating difficulties in this way gives appropriately trained practitioners the means of helping people first to become aware of, then to question, their unhelpful thoughts and assumptions, and finally to plan and practise more effective coping strategies, both cognitive and practical, for dealing with their difficulties in living. As Beck *et al.* (1979) noted:

> Anxious patients in the simplest terms believe, 'Something bad is going to happen that I won't be able to handle.' The cognitive therapist uses three basic strategies or questions to help the patient

---

Table 3.3: Cognitive difficulties (Beck, 1976)

---

1   *Sensory – perceptual*
        Mind: hazy, foggy, dazed
        Feelings of unreality
        Self-consciousness
        Hypervigilant

2   *Thinking difficulties*
        Can't recall important things
        Confused
        Unable to control thinking
        Difficulty in concentrating and reasoning
        Blocking

3   *Conceptual*
        Cognitive distortions
        Fear of losing control
        Fear of not being able to cope
        Fear of negative evaluations
        Frightening visual images
        Repetitive frightening thoughts

---

restructure this thinking. Nearly all of the cognitive therapist's questions can be broken down to one of these questions:

1 'What's the evidence?'
2 'What's another way of looking at the situation?'
3 'So what if it happens?

A wide range of further cognitive approaches is also available: see Table 3.4.

In all the above examples, an attempt is made to help the person in two ways: making them aware of inaccurate or unhelpful thinking patterns so that their impact can be offset by more accurate information; and replacing undermining tendencies to 'rehearse the problem' by more constructive patterns of thinking. These cognitively based processes are unquestionably powerful, as numerous studies have shown (Beck *et al.*, 1985), but this approach can be enhanced even more by incorporating aspects of learning theory, so that a further array of strategies become available (see Table 3.5).

'Solution-focused therapy' (George *et al.*, 1990), familiar to many social workers, seems to have much in common with problem-solving approaches. It is very encouraging that researchers and practitioners working in different contexts have arrived at a common model of cognitive-behavioural practice. Solution-focused approaches will be explored more fully in Chapter 11.

In *all* this work it is essential that there be a strong and supportive 'therapeutic alliance' between practitioner and client; in other words, that the 'core conditions', of empathy, genuineness, warmth and unconditional positive regard obtain. These conditions are the ones summarized by Truax and Carkhuff (1967) in their seminal book *Towards Effective Counselling and Psychotherapy*. It is also the same requirement as described in *Child Protection: Messages from Research* (Department of Health, 1995) which stressed that without consistent, empathic support for the families concerned, efforts to help them to protect children were futile. With this foundation, *which offers people the assurance of safety and respect*, the worker can draw upon a range of approaches for practice from cognitive-behavioural theory. These are *not* manipulatively imposed upon people; on the contrary, the principles can be openly explained and clarified and the ways to make best use of them can be explored and negotiated by all concerned.

Using cognitive-behavioural theory to help families

We saw above (page 58) that much behaviour is *learned*, both by imitation or modelling and in accordance with different contingencies of

Table 3.4: A repertoire of cognitive strategies

Strategy	Definition, function or example
1 *Putting circumstances in a wider context*	Helping people understand that they may be blaming themselves for circumstances beyond their control. For example, helping someone understand that their inability to find a job is attributable to a local economic downturn, not to personal limitations.
2 *Providing a political perspective*	Alerting people to their political rights. For example, helping a black person against whom there is clear evidence of discrimination to decide how to take action about it.
3 *Supportive rational questioning*	Countering irrational beliefs about oneself or other people. For example, pinpointing the source of and questioning a learned but long-held view – 'My teacher was right; I am a hopeless case ...'
4 *Monitoring one's self-talk*	Detecting patterns of negative thinking, self put-downs ('I'll never cope with it') and self-reproach ('How could I have been so stupid?')
5 *Learning positive self-talk*	Countering destructive thoughts or beliefs and controlling panicky feelings. For example, helping someone consciously practise constructive thinking, 'I've coped before and I'll probably cope again', and 'What I did was not stupid; it seemed the right thing to do at the time'.
6 *Testing the evidence*	Examine the validity of one's views or belief by arranging a 'reality check'. For example, helping someone who undervalues herself to test whether her application to college is rejected.
7 *Practising helpful imagery*	Countering fears about competence; for example, imagining oneself dealing calmly with a critical service-user.

Table 3.5: Strategies arising from integrated cognitive-behavioural theory

Strategy	Definition, function or example
1 *Goal-setting*	Breaking down overwhelming tasks into small, attainable goals. For example, a father seeking to control his drinking patterns may be urged to take 'one day at a time' and to break whole days into very brief intervals: a morning, an afternoon and an evening. In this way, a small achievement acts to reinforce the self-control which came before it, and this in turn motivates the person to accomplish the next task. There is increasing agreement that, for maximum effectiveness, goals should be:
	S Specific M Measurable A Attainable R Realistic T Time-limited
2 *Problem solving*	The following steps have repeatedly been found helpful (Spivack *et al.*, 1976):
	• Defining the problem very precisely • Brainstorming a wide range of responses • Exploring each possible solution • Selecting the best solution • Implementing that solution

reward and sanction. This understanding is extremely important: it provides us with the means of analysing, for example, undesirable patterns of children's behaviour to see if they are being maintained by the rewards which are, often unwittingly, being provided by parents or caregivers; alternatively, we can see whether desired patterns of behaviour, which occur only occasionally, are fading away because, unintentionally, parents are punishing them or failing to reward them.

Behaviour analysis

Parents typically make very general complaints about their children: 'Steven is lazy'; 'No one can do anything with Joanne'; 'John's been nothing but trouble since he was born'; 'Sanjay is naughty'. It is sometimes startling for them to be asked, 'Exactly what does Steven/Joanne/John/Sanjay *do* which upsets you so?' They usually find it very difficult to specify exactly what their child *does*, but this is a necessity in using this body of theory. We need to know precisely which *behaviours* the child displays that so upset his parents, his brothers and sisters, his teachers and sometimes himself. With help, parents can eventually work out a 'problem profile' for their child. It may be that he or she:

- Shows aggressiveness: hits other children or parents
- Bites other children or adults
- Tips over furniture
- Is rude to his or her teachers
- Runs about in the classroom
- Refuses to do what parents ask
- Throws things: food, ornaments, kitchen items
- Does not settle to anything for more than a few minutes: short attention span
- Interrupts his or her parent(s).
- Swears at mother or visitors to the house
- Spits at family members

I also ask them if they can identify positive or pleasing aspects of their child's behaviour, aspects that they would like to see more of, and this is sometimes even more difficult for them. Perhaps they can suggest two or three things: Jason's good behaviour when he is alone; Dean's readiness to come for a cuddle; or that Wendy, a terror while awake, sleeps all night through. Sometimes, very sadly, there is nothing that a parent can think of that they like about their child; they have already written him or her off at the age of three and 'can't wait until he goes to school'. Eventually, however, we are usually able to develop a 'positive profile', which may include an acknowledgement that the child:

- Occasionally carries out a request
- Finds things which are lost
- Feeds the dog reliably
- Eats well

This way of analysing what often seems to the affected family to be a blur of continuous misbehaviour by distinguishing its component behaviours can be mystifying to parents, but gradually they come to see the advantages of identifying specific behaviours and addressing them separately. Table 3.6 clarifies the relationship between rewards and penalties even further.

Assessment

A new instrument, the *Strengths and Difficulties Questionnaire* (SDQ), has been published by Dr Robert Goodman (1997) and he has gener-

Table 3.6: Behaviours, consequences and their probable outcomes (Herbert, 1993)

Desirable behaviour + reward	→	More desirable behaviour
Desirable behaviour + no reward	→	Less desirable behaviour
Undesirable behaviour + reward	→	More undesirable behaviour
Undesirable behaviour + no reward	→	Less undesirable behaviour

ously given permission for it to be reprinted as Appendix 5.3 to this book. This is applicable to children from 4 to 16, and can be used by parents or teachers to specify both a child's problem and positive behaviours. Further versions are available from Dr Goodman, including one which can be completed by the young person concerned, and versions in languages other than English. The particular value of such validated questionnaires is that they can be used, if appropriate, as measures before and after a programme of intervention, and indeed at follow-up some months or years later, as a way of testing whether there have been any long-lasting effects of training the parents or caregivers to manage the child's difficulties.

In my own research I asked parents to complete a scale very similar to the SDQ on two occasions, once before and once after my weekly contact with them. I also asked them to collect two sets of behaviour counts: the first showed, on a day-by-day basis, the number of instances of one specific negative behaviour, such as a refusal to follow instructions or requests, while the second, recorded eight weeks later, showed the instances of one specific positive behaviour: carrying out requests (see Table 3.7). The first week's records provided a 'baseline' or benchmark against which to measure subsequent change: a means of judging over the weeks that followed whether behaviour was changing in the desired direction – negative forms of the behaviour decreasing and positive ones increasing. (See Figure 3.1.)

Table 3.7 shows how practitioners can help parents identify both negative and positive forms of a range of behaviours, helping them to recognize and attend to the occasional positive behaviour, so rewarding it, in the expectation that mildly penalizing or ignoring the negative form will lead to its reduction.

Analysing the sequence: Antecedents–Behaviour–Consequence

The relationship between a behaviour and the events in the environment associated with it is called a *contingency*. It includes three com-

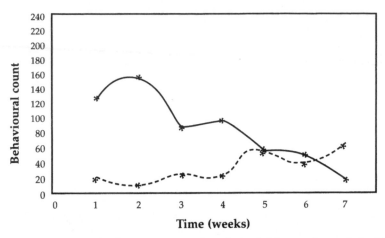

Figure 3.1. Plot of behaviour counts for a little child over the period of this study

Table 3.7: Positive and negative forms of selected specific behaviours

Negative form of behaviour	Positive form of behaviour
Refusal/reluctance to follow requests or instructions (within one minute)	Follows requests or instructions (within one minute)
Aggressiveness; hits or bites others	Kind behaviour; shares/lends toys
Comes downstairs after being put to bed	Settles after being put to bed
Refuses to eat/throwing food	Eats a small amount
Disrupts other children's activities	Plays quietly with other children
Speaks rudely to or shouts at parents	Speaks calmly and quietly to parents

ponents: the behaviour itself, antecedent events, both distant and immediate, and consequent events. It is easy to remember these important terms by referring to them as the A–B–C sequence, standing for Antecedents, Behaviour and Consequences. The term Activator is sometimes clearer to use than Antecedent, and is useful as it has connotations of being a cue or a trigger to behaviour. Since practice using principles of cognitive-behavioural theory involves analysing how behaviour may be affected by its antecedents, by its consequences, or by both together, let us consider some examples of each situation shown in Table 3.8.

Table 3.8: Analysis of behaviour, with a focus upon antecedents

Antecedent	Behaviour	Consequence
1. A family centre worker brings a plate of toast to the table.	The child reaches eagerly for the toast.	The mother frowns
The mother says, 'He doesn't like toast.'	The child draws back his hand.	He throws the toast on the floor.
2. The teacher greets the new child on her second day at school.	The child looks at the toys with interest.	
Granny says 'He didn't want to come.'	The child stops and clings to Granny.	He bursts into tears and screams to be taken home.

You will see that in both the examples in Table 3.8, the child's undesirable behaviour followed directly from what went before, the Antecedent. In effect, the child was cued to behave in the undesirable way. This is no one's fault, or at least there was no intention to cue the child in this way, so there is no point in blaming people for being unaware of something so subtle. It is, however, how learning takes place, so it is helpful if parents and other people who look after children can be brought to see that sometimes we all unintentionally *teach children to behave in undesirable ways* (see Table 3.9).

In all these examples the children have learned from the consequences of their behaviour that it they persist long enough and

Table 3.9: Analysis of behaviour, with a focus upon consequences

Antecedent	Behaviour	Consequence
1. Dad told Danny to put the TV off.	He kept putting it on.	Eventually it was left on to give people a bit of peace.
2. Grandma told Jane to wear her blue jersey	Jane said she wanted to wear her new red one.	Eventually Grandma gave way, so as not to seem horrid
3. Paul was out with Mum. He demanded an ice-cream. Mum refused.	He began to scream, 'I want one, you pig!'	Mum gave way, so that people wouldn't stare at her.

unpleasantly enough in demanding their own way, the adults will eventually give in! We may not be aware of what we are teaching children when we give in to their threats or their rudeness, *but we are ourselves teaching them, just as if we told them in a classroom 'It is right to be rude and threatening to people'.*

A range of strategies for altering consequences or antecedents

If a child is old enough to understand, the intention to use the approaches shown in Table 3.10 should be explained to the child. He or she can then understand what is happening when the parents or teacher begins to do as they said they would.

Using brief withdrawal of attention as an effective sanction

There is, at the time of writing, a national debate about smacking as a form of punishment. It is satisfying to be able to confirm that smacking is both undesirable and ineffective (Leach, 1999). A *far* more effective penalty for pre-school and primary children, where it is clear that the child's behaviour is unacceptable, is to ignore the child by placing them in a situation where they are not receiving and cannot receive any rewarding attention. This is called placing them in 'Time Out', although the term 'Calm-Down Time' is increasingly favoured as explaining more clearly what is meant to happen during the period of being ignored. Webster-Stratton and Herbert (1994) have distinguished three forms of Time Out, of increasing effectiveness (see Table 3.11). As stated above, this sanction should follow immediately after the misbehaviour, or as soon as possible thereafter.

Young children can be placed on a cushion or chair in the corner of the room; older children can be placed in a safe hallway. I myself recall being made to stand in the corner after some small misdemeanour; I was mystified and bored. I don't recall having it explained to me why I was being made to stand in the corner, or what I should do to avoid this boredom on another occasion. It is now known that such an explanation helps a child understand what is happening; and is now built into this work at the Planning stage of the ASPIRE process. Other strategies which work to the same ends and which have been reported as effective to me during training sessions include those shown in Table 3.12.

The principles for using Time Out are shown in Table 3.13.

Table 3.10: Key cognitive-behavioural strategies for responding to children's behaviour

1 Positively reinforcing/rewarding a desirable behaviour
Identifying and praising or commending *immediately it occurs* a specific pattern of behaviour that you wish to happen again; for example, a kind action on the part of a child.

2 Planned ignoring of an undesirable behaviour
Deliberately paying no attention to a behaviour that you wish to discourage; for example, demanding or interrupting behaviour.

3 Rewarding a behaviour opposite to that which you wish to discourage
For example, deliberately providing an opportunity for an aggressive child to show kindness to another child, and then commending him for doing so.

4 'When... then...'
A variant of 1. The reward is offered, but it is dependent upon a specific behaviour having been carried out. 'When you have put your bike away, then we can have tea.'

5 Time Out – sometimes called 'calm-down time'
This is the last resort. The child has to spend 'Time Out' from negative reinforcement – that is, from the attention that often reinforces misbehaviour. The place used for Time Out must be completely safe, but completely dull. See Tables 3.12 and 3.13 below.

Table 3.11: Graded forms of Time Out (In Webster-Stratton, C. and Herbert, M. (1994) *Troubled Families – Problem Children*. Copyright John Wiley and Sons Limited. Reproduced with permission.

Activity Time Out
The child is simply barred from joining in an enjoyable activity but still allowed to observe it – for example, having misbehaved s/he is made to sit out of a game.

Room Time Out
The child is removed from an enjoyable activity, is not allowed to observe this, but is not totally isolated – for example, having misbehaved, he/she is seated at the far end of the sitting room or a classroom.

Exclusion Time Out
The child is briefly isolated in a situation away from the rewarding circumstances – e.g. in a hall way or empty room (unlocked). The place must be safe, dull and boring. There must be nothing to do: no toys, no TV, no jobs. If necessary an adult stays with the child, but pays him or her absolutely no attention.

Table 3.12: Strategies for ignoring a child

1 Holding a child who struggles against being placed in Time Out *very* firmly by the hand or wrist so that he cannot run off but giving 'No speech; no eye contact'. The time period is two to three minutes. This is said to be effective for a young but obstreperous child in understaffed classrooms!
2 Other children in a family or small class are asked actively to ignore the misbehaving child for the Time Out interval each time he misbehaves.
3 The parent herself leaves the child without an audience and goes to the bathroom for the Time Out interval – having checked the room for safety.

Table 3.13: Guidelines for using Time Out/Calm Down

1 If you decide to use Time Out, give one warning only before carrying it out.

2 Never threaten to use Time Out and then fail to follow through.

3 You *must* be consistent. The child cannot learn the rules about how you want him or her to behave unless you are consistent.

4 Never use a frightening place for Time Out, but do use a place that is safe, unrewarding and dull: the foot of the stairs, standing or sitting in a corner facing the wall, an empty room, a hallway.

5 Always check for safety.

6 N*ever* lock a child in a room. Just keep returning him or her to the Time Out place, insisting that the child stays, until the penny drops with the child that you really mean it.

7 A useful rule of thumb for how long that a child should remain in time out is shown below:
   a 2-year-old remains 2 minutes on each occasion
   a 3-year-old remains 3 minutes on each occasion
   a 4–9-year-old remains 4 minutes on each occasion
   a 10-year-old remains 10 minutes on each occasion, and so on

8 There is no point in making the Time Out interval very long. We are trying to help the child learn a new association between misbehaving and the inevitability of the sanction. He will learn this association best from having every instance of misbehaviour followed consistently by a Time Out period.

9 If the child who has been placed in Time Out repeats the misbehaviour on emerging he goes straight back into Time Out/Calm Down. If need be, repeat this frequently, so a new association is learned as soon as possible.

10 Whoever puts the child in Time Out/Calm Down takes him or her out.

11 Keep a simple record of how often you have had to use Time Out/Calm Down day by day. This will show if instances of the misbehaviour are increasing or reducing.

12 *Things may get worse before they get better.* This is important. Having 'ruled the roost' for so long, the child will work hard and misbehave all the more to keep his dominant and controlling position. If you persist, however, the message will eventually be learned: *you* are in charge now.

Further use of the principles

Many strategies for practice have been developed from cognitive-behavioural principles. Table 3.14 draws on the work of Martin and Pear (1992) in clarifying and defining approaches and also includes others which I have found helpful in my own research.

Table 3.14: Cognitive-behavioural procedures (after Martin and Pear, 1992)

Principle	Example
1 Taking account of principles of classical conditioning	A tiny child suddenly screams as her mother approaches the cheese counter in the supermarket. Extensive attempts to understand the cause identify the link between the assistant's white coat and the white coat of the doctor who injected her at a recent hospital admission.
2 Getting a behaviour to occur more often with positive reinforcement or reward	Danny, who hates reading after his clever brother called him a 'dumbo', is helped by a sensitive classroom aide to read a few sentences each day. She always quietly commends his efforts; she never criticizes him, but she does gently correct errors. He soon begins to choose reading as an activity.
3 Encouraging perseverance through intermittent reinforcement (occasional reward)	Jason, who has learning disabilities, has gained the skill of dressing himself. He still prefers his mother to dress him, but she remembers to give him occasional warm encouragement for his achievement. Jason maintains his skill and develops it .

Table 3.14: (continued)

4	Rewarding undesirable behaviour through occasional reward (inconsistency)	Carl is told he can't go to the late-night party. He shouts and complains and nags and nags. Eventually, his mum, worn down by his nagging, gives in. From then on, Carl nags and grumbles about everything he is told he can't do in the hope of getting his own way again.
5	Getting a behaviour to occur less often by avoiding rewarding it so that it extinguishes	Amanda, aged 5, interrupts and makes demands whenever her mother is on the phone. Her mother turns her back on her and completely ignores her. Amanda stops interrupting in less than a week.
6	Getting a behaviour to occur less often by actively penalizing it	Wendy keeps getting down from her seat at meal times. Her mother, having tried for several days to get Wendy to eat by following her round with a bowl, feeding her with spoonfuls, now warns her little girl that if she gets down her plate will be removed and not replaced. Within three days, Wendy is staying at the table and finishing her meals promptly.
7	Getting a behaviour to occur less often by 'response cost'	Rosemary is exasperated by the way in which her children leave their possessions all over the house. They receive weekly pocket-money, so she institutes a system of fines. Any clothes, sportsgear or other possessions which are left about are confiscated. It

Table 3.14: (continued)

		10 pence to recover each item. The money is given to Oxfam.
8	Using modelling and rehearsal to affect behaviour	Samantha's friends keep trying to make her drink more than she wants to. Her school counsellor and she work out by role-play how she can resist this pressure. They rehearse what might happen, what she wants to say and whom she might use as an example to follow in resisting pressure to drink.
9	Helping an individual child or young person to develop self-discipline	James, 12, wants a computer. His mum and dad encourage him, but say they cannot afford to buy it for him; he will have to save up for it. James does so, by doing household chores for which he is paid a fair rate.
10	Helping children and parents 'take charge of their own patterns of thinking	Maxine, aged 18 and with two children under 3, thinks of herself as 'a bad mother'. She is helped to realize how well she has cared for her children, whom she cuddles and who love to sit on her lap – even if sometimes their clothes are grubby and have seen better days. She is helped to remind herself daily, 'I am a *good* mother. My children are happy and healthy. *I* have achieved this'.

Table 3.14: (continued)

11	Using problem-solving (Spivack *et al.*, 1976)	1. Pinpoint the problem.
		2. Gather all the relevant facts about the problem.
		3. Formulate the difficulty as a problem to be solved.
		4 Generate potential solutions by means of a 'brainstorm'. Any ideas may be proposed. Criticism is deliberately withheld.
		5. Examine the potential consequences of each solution. Agree on the best strategy.
		6. Plan how to implement the strategy.
		7. Put the plan into action.
		8. Review and evaluate the effectiveness of the plan. Adapt it as necessary.

Summary of some key principles of cognitive-behavioural theory

The following list shows well tested principles arising from this body of theory:

Principle 1	A behaviour which is rewarded is more likely to be repeated.
Principle 2	A behaviour which is penalized is less likely to be repeated.
Principle 3	A behaviour which is consistently ignored or penalized is likely to extinguish.
Principle 4	A behaviour which has been established, then ignored but is then rewarded again, is likely to start all over again.
Principle 5	A behaviour may be learned because it occurs in association with another behaviour.
Principle 6	A behaviour may be learned by imitating another's behaviour.
Principle 7	A behaviour may be acquired by thinking it through and practising it beforehand.

Reference will be made to these principles in later parts of this book.

Ethical issues

To some, the introduction and recommendation of the principles set out in this chapter will cause profound disquiet. To them, the application of principles of systematic reward and penalty to vulnerable young children sounds like a crude process of manipulation. When one adds to these moral objections the evidence of gross abuse of behavioural principles in a number of scandals in Britain, one may ask how the use of behavioural concepts can be tolerated at all, let alone taught in universities and colleges.

To these objections I would offer the following responses:

1 Yes, the principles can be and have been abused. It is, therefore, essential for practitioners who are persuaded by research that cognitive-behavioural methods have much to offer in the relief of human suffering to devise ethical codes which impose high standards of practice. Such a code has been devised by the British Association for Behavioural and Cognitive Psychotherapy, and is set out as Appendix 3.1.
2 These principles are applied whether one is aware of, and approves of, them or not. Every teacher who commends or fails to commend a child's efforts to learn to read, every driving instructor who commends or fails to commend the learner's efforts to pick up a new skill is employing these same principles. It is time that teachers and instructors understood better some fundamental principles of giving feedback to their pupils and students.
3 As set out in the BABCP Code, the goals of the work should be made clear to everyone involved – and where possible negotiated with them. This means that the processes can and should be used as transparently as possible; people actively collaborating in the work both of identifying specific goals and working with practitioners towards achieving them.

All readers of this book who venture to employ some behavioural principles are asked to adhere to the code throughout their work.

Summary points

❑ In order to grapple with the complexity of the human condition, social scientists have developed many ways of thinking about it. One way is to think of human beings as part of other systems; a second is to take a number of perspectives on the human being, that is, to think of them in different ways: as biological phenomena, with innate features; as creatures with powerful feelings, both conscious and unconscious; as beings who learn from their environments and from what happens to them; as beings who think, make judgements and arrive at opinions and beliefs; as beings who have the potential for growth and development.

❐ Research shows that we respond positively to being treated with unconditional respect, warmth and empathy by people whom we feel to be sincere and genuine.

❐ Research has identified four main ways of learning: by classical conditioning, by operant conditioning, by the observation of others, and by cognitive or intellectual processes.

❐ Within operant conditioning, a number of key processes have been identified including: positive reinforcement or reward, penalty, the effects of different timings of rewards and penalties, generalization of a behaviour, desensitization, and extinction of a behaviour.

❐ Cognitive processes are increasingly recognized as of great importance, and many workers use a repertoire of cognitive strategies to help family members they work with. These strategies include: exploring the evidence for a viewpoint, learning to talk positively to oneself, testing the evidence for a belief and practising helpful imagery.

❐ Integrated cognitive-behavioural approaches include: goal setting, problem solving and solution-focused work.

❐ Research on the cognitive-behavioural approach has established the usefulness of behaviour analysis, record keeping of negative and positive behaviours and the application of a repertoire of cognitive-behavioural skills to help families promote positive behaviours and discourage negative ones.

4

Engaging with families:
issues relevant to all disciplines

It is difficult enough for one agency, such as a voluntary organization, to deal with one family and to engage its members in collaborative plans to help children: when several agencies are involved the task is extremely complex. From the point of view of the family, it is often confusing and frustrating to cope with practitioners from more than one agency. Taking the family's point of view first, then, let us consider some of the difficulties which confront them in trying to bring up their children.

Children and parents coping with stress and disadvantage

Many troubled children come from deeply disadvantaged back-grounds. We saw in Chapter 1 that Blanz *et al.* (1991) in Germany, had found a clear association between high scores on Rutter's scale of social adversity and emotional and behavioural difficulties in the children. Of children excluded from school in England and Wales, it has been noted by Gardiner (1996) that at that time 25.7 per cent were from minority groups and that about two-thirds of the children excluded were in the care of the local authority. Thus, those children who have experienced multiple stressors are those who show greatest evidence of disturbance. There is no mystery here.

Reaching and engaging with these children and their parents poses a huge challenge to practitioners. Many children have had multiple changes of caregivers, for, as a recent study by Barnardo's found:

> of 145 children in seven projects in Scotland [we] found that they averaged 3.7 moves each while being looked after by local authorities. Thirty one of them had experienced more than five moves.
>
> (Warren, 1997)

The children have *learned* not to trust, to be suspicious of adults and their strategies. In terms of the fight–flight–freeze response, some have learned to challenge and confront those who seem to threaten them;

others have learned to withdraw from threatening situations. As a youngster said to a student on placement who tried to extend the hand of friendship to him, 'Why should I talk to you? You'll only tell other care staff what I say – and you'll be gone in two months anyway.'

To reach and engage with their parents is no less demanding. Many will have had horrifying experiences as children, of abuse – physical, sexual or emotional and sometimes of all three – and also of neglect. Some children will be survivors of trauma from natural disasters or wars. A common characteristic of all such traumatized individuals is that they experience continuing high levels of stress; they are all, therefore, particularly vulnerable to further stress. This vulnerability may make them particularly likely to use smoking, drinking or drugs as a means of coping with tension or loneliness. Many have become parents at a very young age, sometimes in the belief that the intimacy of the sexual relationship will provide long-term security. They are likely to be very suspicious of people in authority, not least because of the fear that their children, the one source of close relationships which may be left to them, will be removed from their care.

Engaging with parents

Parents whose children have emotional and/or behavioural difficulties need opportunities to pour out the feelings of frustration, rejection and despair which these difficulties arouse in them. As Webster-Stratton and Herbert (1994) have vividly described, it is not only their child's behaviour which has caused them heartache and embarrassment but also the response of family and friends. The challenge is all the greater if, as is often the case, the parents of children with emotional and behavioural problems see the difficulty as located *in* the child. It is not surprising that they do so: if a child is throwing him- or herself about, is screaming at visitors to the house or, conversely, is very withdrawn and reluctant to enter into any conversation, it is utterly natural to see the child as being, or having, a problem. The interactional origin of many difficulties is not generally understood – and it will be a long time before it is.

As in the field of counselling, it is essential to spend considerable time building a supportive relationship or therapeutic alliance with the family members concerned. This is likely to be composed of the key therapeutic ingredients which Rogers (1951) and Maslow (1970) found to be so helpful and productive. They are reiterated in Table 4.1 because of their great importance.

It is deeply helpful to our work if we are show respect, genuineness, empathy and warmth to the families we work with, and if there is real concern for the well-being of all family members. If, in addition, we set aside time for meetings with individual family members and allow

Table 4.1: Core therapeutic elements of counselling (Rogers, 1951; Truax and Carkhuff, 1967)

1 *Respect*: recognizing the dignity and worth of the person concerned
2 *Genuineness*: being oneself, not acting a part
3 *Empathy*: showing an ability accurately to enter into the feelings of the person
4 *Warmth*: showing friendliness and kindness to the person concerned

them to express feelings of anger, frustration, depression, guilt and despair, and harsh and critical statements about children, away from the children's hearing, then this can be extremely therapeutic. The early stages of work, in particular, must not be rushed. Recently, a health visitor told me that it had taken her five visits to a family, visits during which the mother had voiced a litany of complaints, fears, resentments and despair about her child, and during which the health visitor had listened in a supportive and non-judgemental way, before she judged it possible to move on and to begin to draw the mother into a shared assessment of the child's difficulties. Such time as this is not always available, but it may be a prerequisite of progress.

In some families the level of the parent's depression is so great that it is fruitless to attempt any kind of assessment until this depression is addressed. Multidisciplinary work should make it possible for practitioners to gain access to such scales as the Beck Depression Inventory, the Edinburgh Post-Natal Depression Scale and the Hospital Anxiety and Depression Scale. In my own work I asked parents, mainly mothers, to complete the Beck Depression Inventory and found that eleven of the twenty-three participants had scores equal to or more than 15, the criterion for clinical depression with this Inventory. Empowering them by giving support and by teaching them skills of managing their children's behaviour was successful to the extent that at post-intervention only two mothers had scores above 15 (Sutton, 1995).

Another strategy is to attempt to raise the mother's morale by raising her self-esteem as a separate task before embarking upon any focused work in parenting. While I did not do this in my own work, since it was a research study and so required a similar approach to all mothers, I recommend to other practitioners that they offer parents the option of receiving some individualized counselling and support before embarking on a demanding course of work with their child. The usefulness of this two-staged approach should be evaluated in a rigorously controlled study.

In my own work I encountered many families who were at their wits' end about their child. One of them said, 'I'll swing for him...', another said, 'I was on the point of ringing social services and saying, "Take him..."', while a third reported, 'I've leathered him fifteen times, and it makes not a bit of difference.' These families were desperate to know what to do to manage their child's behaviour. Simply listening empathically and in a non-judgemental way laid down the foundations of our work together (Sutton, 1992).

Support for fathers

If it is difficult for mothers to seek support in managing their children, it is even harder for fathers. The role of the father in many communities is typically that of the disciplinarian, and if the strategy of administering discipline, be it verbal or physical, is unsuccessful – in that the child still fails to conform – then the tendency of the father seems to be to administer ever harsher and harsher discipline. Any approach which suggests an alternative strategy is likely to seem ridiculously weak, and completely unacceptable to parents who have themselves been brought up by means of strict discipline. In fact, suggesting a move to a strategy of managing children based upon praise and encouragement is likely to be ridiculed from the start.

I found in my own work that only two fathers attended the group which I arranged, and then only the two earliest sessions. I had believed that since the group was held at a university, its credibility was enhanced, but, despite my best efforts to make them welcome, they did not return for the subsequent sessions. One father, who had been reluctant for his wife to attend, continued actively to discourage her from attending and she eventually stopped coming before the end of the series of group meetings. I had already visited his wife at home, to explain the nature of the group and what it was trying to achieve, but he was not available to meet me. With hindsight, I should have made efforts to visit all families at times when both parents were available so that I could let them meet me at first hand and put questions to me.

Some practitioners, aware of the difficulties posed to many cultures by principles of Parenting Positively, have pointed out that the *setting* of meetings for fathers should be given much careful thought. Ever-mindful that the locations in which meetings are held carry connotations, workers have put forward several suggestions for venues. Perhaps the best is booking a room at the local school or community college, which has connotations of continuing education. Even colleges, however, have unpleasant associations for some parents because of difficult experiences at school. Other suggestions have been a GP's surgery, a health centre, a working men's club or a room booked in a pub.

It is particularly important for there to be male practitioners to support fathers, uncles or older brothers who are willing to attend groups or who are involved in one-to-one work. Whether we accept it or not, it is really difficult for men to attend groups or other activities where all the other participants, including the facilitator, are women. Many practitioners with whom I work agree that fathers need male health visitors, social workers and therapists. In this connection, I make a plea that 'Mums' and toddlers' groups' should be renamed 'Parents' and toddlers' groups'. We should do all we can to facilitate fathers in strengthening their roles in family and community life.

As we shall see there is increasing evidence of the importance of the role of fathers or another dependable male in bringing up children. The concept of the Highly Involved Male, that is, a male figure who actively takes a totally trustworthy, supportive and non-threatening interest in a child's developing confidence and performance at school, is likely to figure more and more centrally in policy documents and initiatives promoting the well-being of children and young people.

Support for families belonging to minority groups

If it is difficult for fathers to participate confidently in meetings which are primarily attended by women, how much more difficult must it be for parents from minority communities in Britain to participate in experiences primarily attended by the dominant community – white people. To people belonging to many minority ethnic groups, and to those belonging to other cultural minorities such as travellers, the prospect of talking about such intimate matters as how one brings up one's children is extremely distasteful – quite enough to discourage attendance at a group. It may be less daunting to receive a worker at home and to participate in a programme personally tailored to one's circumstances, but practitioners need to remember that while the visit of a doctor may be acceptable in many households, the concept of a practitioner offering guidance on a child's emotional or behavioural difficulties is likely to be even more threatening to minority ethnic families than it is to majority ones.

It is natural that people from minority groups should seek members of their own communities to act as facilitators of groups and visitors to their homes when highly sensitive matters such as the behaviour of their children is under discussion. There are still relatively few practitioners trained to help parents acquire the skills of managing emotional and behavioural difficulties, and even fewer who belong to minority groups. If we are to reduce the feelings of acute vulnerability and isolation which these parents feel when seeking help for their children, it is vital that we engage and support appropriately trained practitioners from a wide range of minority groups. This is anti-discriminatory practice in action.

It follows that training resources, posters and booklets should be translated into the parents' first language. Key principles may be illustrated by cartoons and line drawings in all resource materials, of course.

In this connection, the questions devised by Forehand and Kotchik (1996) which enable practitioners to gain information from potential participants about matters and attitudes which would affect their participation in a programme are very instructive. (see Table 4.2).

Comparable considerations must apply to supporting families where one or both of the parents suffers from a disability. Many buildings which might otherwise be suitable meeting-places for groups of parents are still not adapted to accommodate wheelchairs, or do not have audio loops built in for people with hearing impairments. Yet many parents with disabilities are interested in participating in groups, and may prefer this arrangement to home visits. Practitioners may need to prepare themselves, too, for working with hearing-impaired people who are accompanied by their signers, that is, trained workers who translate the teaching or training activity into sign language.

Engaging with parents obliged to participate: Parenting Orders

Magistrates in England and Wales can now make Parenting Orders, a ruling which requires parents of troublesome children and young people to receive counselling on how to manage their children. While parents can be invited to participate voluntarily, if they refuse an Order

---

Table 4.2: Questions to alert practitioners to parents' needs in a diversity of cultures (after Forehand and Kotchik, 1996)

---

1   How do you feel about going to a professional to help you deal with your children's difficulties?
2   What child behaviours do you most like in your child?
3   What child behaviours are most difficult for you as a parent?
4   What parenting behaviours work best in changing your child's behaviours?
5   What parenting behaviours do not work so well in changing your child's behaviours?
6   What might be some of the things that might keep you from taking part in a parenting programme?
7   What would make it more likely that you would take part in parent training?
8   Are there any really important things which we ought to bear in mind in trying to help you deal with your child?
9   How do family members feel about your seeking help in dealing with your child?
10 What is the best way to teach parenting skills to you?
11 What are the stresses that keep you from doing your best as a parent?
12 What are the most important characteristics that you would like in someone who helps you deal with your child's problems?

---

can be made. If they still refuse they can be fined. In my view, extensive preliminary work, achieved by visiting the young person's home and gaining the confidence of parents and youngster, is necessary; if this goes well, it may be possible to engage the parent(s) in a group.

The skills of the practitioner selected to work with these parents must be exceptional. He or she may have to gain the cooperation of people characterized by:

1 Active hostility to the agency representative, school, court, etc.
2 Active refusal to participate in discussion about the child concerned.
3 Blaming of the child or young person for all the difficulties.
4 Refusal to consider that anyone other than the child or young person is contributing to the difficulties which have arisen.
5 Resentment about the prospect of a more serious fine if parents do not attend.

While firmness is obviously vital, high levels of empathy, warmth and respect for the parents are the initial primary tools of the work.

Stages of becoming involved in parenting work

In this situation we have much to learn from psychological research into the processes and stages through which people pass as they gradually change counter-productive ways of behaving to more constructive and helpful ones. A major contribution has been made by Miller and Rollnick (1991) through their enquiry into these processes among addicts.

Miller and Rollnick explored these stages of change in great detail – both in people undergoing therapy and in those deciding to change some aspect of themselves, such as their patterns of substance abuse. They started with the approach of two earlier researchers, Prochaska and DiClemente (1982). Figure 4.1 shows the six stages of change distinguished by these two earlier writers.

Miller and Rollnick comment on the model in Figure 4.1 as follows:

> Before we describe the six specific stages of change, notice several aspects of this wheel. First, the fact that it is a wheel, a circle, reflects the reality that in almost any change process, it is normal for the person to go round the process several times before achieving a stable change.... This wheel also thereby recognizes relapse as a normal occurrence or stage of change

In the field of parent education, I consider it helpful to rename the stages, as shown in Table 4.3.

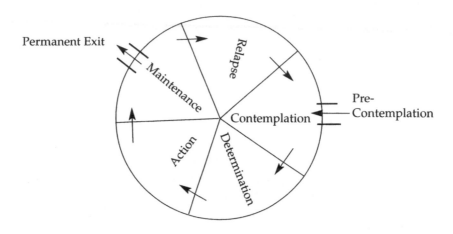

Figure 4.1. Prochaska and DiClemente's stages of change

Table 4.3: Stages of parent involvement in skills training (after Prochaska and DiClemente, 1982)

Stage	Characteristic situation or developments
1 *Pre-contemplation*:	The person(s) concerned are not even considering changing their parenting style.
2 *Contemplation*	The practitioner has gently brought them to the point of contemplating change; for example, by learning new skills for handling misbehaviour. However, they 'see-saw' back and forth about whether to commit themselves or not.
3 *Determination*	At least one parent makes a decision to commit him- or herself to the programme.
4 *Participation*	The parent(s) take part in the programme, which often lasts at least 8 weeks, during which much support is given.
5 *Continuation*	The parents continue to try to maintain the skills and approaches taught on the programme, but often lapse into old habits.
6 *Disillusion*	The parents become demoralized. They slip back into old habits of criticizing their child and into old habits of blaming him or her for the problems. They claim that the new ways of dealing with the child or young person 'don't work'.
7 *Re-motivation*	The parents are re-enthused and re-supported by the practitioner, who offers ongoing encouragement.

Table 4.4: Practitioner's tasks at various stages of work with parents (after Miller and Rollnick , 1991)

Client/parent stage	Practitioner's tasks in motivating parents
1 *Pre-contemplation*	Raise doubt. Increase the client's perception of the risks and problems associated with current behaviour. Confirm that without help the problems are not likely to improve, especially the more serious misbehaviours.
2 *Contemplation*	Tip the balance – evoke reasons for changing and risks of not changing; strengthen the parent's self-efficacy for changing current behaviour.
3 *Determination*	Help the parent to determine the best course of action to take in seeking to change his or her parenting style.
4 *Participation*	Help him or her to take steps towards change. Actively welcome and reward their involvement and efforts to cooperate with the programme.
5 *Continuation*	Help the parent(s) to identify and use strategies to prevent relapse. Warn them that lapses may occur and that they should not be too disappointed if they do.
6 *Disillusion*	The parents lose heart. They find dealing positively with their challenging youngster too demanding and that there are few encouraging signs of improvement. They say 'It doesn't work ...'. They say they can't carry on ...
7 *Re-motivation*	Help the parents to renew the processes of contemplation, determination and participation, without becoming stuck or demoralized. Remind them that you warned them that lapses might occur, and say, 'It's two steps forward and one step back'.

Miller and Rollnick then set out a summary of the stages of change and the associated tasks for the therapist or practitioner (see Table 4.4). I briefly discuss these stages below, and examine their implications for the parent educator:

1 *Pre-contemplation:* Just as people at this stage of their drinking or drug-taking difficulties are not even considering making any changes in their patterns of behaviour, as there is no recognition that they are desirable or necessary, so parents at this point are not even considering changing. Those concerned may have been referred by a court, or may be present as a requirement of a probation or other order. A spouse or partner may have made attendance at a group a requirement of continuing the relationship. Those who have experienced these or

similar pressures to attend are likely to be resentful, resistant to the practitioner and able to justify their current practice or life-style.

Parents who are in this stage are likely to be even more inaccessible than people with alcohol or drug problems. This may be for several reasons: First, they may see the problems as located exclusively *in* the child concerned, so they may say, 'It's a medical problem: he needs some treatment', or 'There's something wrong with her: she needs sorting out.' Second, they may feel that they have done their best to manage their difficult child and claim, 'Nothing's worked... We've tried everything we can; and now we've had enough'. Third, the parents of older youngsters may no longer see themselves as having any responsibility for or power over the young person concerned. All these parents may be very resistant indeed to the notion of involving them in strategies to change their parenting style. There is an element of threat implicit in even the suggestion of change: 'So you're blaming me for how he is, are you?'!

2   *Contemplation:* The person in this stage 'both considers change and rejects it', as Miller and Rollnick describe it. Given the opportunity for giving up heavy drinking, smoking or substance abuse, the person 'seesaws' between the pros and cons of changing their behaviour. This stage may continue for several weeks or even months. It is a mistake to try to pressurize the person during this period; he or she needs to arrive at their own decision to make a change or not. However, the worker can judiciously help the person concerned carry out a cost–benefit analysis of their current course of behaviour, for example, in the case of smoking, setting the expense and health costs against the short-term benefit of the reduction of tension brought by smoking.

The difficulties for the parent educator at this stage are even greater. Whereas the smoker knows that he or she alone is ultimately responsible for making the change or not, the parents of children with emotional and behavioural problems do not, typically, accept this responsibility. Indeed, as discussed above, they may not accept that they have any responsibility at all for their child's difficulties. They may well have come to the conclusion that he is either bad or, just possibly, mad, and in any case is now someone else's responsibility.

An approach which is likely to help to engage family members, be they attending voluntarily or obliged to participate, is to offer empathic support in the difficulties they are encountering with their child or young person. To acknowledge the depth of feeling, anger, shame, embarrassment or hopelessness which parents, however hostile on the surface, may be experiencing is to offer understanding and non-critical support. Indeed, we can almost take it for granted that these feelings do underlie the surface hostility – although we may need to give more time than we have at our disposal to enable it to be acknowledged. *Time is so very important: the building of trust cannot be rushed.*

Empathetic responses that skilled practitioners have found helpful include:

- All this has really distressed you...; am I right?
- Your son's being excluded from school is just the last straw, isn't it?
- Having to go to court about Chris has upset the whole family, hasn't it?
- It distresses you to see your child so unhappy, doesn't it?
- This situation makes you feel completely hopeless; have I got it right?

Using these tentative suggestions allows people to correct you if you are wrong, but also to feel able to express whatever emotions they *are* experiencing, without fear of criticism. Other phrases may be equally helpful.

Coping with objections: As contact proceeds, we make suggestions which the families we are working with may reject. It is helpful to have some considered responses to these objections. Table 4.5 shows some commonly offered important objections and a few responses which other practitioners have found useful. The responses of the practitioner at this stage are crucially important if the parents are eventually to be successfully involved. It would misguided to challenge their perceptions or their stance at this point. Even to do so unintentionally would be counter-productive as I once discovered to my cost.

I had arranged to meet in one room the parents of some children who were causing difficulties, while a nursery nurse looked after the children themselves in an adjoining room. I had already visited all the parents at home but had not met all the children, although they had been screened for organic or other difficulties by health professionals as a requirement for their entry into the study. I made the introductions and was starting on the programme for the first session when one of the mothers demanded, 'But when are you going to see the children?' 'Oh', I replied, confidently, 'I don't really need to see the children. It's you I want to work with...' The tension in the room became almost palpable. Out of inexperience and ignorance, I had implied that it was the fault of the parents that their children had difficulties. Fortunately, I realized my error from the body language and facial expressions of the mothers and was able to retrieve the situation by assuring them that I would observe the children soon – as of course I should have done in the first place.

What I learned from this, and this lesson has been confirmed in all my subsequent work, is just how acutely anxious parents are about the behaviour of their children; how they are embarrassed by their rudeness or their shrinking shyness; how some dread the postman because of the letters of complaint which may arrive; and how others begin to

Table 4.5: Coping with objections

Objection	Possible solution/response
1 Nothing works; we've tried everything.	Exactly what have they tried? • ask them to tell you *precisely*. • for how long did they try each approach?
2 My husband/wife/ partner won't co-operate.	Ask if you may meet this person. If you cannot involve him or her, negotiate his/her support or his/her agreement not to undermine the plan for, say, 4–6 weeks, while you work with the other parent.
3 The grandparents won't agree.	As 2, above.
4 I haven't got time to do what you're suggesting.	Explain that in the long run, what you are recommending will *save* time.
5 I haven't the energy to try again.	Empathize, but promise regular personal support.
6 That's not how we do things in our community.	Has that way of doing things been successful with your child?

avoid going out during daylight hours because they may meet people who look at them askance as 'the parents of that awful child'.

An approach which does seem to be constructive, however, is to emphasize that we may be able to teach parents some *skills* for dealing with their child. We can say, as is true, that children come into the world differently, each with a different genetic endowment, and it is wrong, as well as unhelpful, for parents to blame themselves for all their child's difficulties. On the other hand, most parents want to do their best for the child and it is now known that there are skills, which they can learn like other skills such as driving or learning to play a musical instrument, for dealing with children's behaviour problems. Our wisest course in this contemplation stage, then, is to convey real empathy for the difficulties they are experiencing, and emphasize that, while we have skills we can teach, it *is* necessary for them to wish to learn the skills. Many practitioners ask for a week's baseline counts of a given behaviour (see, for example, Chapter 9) to be collected as an indication of the parent's commitment. We should not convey that the way forward will be smooth; rather its challenges should be made clear.

3 *Determination; commitment to action*: This is the point at which the parent makes the decision that he or she will embark upon the course which the practitioner is exploring with them. The feeling may well be, 'What have we got to lose? Things can't get any worse than they are now.' Miller and Rodnick comment about this stage: 'Anticipation of problems and pitfalls appears to be a solid problem-solving skill. Subjects who are ready for action would do well to examine these barriers.'

For the parent educator, this is just the beginning. For example, it may well be that only one parent and not the other, or only the parents and not the young person, have reached the point of determination. Below are some further factors, arising from research, which parent educators would do well to consider.

- Does the parent have active support from *someone?* In my own research (Sutton, 1992) I found that while many lone parents were successful, those who were living with a partner or relative who actively mocked or undermined her attempts to follow my guidance were almost doomed to failure. Successful families were typically those in which the main person undertaking the strategies received support and encouragement, if not from a husband or partner, then from a sister, mother or even a teenage son or daughter.
- Have the parents given an indication of their intention to undertake the programme by collecting at least one week's baseline counts of a specific, identified behaviour?
- Have the parents thought through *when* they might begin to undertake a programme of behaviour change? It is unwise to begin on a programme which will be totally disrupted by, say, a family holiday or Christmas.

4 *Participation*: For the practitioner working in, say, the field of alcohol or drug misuse the task ahead is relatively clear. He or she has to offer that support and guidance which, according to the research, will help the person concerned to gain control of his or her self-defeating patterns of behaviour, smoking, alcohol or substance abuse.

The parent educator has a more demanding task. She has to teach skills to parents to use in *interacting* with another active, participating person, their child, who may already be alienated, resentful and hostile. The parents have to learn new and unfamiliar skills which may be alien to their culture. This is a huge challenge to the practitioner, who will need his or her own support.

It is during this stage that the assessment of the family's particular circumstance will be completed and planning undertaken. These steps will be examined in detail in Chapters 5 and 6 respectively.

5 *Continuation*: For a practitioner helping someone seeking to control drinking, the task at this stage is not only to deal with the

repeated impulse to drink, but also to develop strategies for dealing with the social pressures to continue long-established habits and to help find alternative ways of spending time previously spent with drinking companions. Complete changes of life style may be required.

The parent educator has to support parents in changes which are quite as demanding and which may seem alien not only to the parents but also to their family or neighbourhood culture. Below are a few of the supportive tasks required of parent educators; they will be explored in more detail in Chapter 6.

- Implementing the details of the plan negotiated earlier.
- Encouraging parents to practise a positive approach to their child
- Working towards helping them grasp the principles of interacting with their child in this way – so that they can apply these principles to a wide range of situations.
- Helping parents practise being consistent: of making only those threats and promises which they are prepared to keep.
- Supporting them through the period when the child's difficulties become worse before they begin to improve.

6 *Disillusion*: Miller and Rollnick make a particularly helpful contribution in reporting that their research showed *the probability of relapse as a routine part of the process of clients learning to control their addictive behaviours.* Therapists working in this field are so familiar with this phenomenon that they routinely take it into account when developing plans with those whom they try to help.

Relapse, in the form of abandoning attempts to remain positive with their child, or in failing to keep an appointment, will almost certainly occur. Indeed while we should not *expect* that there will be relapse, we should discuss this possibility when developing plans with parents. Knowing beforehand that progress is likely to be 'two steps forward and one step back' is likely to reassure all concerned when family members have a blazing row or when dad refuses to have anything further to do with the approach. The role of the practitioner at this stage is to remain confident that there can be progress, to be undismayed by the backsliding and to work to enabling the parents to re-enter the contemplation and subsequent stages again.

An example of this occurred in my work with a family in which, with patience and hard work, the lone mother had managed to bring about a firm and consistent style of parenting her little daughter, with major improvements for them both. After some five weeks, the little girl had to be admitted to hospital and her return home was accompanied by a resurgence of the hitting, abusive language, temper tantrums and non-compliance which had led her mother to contact me in the first place. The mother was totally demoralized.

7 *Re-motivation*: So was I, initially, until I remembered my role as re-motivator. I asked the mother to re-establish the limits to behaviour which she had worked out earlier, to explain to her little girl that she would not accept the horrible, abusive language which she was again using and, in a nutshell, to start again from the beginning. To our mutual delight, within three days the little girl had again begun to comply, was speaking politely to her mother and had again stopped hitting her. It took much less time on this second cycle of using the approach to 'get back on track'.

This re-motivation will probably be necessary on later occasions after the end of the main course of training, as old habits of parenting reassert themselves and the newly learned patterns of Parenting Positively tend to extinguish. Indeed, I consider it absolutely essential that practitioners should build in occasions for 'boosters' for parents at, say, monthly intervals, so that we use the theory to practise the theory: that is, we offer intermittent or occasional reinforcement to maintain the newly learned skills.

Summary points

☐ Many children and parents with whom professionals work are coping with profound stress and disadvantage; those children who have experienced multiple stressors are those who show the greatest evidence of disturbance.

☐ The core elements of respect, empathy, genuineness and warmth are likely to be absolutely central in gaining the trust of people who have been bruised by life events.

☐ Listening with patience and a wish really to understand is likely to be of great benefit to parents before there is any explicit focus upon parenting.

☐ For some parents, individual counselling may be a necessary precursor to any focus upon parenting.

☐ Fathers are likely to need male practitioners.

☐ Families from minority ethnic communities are likely to have more confidence in practitioners from those communities.

☐ Researchers in the field of addictive behaviours have identified a number of stages through which people considering change may pass: pre-contemplation, contemplation (of change), determination, action, maintenance, relapse. Parents reluctant to engage in discussions about parenting may pass through similar stages.

PART III

ASPIRE: A PROCESS FOR INTERVENTION

5

Assessment of children's emotional and behavioural difficulties: a multidisciplinary approach

Before any assessment can take place, children and young people have to be identified as in need of assessment. There also has to be a willingness on the part of their parents and indeed of the children, when older, and young people themselves to cooperate with the process of assessment. This is not always as straightforward a matter as it sounds. Among deeply disadvantaged families there is often great fear of the 'authorities', be they social workers, education welfare officers, teachers, nurses or doctors. Health visitors seem to be less frightening because, as every family in Britain is entitled to the support of a health visitor or similar professional after the birth of a baby, and as each young child is normally screened on at least three occasions during the early years of life, it is not stigmatizing to receive visits from these practitioners. There is always the fear, however, that *any* worker may consider that a child shows signs of neglect, physical or sexual abuse, or, much more difficult to establish, emotional abuse; as we saw in Chapter 1, there is abundant evidence that these abuses are rife.

In this book we are concerned not so much with children who may be referred to social workers because of concern that they may be being abused, as with children who show signs of emotional or behavioural difficulties. In some cases there may be evidence of both emotional or behavioural difficulties *and* some form of abuse, but our focus here will not primarily be on families deeply involved with social services departments.

Apart from parents, the people most likely to refer children for assessment are health visitors, nursery nurses, playgroup workers, teachers, doctors, neighbours and volunteer family visitors. These are the people closest to the children, both literally and figuratively, and they will probably discern the indications of distress, isolation, overactivity or failure to reach developmental milestones which lead to seeking the parents' permission for a referral. Parents do often initiate a referral, but children can be referred anonymously to social services departments and, whether the parents cooperate or not, each referral must be investigated.

What is being assessed?

The answer to this question typically rests on the perspective of the initial assessing agency. Educational welfare officers are likely to be primarily concerned with the child's school progress; health visitors with weight gain and the child's holistic development, all must be concerned with matters of child protection. If there are concerns about a child's physical, emotional or sexual well-being, then the responsible statutory body is the social services department. Of course, if there were no limits upon our time, we should all be seeking to make a multidisciplinary assessment – that is, many disciplines contributing to the overall picture – of the child in his or her family system, taking into account the parenting skills of the parents or caregivers, their personal histories, life circumstances and so on. As it is, our time is usually limited and, in view of the numbers of troubled children, is likely to remain so for the foreseeable future.

If we have the opportunity to make an assessment of the parenting skills of the people who care for the focus-child, then we can now use a new instrument, designed explicitly to be used in a multidisciplinary way. This is the *Parent Assessment Manual* (1999), written after extensive research by Sue McGaw and members of her team. The manual was designed for multidisciplinary use, and so enables workers from any professional grouping or discipline to use the same screening instruments to assess key parenting skills, in a way which provides both a child profile and a parent profile. Table 5.1 shows the ten core domains, grouped into three main categories in respect of the child. Full details are shown in Appendix 5.1, 'Initial Screening Tool'.

A particularly attractive feature of the manual is that it permits the parents, both mother and father if they are willing, to state their own views of their parenting skills and to identify perceived areas of need, as in Appendix 5.2, 'I need help'.

The manual was developed mainly with the needs of particularly vulnerable parents in mind, such as those with learning disabilities, but can be used for any family whose children show emotional or behavioural difficulties. It provides extensive resources to support parents in caring for their children, of any age from newly-born to 19. Further information on the availability and use of the manual can be obtained from Dr McGaw at the address given in the Appendices.

It may be, however, that we are not in a position to undertake a full assessment of the skills of the parents involved, and find ourselves having to focus much more narrowly upon a child's specific difficulties. We may also be responsible, having carried out the assessment, for putting a coordinated intervention into effect and evaluating its impact. In that case the steps of the ASPIRE process may offer a useful guide (see Figure 5.1 and Table 5.2).

The ASPIRE process

ASPIRE is a mnemonic acronym composed of the first letters of five words:

AS   Assessment
P   Planning
I   Implementation (of plan)
R   Review
E   Evaluation

Any intervention can be structured in this way. Figure 5.1 shows the key tasks associated with each stage of what is essentially a cyclical process.

Table 5.1 shows an outline of the steps for undertaking an assessment where there is one key worker (Sutton, 1999). In a multidisciplinary team, several practitioners are likely to be involved and to contribute at every level. For clarity, the stages under Planning, Implementation, Review and Evaluation are also included, although they will not be discussed in more detail until Chapter 6.

Table 5.1: Child profile: domains within the Parent Assessment Manual (McGaw *et al.*, 1999)

Physical health and development

1   Feeding
2   Health care: general
3   Health care: hygiene
4   Health care: warmth

Emotional care and development

5   Parental responsiveness

Development

6   Stimulation: visual
7   Stimulation: motor
8   Stimulation: language
9   Guidance and control
10 Responsibility and independence

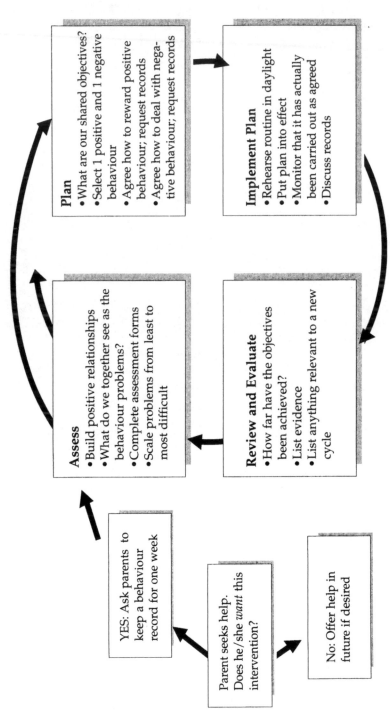

Figure 5.1. ASPIRE: a process for practice

Table 5.2: The ASPIRE process for helping children with emotional and behavioural disorders: the whole 10-step sequence is given for the sake of clarity

Step 1	Introduce yourself: build supportive and empathic relationships.
Step 2	*Assessment*: (AS of ASPIRE process) Gather information for an holistic assessment With permission, liaise with other services Help family to identify stressors in child's life in parents' life
Step 3	Identify problem behaviours: i.e. problem profile What are the difficulties? Which are the priority problems? ⎫ When do they occur? ⎬ Use scales to identify Who is involved? ⎬ problems if appropriate. Why do parents think they happen? ⎭
Step 4	Identify positive profile: What behaviours would parents like to see more of?
Step 5	Discover desired outcomes; write them down for future reference.
Step 6	Explore tentative rationale for child's/family's difficulties 1 stressful events in child's/parents' earlier experiences 2 factors intrinsic to the child; e.g. hearing impairment 3 day-to-day difficulties: suggest you can offer useful skills to help parents manage these.
Step 7	Ask for one week's counts of one negative behaviour ⎫ Introduce and one positive behaviour: ⎬ A–B–C
Step 8	*Planning*: (P of ASPIRE process). Empower parents by exploring plans: 1 to relieve any specific stressor for child/parent 2 to deal with factors intrinsic to the child e.g. hearing check 3 to practise skills for managing day-to-day difficulties Teach the A–B–C sequence – lots of examples – no blame to parents Explain which skill to use when negative behaviours happen when positive behaviours happen.
Step 9	*Implement* plan (I of ASPIRE process) Put plan into action: lots of encouragement for parents Ask parents/caregivers to continue to keep records Trouble-shoot difficulties.
Step 10	*Review and Evaluate* (R and E of ASPIRE process) Provide boosters to maintain progress.

These steps have been examined in more detail in one of my earlier books, *Helping Families with Troubled Children: a Preventive Approach*, so only key points will be noted here, with a focus on multidisciplinary approaches.

Step 1: Build supportive and empathic relationships

- Our support must convey empathy, warmth and respect, key characteristics of effective counsellors (Truax and Carkhuff, 1967).
- Listen.
- We must offer a 'no blame' approach; parents have been criticized enough.
- We must seek to raise parents' self-esteem by demonstrating respect for them, by highlighting their existing achievements in bringing up their child, and by helping them gain confidence and pride.

Step 2: Gather information for the initial assessment

- It is likely that one member of a multidisciplinary team will carry out the main assessment, with the option of making referrals to, and drawing on the skills of, a larger team. If the family comes from a minority community, or one where English is not the first language, then every effort should be made to obtain the services of an interpreter, if needed, to assist in the task of assessment.
- We seek information about predisposing factors, such as 'life events' for the child and the parents. These may have triggered, or be compounding, the child's difficulties.
- We also need information on organic or developmental factors, even though one of the specialist agencies, such as GPs, paediatricians or other medically trained practitioners may identify these in greater depth.
- We need to be alert to poor receptive language abilities (Cross, 1997).
- Similarly, we need to establish whether the child has suffered from teasing, bullying, racism or discrimination at home or at school.
- We can use a range of resources such as the open-ended questions for children who naturally find it difficult to articulate their worries. See Herbert (1991).
- It may be appropriate to use the Strengths and Difficulties Questionnaire (Goodman, 1997; see Appendix 5.3).
- We may use a formal questionnaire to ascertain the child's level of self-esteem. One developed in the UK is named B/G-Steem: this may be useful in gaining an impression of a child's or young person's sense of self-worth (Maines and Robinson, 1988). Such scales, however, may not be suitable for children from minority ethnic groups, and in any case they always demand sensitivity in their administration.

Step 3: Develop a problem profile

- Identify the specific *behaviours* which are causing difficulties: e.g. hitting the parents or other children, not settling to any task for more than 3 minutes, constantly complaining, rushing about.
- Difficult behaviours should be scaled, (placed in a hierarchical order) from the least worrying to parents, such as complaining, to the most, such as hitting themselves or other children. *We need to build in success for the family and for ourselves,* so would be wise to negotiate starting with minor misbehaviours which can either be ignored or mildly penalized.

Step 4: Develop a positive profile

- Identify specific behaviours which the parents like, and would like to see more of: e.g. finding something which is lost; sharing or lending something belonging to the child in question; comforting another child.
- This helps the parents begin to attend to their child's strengths and positive behaviours.

Step 5: Discover parents' desired outcomes: target hoped-for behaviours

At this point, we help parents to think forward, not back. We help them to identify very precisely how they would like their child to behave at the end of our shared work together. This list acts as a set of goals for us to work towards. For example, the parents of an aggressive child might specify of their 7-year-old 'We want him to stop hitting us and his brother and sister at any time at all'. The parents of a disruptive child might agree, 'We want him to occupy himself for two spells of 15 minutes each day'. The lone mother of a very withdrawn child might say, 'I want her to let me leave her with the childminder for an hour twice a week'.

Step 6: Attempting a formulation; making sense of the child's troubles

This demanding step involves bringing together all the information available in such a way as to make some sort of sense to the parents or caregivers. It will include:

- Taking account of the stresses experienced by child and parents: the birth of new siblings, bereavements, separations, bullying, discrimination or name-calling.

- Ensuring that information from the multidisciplinary team members is taken into account.
- Taking account of any organic or developmental factors which may be contributing to the situation: for example, an asthmatic condition.
- Explaining that children can sometimes learn to 'behave badly'.
- Explaining that there are skills of managing children who are experiencing stressors which we can help teach the parent.

Step 7: Request 'baseline data' for one negative and one positive behaviour

Instructing families how to record counts of a child's target behaviours, either by using a chart or by placing buttons in two jars, one for the desired target behaviour and one for the undesired target behaviour; for example:

- Negative: e.g. instances of nagging and pestering.
- Positive: e.g. instances of helping a parent with a household task, such as clearing the table.

The sections on Planning, Implementation of the plan, Review and Evaluation will be in the next chapter. See page 124.

Approaches to assessment across a range of disciplines

Assessment is an increasingly important focus of attention within many the disciplines concerned with children's well-being. Each discipline is developing questionnaires, scales and instruments which address a child's difficulties from its own perspective, so there is a profusion of discipline-specific materials. The rest of this chapter will first consider some of the major disciplines and organizations which may assess children's well-being or difficulties, and then the necessity for setting all assessment within a developmental context. The next section will include the classification by Kazdin (1995) of the types of assessment modes and scales which are available and also an examination of some of the scales and instruments most frequently used by practitioners of the main disciplines.

Disciplines involved in assessment

The following are some of the disciplines which typically may assess a child with emotional or behavioural difficulties and the child's family.

Each discipline may have its own tools for assessment, leading to serious overlap and duplication of work. The disciplines may include:

- Art therapy
- Clinical child psychology
- Child psychiatry
- Counselling e.g. bereavement
- Educational psychology
- Education welfare
- General practitioners (GPs)
- Health visiting
- Nutrition services
- Paediatric services
- Play therapy
- School health
- Speech therapy
- Teaching, specialist

It is because of the danger of duplication of work that I am concerned to disseminate such brief but comprehensive scales as the Strengths and Difficulties Questionnaire (Goodman, 1997), of which the main version will be found as Appendix 5.3 to this book and which is discussed further below (page 115).

Setting all assessment within a developmental framework

Four reasons for the importance of setting all assessment within a child-developmental framework have been set out by Cox (1995), who writes from the standpoint of psychiatry:

a) Children behave differently at different ages and the clinician needs to know the range of behaviours expected at each age to judge what is normal and abnormal.
b) In order to assess the severity of... disturbance, it is useful to consider how far there has been interference with the normal course of psychological development.
c) Different phases of development are associated with different stresses... for example, the toddler age period is the time when children are most likely to be adversely affected by hospital admission and separation experiences.
d) If clinicians are to understand how problems have arisen, they must understand the processes that underlie both normal and abnormal development.

This knowledge and experience of recognizing the indications of normal development and departures from that normality must underpin the assessment practices of each discipline, be it health, education, social services or other contributory profession. Each practitioner encountering a child should consider whether he or she falls within the limits of the normal range of development for a child of his or her age, background and ethnicity. In the UK the primary concern is whether a child keeps within standardized centiles for gaining weight and height as he or she develops.

Types of assessment approach

Kazdin (1995) has grouped the various means of assessment under a number of heads, as follows:

Meetings with parents

The information supplied by parents is obviously of the greatest importance. Most of such information will be factual and qualitative rather than quantitative in format, but it will include such crucial material as major events in the life of the child and the family, including developmental milestones and medical details.

Parents need time and space first to 'tell their story in their own way' (Cox, 1995). The parents I worked with (Sutton, 1992; 1995) without exception wanted to vent their distress, anger, confusion and frustration before they could move on to talk in a calmer manner about their child. This can be extremely time-consuming, but it is time well spent. For when the parent(s) have become less agitated, having expressed their feelings and fears and having had them acknowledged in an empathic and non-judgemental way, they are then better able, both physiologically and psychologically, to enter into a calmer and more objective discussion of their child's difficulties.

Taking a history

This exercise can usefully start with devising a genogram, which can be in greater or lesser detail according to the time available. A typical genogram is shown as Appendix 5.4. Thereafter for the parents of young people a semi-structured questionnaire (see Appendix 5.8), with space to accommodate details seen as particularly important by the parents and/or child, can provide a helpful structure. One particular area of information, now known to be associated with cognitive delay and behavioural disturbance in children, is the experience of postnatal depression by the mother. We shall be considering this in some depth in Chapter 7 so suffice it here to highlight the evidence of the serious impact of postnatal depression on both mother and child.

An informal questionnaire is shown in Table 5.3. This can be completed by parents, by any child or young person and by teachers. In appropriate contexts, a comparison of the results of completing the questionnaire by several people who know the child well is often very illuminating. The questionnaire can be used at, for example, three monthly intervals, to monitor change over time.

Table 5.3: An initial screening questionnaire for children and young people. With acknowledgments to its unknown originator

Area of difficulty	*No difficulties*	*Minor difficulties*	*Considerable difficulties*	*Major difficulties*
1 Family relationships				
1.1 With mother				
1.2 With father				
1.3 With siblings				
1.4 With other				
2 Difficulties with friends/ friendlessness				
2.1 At school				
2.2 At home				
2.3 In other places				
3 School or college				
3.1 Educational achievement				
3.2 Behaviour in school				
3.3 Truancy				
3.4 Other				
4 Self-esteem				
4.1 Confidence				
4.2 Self-understanding				

Talking with the children themselves; self report

Even quite young troubled children can, once their trust has been gained, reveal to sensitive listeners the feelings and situations which underpin their distress. A range of approaches are available to support this. See, for example, Herbert (1991) for a number of sentences for completion by the child (see Table 5.4).

Life Stream

A further informal but informative approach is the Life Stream (see Figure 5.2). Dates can be entered, and although some children may not be able accurately to locate the precise date of a major event in their lives, they will be able to identify roughly what those events were and the circumstances in which they took place. If this approach is used, the following factors should be borne in mind:

- Time should be set aside for the child to meet with a trusted worker; there should be no interruptions. Needed will be one or two large sheets of paper, coloured pens, glue and coloured paper. A box of tissues should be available.

- These sessions can be very upsetting for children, as well as helping them understand better some events in their lives; they must be handled with great sensitivity.

- The worker is the *facilitator* of the child's creative experience in making sense of the past.

Table 5.4: Sentences for completion by children and young people (Herbert, 1991)

1 I like to . . . .

2 What I most dislike . . . .

3 My best friend . . . .

4 I wish . . . .

5 My dad . . . .

6 My mum . . . .

7 If only . . . .

8 In my home the nicest thing is . . . .

9 The worst thing is . . . .

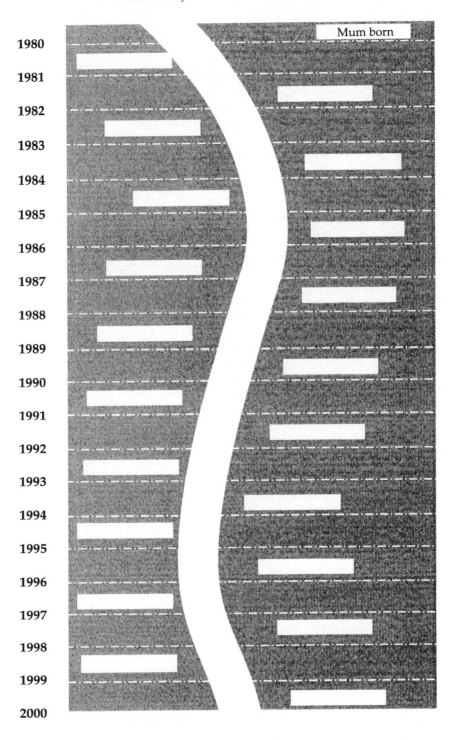

Figure 5.2. The Life Stream: a way of helping to make sense of life events

- The child should set the pace: that is, he or she should be the one to say whether or not to continue.

- The approach can be used in conjunction with devising a genogram.

- A relatively light-hearted approach is often appropriate, with happy memories recorded aongside more troubled ones.

- The child should say how events are to be recorded; for example drawing his or her first house as he or she recalls it, rather than the worker.

- The worker should give accurate information, handling sensitive areas with great care.

- The child will probably need support after the session.

- The impact of the experience may well carry over into dealings with other people, such as foster parents or teachers.

This also enables children to talk of the feelings and meanings of these events for them: their memories of rejection, their fears about being fostered, their homesickness, their longing for home despite the impossibility of returning there and so on. Sensitive listening can unleash a tide of feelings of distress in a constructive way and can also lead to opportunities gently to correct misunderstandings or inaccuracies or to provide missing information.

Direct observation

This involves the worker physically being present with the child or young person and seeing at first hand the patterns of behaviour and interaction which cause concern. Kazdin notes:

> The key ingredients of direct observation are defining behaviour carefully, identifying the situations in which the behaviour will be observed, sending observers to record the behaviours and ensuring that the behaviour is observed accurately and reliably.

Kazdin acknowledges that such observations are hard to obtain, and that often parents can be relied upon to make the necessary observations, but he concludes: 'An advantage of direct observations is that they provide samples of the actual frequency of occurrences of particular antisocial or prosocial behaviours.' Such observations need not be carried out for 24 hours a day: for high-frequency behaviours, such as whining, threatening and pestering, data gathered between 5.00 and 7.00 p.m. on two evenings a week may provide a suitable baseline, while for low-frequency behaviours, such as known instances of taking money from the parent's purse or wallet, may be gathered as they occur over, say, one month.

Asking parents to record instances of misbehaving pre-school children complying or otherwise with instructions was a practice which I myself followed in my research; I continue to find it relevant.

Using questionnaires, inventories and scales to aid assessment

The increase in the number of instruments and schedules available to professional workers is to be given a cautious welcome. It is highly desirable that more objective means of gathering data should be made available, but some coordination is called for, so that only scales and questionnaires which are valid and reliable are used. Some of the main areas are considered briefly below.

Increasingly, the approach of gathering factual information from parents together with their views upon their children's difficulties is being supplemented by the use of validated questionnaires. For example, the Strengths and Difficulties Questionnaire (Goodman, 1997) is an extremely valuable addition to the range of tools for assessment (see Appendix 5.3). It comprises 25 questions, divided into 4 sub-scales of 5 questions each, concerning the child's common areas of difficulty: conduct difficulties, emotional difficulties, peer relationship problems, and hyperactivity, together with an additional sub-scale which indicates a child's strengths or positive behaviours

The inclusion of this last sub-scale of five questions concerning the child's areas of strength is a particularly welcome innovation. These can be identified and referred to as a means of offsetting the all-too-common emphasis on the child's negative characteristics. The questionnaire, which is relevant for children aged 4 to 16, has at least three other useful features: first, it is published in forms which can be completed not only by the child's parents but also by his or her teachers; second, for children of 11 to 16, it can be completed by the young person him or herself, and; third, versions are also available from Dr Goodman in a range of minority ethnic languages. These details are available from Dr Goodman at the address given in Appendix 5.3. The particular value of such validated questionnaires is that they can be used, if appropriate, as measures before and after a programme of intervention and indeed at follow-up some months or years later to measure the benefits of training the parents or caregivers in managing the child's difficulties and to test whether any improvement has persisted.

Other scales for completion by parents include the Conners (Conners, 1973) scale for hyperactivity; this, too, has a form for completion by teachers to enable comparisons to be made on a child's areas of difficulty.

The Edinburgh Postnatal Depression Scale (EPDS; Cox *et al.*, 1987) is a short and simple means of identifying women who have recently given birth and who are still experiencing serious emotional distress (see Appendix 5.5). It comprises ten sets of three statements: the women concerned are asked to tick one of the three statements in each set. The scale can be completed in less than five minutes. Cox and Holden (1994), provides a full introduction to the scale, its history and clinical applications.

Components of a holistic assessment

Assessment of health

The holistic assessment of a troubled child or young person should routinely include a medical examination. A general practitioner or paediatrician may be able to diagnose a number of organic or physical factors contributing in whole or in part to a child's difficulties. For example, enuresis, while not of itself an emotional disorder, can be the focus of much distress and anxiety on the part of the child concerned as well as the parents. Many paediatricians arrange a test for urinary infections in children wet in the day and in those wet at night who do not respond to treatment by about age five or six.

It is not a straightforward matter to diagnose Attention Deficit Hyperactivity Disorder (ADHD), but where other explanations for a child's overactivity have been excluded, a genetic component is often involved (Barkley, 1995). Some paediatricians also consider that where serious behaviour problems are associated with ADHD, or where conduct disorders have been life-long, there is evidence of a genetic influence (Moore, 2000).

Assessment of mental health

This is a specialized area. While the Strengths and Difficulties Questionnaire will give an indication of emotional difficulties, a child who is displaying depression or anxiety to the extent that this disrupts their day-to-day life at home or at school needs assessment by an appropriately qualified professional. Appendix 5.6 (Herbert, 1993, p. 79) is a list of screening tests which many psychologists, clinical and educational, have found useful in ascertaining whether aspects of a child's mental health need individualized attention.

Educational assessment

This branch of assessment will, of course, have to be carried out by an appropriately qualified psychologist and, because of the shortage of educational psychologists, this may be hard to achieve. It is becoming apparent, however, that so many children's difficulties in school have not been picked up early enough for them to be assessed by the small number of educational psychologists available that, even if a child has been 'statemented' under the Education Act 1981, it is still not certain that they will receive adequate educational support.

Social work assessment

In view of what is known about social adversity and its impact upon a child's well-being, it is imperative that clinical assessment should be balanced by an assessment which takes account of a child's social circumstances. Part of this information may already have been gathered by other practitioners but it is addressed specifically here as this is the particular area of contribution of social workers. Appendix 5.7 is a pro forma showing a possible multidisciplinary assessment, including social work.

Assessments by other professionals

It is likely that other professional groups, notably speech therapists and physiotherapists will also be involved in contributing to a holistic assessment of a troubled child. It has been shown, for example, by Cross (1997) that many children with behaviour difficulties have poor receptive language and that this prevents them from gaining a clear understanding of the instructions which their parents may be giving them.

Bringing together and integrating information

Now that we have considered at least some of the main contributory assessments from which information and data will contribute towards a holistic assessment of a given child, we must consider how it can all be brought together. I make some suggestions below.

One agency should accept the role of key agency for a given child

The idea that families with a child in need of services should have a named key worker who takes responsibility for coordination is widely accepted in principle. The role has been most widely developed in relation to children with learning disabilities, where the key worker takes responsibility for, at least, the following:

a) Being the main point of contact for the family concerned.
b) Clarifying services and other entitlements due to the family or child.
c) Liaising on the family's behalf with other agencies.

Recent research, however, shows that even for children with disabilities, fewer than one-third of families investigated had a key worker (Mukherjee *et al.*, 1999). Their work, arising from a multiagency pilot project in which researchers, managers and practitioners collaborated to establish this kind of support, provides us with important insights into the conditions necessary to provide effective services to the families concerned. They write:

> Our evaluation of the project showed that the distinguishing features of a good key worker service for families were:
> • working across agencies
> • working with families' strengths and ways of coping
> • working for the family, as opposed to the agency.

Mukherjee *et al.* go on to report that the service varied both within and between areas. The ease or difficulty with which the key workers were able to take on the role was dependent on two factors:

> First, the organizational context needs to be one in which some degree of joint working exists, and there is commitment to promote and support multiagency working. Second, the initial and ongoing training and supervision needs of key workers must be identified and addressed. It is important that this includes clarity about the role of a key worker.
> Key workers also need protected time for the role and agencies need to act as an independent advocate for the family.

The authors make it clear that the parents of the children concerned were closely involved in devising the report and clarifying their needs. This is the point of the whole exercise.

For children with emotional and behavioural difficulties, particularly where they receive multiple assessments, I propose that a *key agency* should accept responsibility for the coordination of services for a family. It may occasionally be possible for a key worker to be appointed to the family concerned, and this is the ideal towards which we should work, but at the very least each family with a child with emotional or behavioural difficulties should be able to turn to one dependable agency. This might be any one of the many agencies responsible for working with the family, not necessarily the one with the most frequent contact. Thus for a child with both educational and health difficulties, the coordinating agency might be health, since the child was initially identified as displaying aspects of developmental delay by the health visitor. It might, however, be education, since the greatest part in the care plan for the child is being played by that service.

Parents' permission to be sought for key information to be held on a centralized computer

As we move deeper into the information age, it becomes possible to bring together a great deal of information into one store. It is logical that, for a given child, this information should be located in a central database to which professionals concerned with the family should have access. The permission of parents to allow access to their child's records across agencies by designated practitioners using a special password would of course be crucial. Collaboration would be coordinated by the key agency.

We may note the following points:

a) The technical means for setting up centralized data bases already exists: it will become more sophisticated in the twenty-first century.
b) Organizations, notably the medical professions and insurance companies, already hold a great deal of personal information about members of the public upon their computers. This information is already the focus of data-protection legislation. Such legislation would of course apply to information concerning children's well-being.
c) The awareness that parents would be able to read material written about them would impose a desirable discipline on professionals to couch the information which they record accurately, succinctly and positively. Practitioners would have to be able to support their entries in the records by evidence, and they would have to distinguish between fact and opinion.
d) The principle of parents holding their children's health records was established in many parts of the UK following research into the viability allowing them this responsibility. It was found that parents were highly responsible in taking care of their child's health records

in booklet format; in many health authorities these booklets are the standard means of recording a child's progress. Duplicate documents are usually held by health authorities. All I am suggesting, therefore, is an extension of this principle so that parents could hold a 'read-only' disc, giving them basic information about the care plan for their child with emotional or behavioural difficulties.

Exploring a formulation: developing a provisional shared understanding of the child's difficulties

It is vital that we should be cautious. The teaching of skills in gathering evidence about factors contributing to children's difficulties, of whatever kind, is now common on professional training courses. A much more difficult skill is that of weighing this evidence and arriving at a *formulation which can be explored with the child's parents.* For we might so easily be wrong. Readers will be familiar with the story of the views of Bowlby (1953) – that mothers must be the full-time carers of their children – which were subsequently shown to be misguided, though not before much damage had been done. Similarly, they will be aware that wrongfully placing responsibility for autism upon so called 'schizophregenic mothers' was responsible for much suffering and anguish among those innocent women. Finally, they will be aware that the flawed doctrine that maternal bonding occurred in a once and for all fashion soon after birth caused untold damage to mothers who believed that, because circumstances prevented their bonding in this way with their newborn children, these children were irreparably harmed. We must learn a fitting humility and caution in our efforts to help others.

The tentative, collaborative nature of developing a formulation

With these cautions in mind, workers can explore with parents a provisional *formulation* of the child's difficulties. This is the vital step of attempting to make sense, in discussion with those concerned, of the difficulties being experienced by a troubled child. That is, the practitioner explores with them the key events or factors which *appear to* have contributed to the child's difficulties. These may be life experiences affecting the whole family, such as a bereavement or major illness, or events which, while they affected only the mother, such as an episode of postnatal depression, had serious effects upon the child. They may include events in the child's experience, such as a family separation or a road accident. Alternatively, they may be organic, such as an inherited disorder or a hearing or speech difficulty. All these factors interact, and one of them may 'potentiate', that is make more influential, other factors.

In addition there are likely to be effects which lend themselves to an analysis in terms of social-learning theory. As discussed in Chapter 2, parents may unwittingly be reinforcing bad behaviour by sometimes rewarding and sometimes penalizing unacceptable rudeness or aggressiveness; they may get into long arguments with their unruly children which have the effect of rewarding that behaviour; or they may have, understandably, given up on any attempt to manage their children. While family members may not readily accept that they themselves play any part at all in their children's behavioural problems, a vast research literature shows that many problems respond to parents' managing their children in more constructive ways. At this stage, it would not be appropriate to insist upon this aspect of the formulation; instead we might say something which alerts family members to the idea that they need help in dealing with the situation. Something along the lines of, 'and we may be able to help you gain some skills in managing Craig when he becomes so aggressive' will suffice at this stage.

This first formulation is undertaken in a provisional and tentative way, because it is always possible that new information may come to light. It is also undertaken in a non-judgemental way, one which takes account of the parents' view of the situation.

The overall or holistic assessment is the responsibility of a practitioner from the key agency for the child, for example a paediatrician or a social worker. Practitioners from each agency where a child has been seen offer their specific contribution to the integrated assessment. That is, professionals within each agency, after screening and assessing the child using standardized schedules and questionnaires, and in the light of published evidence and their own experience, identify factors which may contribute to the formulation of the child's difficulties. As the education of professionals in such disciplines as psychology, psychiatry and social work improves, and as ever-more-sophisticated research teases out more and more accurately the variables contributing to children's difficulties, so there is likely to be greater agreement between professionals on these factors. For example, we must never lose sight of the research by Blanz *et al.* (1991) on the impact of social adversity (see Chapter 1), and such factors should be explicitly acknowledged when trying to arrive at a shared understanding of a given child's difficulties with his or her parents.

The value of the concept of 'stress'

When struggling to arrive at a shared understanding with families, I have found two ideas particularly useful:

a) The concept of 'stress'
We all know this term and are aware that it is bad for us to have to cope

with too much stress. Newspapers and magazines contain articles and questionnaires to help us to determine how much stress we are subject to, as well as suggestions for dealing with it: relaxation, dancing, swimming and so on – though not smoking and not alcohol, except in moderation. All parents, moreover, will know that they are stressed, both in relation to their child's difficulties and in relation to all the other pressures upon them. For some, these will include being on Income Support, having poor housing, being a lone parent and having one or more children with a disability.

So to talk with parents about their child being 'stressed' is likely to make sense to them. Then we can clarify, on the basis of what has emerged in the assessment, what we believe some of the main stressors to be:

- Chris is finding it very difficult to learn to read
- It may be that he is dyslexic: this will have to be investigated
- He reacts to these difficulties by messing about in class or by truanting.

The parents and the child can then add their views to this formulation. The parents may say: 'Chris has been upset by the fact that we have considered separating. We have tried to keep it quiet, but he may have suspected something.' If this is explored with Chris on another occasion, he may say, 'Yes, I did know. What will happen to me if you two split up?'

Parents may feel that they are learning little new about their child, but exploring these stressors with them in a structured way can help them feel that they have moved forward – particularly if this is accompanied by a clear statement of the plan which the practitioner intends to set in train.

b) The idea of helping them gain skills in managing their child

The idea of gaining skills is increasingly acceptable these days. We gain skills in driving, cooking, playing an instrument, using a computer and so on. Who does not have the potential for gaining new skills in something? So the notion of gaining additional skills for managing a troubled child can be placed directly alongside these other everyday skills. If we talk of 'therapy' we may well lose people: if we talk of 'gaining skills' we are all in the same boat.

Developing this provisional assessment in conjunction with the parents and taking their ideas into account enables us to move on to the stages of planning and, in due course, implementing a plan devised by a multidisciplinary team.

Summary points

❑ Although different professionals inevitably have different perspectives and emphases, all are contributing to a holistic assessment.

❑ Listening and respecting parents' views and strengths is a core feature of the process of making an assessment.

❑ Means of assessment include the following: meetings with parents, so that they can tell their story in their own way and to enable a history to be taken; meetings with children; direct observations; as well as using questionnaires, inventories and scales.

❑ Components of a holistic assessment are likely to include separate assessments of health and educational progress including, as appropriate, assessments of mental health, hearing, speech and language.

❑ It is highly desirable that one agency should accept the role of key agency for a given child. Within that agency a key worker should coordinate care plans for the child.

❑ In order to coordinate information and care plans, it is desirable, so long as parents are in agreement and data is protected, for particulars concerning the assessments carried out by a range of professionals to be held upon a central computer. Parents could themselves carry a disc giving them basic information about the proposed care plan and the names of those cooperating in carrying it out.

6

Issues of planning, implementation, review and evaluation

The last chapter focused on the initial assessments likely to be undertaken on a given child with emotional and/or behavioural difficulties, and on the necessity for a coordinated approach and plan. This chapter will address some of the many issues which arise when devising such a plan and putting it into effect.

ASPIRE: Planning

Multidisciplinary work in the complex field of practice with troubled children and their families can be helped by a coordinated plan drawn up by all concerned – field social workers, parents, teachers, youth workers, family centre staff or GPs.

We start this chapter, therefore, with a summary of the later stages in the ASPIRE process following the section on assessment (see page 101), and then go on to explore the concept of coordinated planning.

Later stages in the ASPIRE process

Step 8: Planning

This may involve working on several 'fronts', for example:

Front 1: Efforts to reduce family stress: examples
- discussing with parents how to try to deal with family stressors: for example, contact with absent parent, bullying, fears of family break-up;
- liaison with other members of a multidisciplinary or network who may have access to the following or additional resources:
  - gaining the involvement of a home visitor to support parent(s);

- support from workers within a minority community;
- training in anger management;
- support for parents with mental health difficulties;
- counselling support;
- support relating to alcohol/substance abuse.

Front 2: Efforts to support the specific child in difficulty: examples
- specific tests of, for example, hearing impairment;
- specific educational testing;
- provision of help with special needs;
- help from play therapist.

Front 3: Clarifying the A–B–C sequence: examples
- Demonstrating the impact of praise for a specific behaviour.
- Providing parents with a model for practice: actually showing them how to give a clear (antecedent) instruction:
  for a young child: get down to the child's eye level; gain child's attention; place hands on shoulders; say child's name; state firmly what is to be done: e.g., 'John, I want you to start putting the cars and lorries away now.' When the child begins to comply, say: 'Thank you, John'.
- Using key ideas for parents: the importance of practical guidelines.
- Helping parents plan to be consistent:
  - providing 'predictable consequences';
  - following through on promises and threats;
  - backing up what another parent/relative has said;
  - developing family rules/guidelines.

Step 9: Implementation

This is the stage of putting the plan into practice.

- Make preparations to start on a given day.
- If necessary, rehearse steps with both parents, such as managing bedtimes.
- Explain the plan to the child and build in his or her ideas wherever possible.
- Provide the family with charts and relevant papers, etc.
- Offer frequent, early and ongoing support and encouragement to parents.
- Expect some setbacks and lapses: see Chapter 4. Use trouble-shooting skills.
- Monitor how the plan is working; build in much support.

Step 10: Review and evaluation

- Examine the evidence against the objective of increasing a positive behaviour and decreasing a negative one.
- Identify specific achievements and how to deal with specific difficulties.
- Where behaviour scales have been used, ask for them to be completed again.
- Adapt the plan in line with the evidence and start a fresh cycle.

The use of coordinated plans

An overall plan is likely to contain a number of sub-plans, devised by the various agencies who have contributed to the assessment of the child. The main agencies will include: health, and mental health, education, social services and voluntary organizations. Each of these main agencies may have its own specialist workers who can provide particular services. Appendices 6.1 and 6.2 show some of the specific areas of practice of a range of clinical psychologists and educational psychologists who work with children and young people.

Some of the most encouraging practice reported in the field of planning with parents has been multidisciplinary work. The Children Act, 1989, and the Department of Health guidance *Working Together* (Department of Health, 1991; 1.8) require social workers to follow a multidisciplinary approach in respect of children considered to be at risk (S 47) or in need (S 17). Legislation also requires social workers to involve parents in the decision-making and planning for their children's future (Iwaniec, 1995). Accordingly, I shall take such practice as a model when discussing work with children with emotional and behavioural difficulties.

If a case conference, having considered the evidence about a given child in the context of the family, considers him or her to be in danger of significant harm, it is likely that this child will be placed on the Child Protection Register (CPR) and that a written plan of care will be devised. A similar care plan is required for many other children whose vulnerability is not so great as to require being placed on the CPR, but whose well-being nevertheless requires monitoring. The responsibility for coordinating the overall plan and the sub-sections of the plan is placed on a key worker in a key agency. To those who contend that this responsibility is too great for individual workers, whatever the resources made available in support, I would respond that this model has been formally in place since the passing of the Children Act, 1989, and informally long before that. To assist social workers who carry these huge statutory responsibilities, the Department of Health requires that not only the name of the key worker but also the names of 'Other agencies providing services to the child and family, including identification of core group' (Department of Health, 1991, p. 107) shall be recorded on the Register. This ensures that all workers responsible for practice with a given child on the Register meet together regularly to liaise and coordinate their work.

With huge pressures on them, social workers have necessarily developed clear procedures for practice. While the public tends to hear only of instances when such procedures and plans are not effectively implemented, many hundreds of children who are the subject of protection plans are safeguarded as a result of being placed on the CPR. Each is provided with a care plan. Here we shall consider how such care plans can also be implemented by agencies supporting children with emotional and behavioural problems and how some of the inevitable difficulties which arise can be surmounted.

Each of the agencies involved will have the responsibility for identifying its contribution to the overall plan for the child. This is likely to be expressed in terms of specific objectives which it is intended that either its own workers, or the workers of an agency which it has specifically commissioned, will meet. The following guidance is given about dealing with children placed on the Child Protection Register. I quote it here because I believe that all members of multidisciplinary teams, not just those in social services departments, can learn from it.

NEED FOR A WRITTEN PLAN

5.17.1   A written plan will need to be constructed with the involvement of the carers/parents and in the light of each agency's statutory duties and will identify the contributions each will make [to] the child, to the other family members and the abuser. It will make clear the part to be played by parents, what expectations they may have of agencies and what expectations agencies may have of them...

5.17.2   Once the plan has been agreed, it will be the responsibility of individual agencies to implement the parts of the plan relating to them and to communicate with the key worker and others as necessary. The key worker will have the responsibility for pulling together and coordinating the contributions of different agencies.

5.17.3   The production of the protection plan must include consideration of the wishes of the child and parents, local resources, the suitability of specialist facilities, their availability for addressing the particular needs of the child and his or her family. Special attention will need to be given to ensuring the services provided under the plan are coordinated, structured and ethically and culturally appropriate

for the child and family, with built-in mechanisms for programme reviews and crisis management.

5.17.4   Children and parents should be given clear information
about the purposes and nature of any intervention together
with a copy of the plan. Every effort should be made to
ensure that they have a clear understanding of the objectives of the plan, that they accept it and are willing to work
to it. If the families' preferences about how the work to protect the child should be conducted are not accepted, the reasons for this should be explained, as should their right to
complain and make representations.

(Department of Health, 1991, p. 32)

I submit that these guidelines offer all practitioners in the helping agencies an excellent model to follow in situations where we seek to support
families with troubled children. The main point is that while compiling
and working to these guidelines may be time-consuming initially, ultimately they offer support and a sense of direction to all concerned.

An example of a child-care action plan

Iwaniec (1995), writing from the standpoint of child protection, gives
an example in respect of a child seen as having very low self-esteem
and identified as showing serious developmental delay due to the lack
of parental nurturing. A case conference was called and the multidisciplinary plan outlined in Table 6.1 was developed.

Supporting a plan by a written agreement

As research in the field of helping troubled children increases, it
becomes apparent that there are major problems in helping parents
alter their patterns of interacting with their children. In response, a
number of researchers, such as Herbert (1981) and Hudson and Macdonald (1986) have advocated devising agreements, discussed and
signed by all those participants who are old enough to understand,
which have the effect of encouraging the signatories to follow through
on agreed courses of action.

The evidence in favour of agreements in supporting parents is substantial. Hazel (1980) demonstrated their usefulness in enabling young
people to move from residential care to foster care, and showed that
written agreements reduced the level of breakdown of the foster placements, while Sheldon (1980) has made a very strong case, with clear
examples, for the benefits of a range of different contracts devised
between two or more participants.

Table 6.1: Multidisciplinary action plan drawn up by a case conference for a child who had experienced significant harm. (Iwaniec, D. (1995) *The Emotionally Abused and Neglected Child*. © John Wiley and Sons Limited. Reproduced with permission.

1 General Practitioner to refer John to the paediatrician to investigate any possible organic reason for the child's poor growth and development (for immediate action).

2 Comprehensive psychosocial assessment to be undertaken by the social worker.

3 Child's weight to be monitored by the health visitor or the General Practitioner on a fortnightly basis (after medical investigation).

4 Help, advice and supervision regarding eating (nutritional provision and appropriate management during this process) to be provided by the health visitor.

5 Developmental counselling to be provided by the health visitor.

6 Attendance of the child at the Family Centre or day nursery to be organized on a part-time basis (two days a week) to help the child with its developmental deficit.

7 Social worker to help to improve... relationship between mother and child, and to work towards better family functioning and fair role-distribution between parents.

8 To review the case in three months' time (or earlier if the key worker or any other person involved requests to do so if there is serious concern).

9 To allocate a key worker responsible for coordination for this case.

There are a number of important features intrinsic to agreements. First, they are based on the notion that people carry out a 'cost–benefit analysis' when deciding on their actions; that is, that people are motivated to behave in ways which increase their benefits, perhaps in material terms, or in terms of moving towards attainments which matter to them, or in terms of the advancing their values – for example, the well-being of people important to them or, indeed, the well-being of the planet. Thus, everybody who participates in writing an agreement should be able to anticipate gaining something from it. This is why writing an agreement may take a long time. Even so, it is better to ensure that everybody is satisfied at the outset of an agreed action, rather than trying to save time planning or drawing up an agreement at the risk of being unclear or of failing to think of what might go wrong. Second, agreements are generally expressed in positive terms, that is, in terms of what people agree that they *will* do rather than what they will not do. With practice, it becomes possible to express almost anything in a positive form! Third, the agreement should be devised in such a way as to enable participants to advance by way of small successes. Agreements do not typically bring about dramatic overnight changes; they provide a strategy for people to achieve small gains, which gradually add up to improvement. There are bound to be failures and disappointments, but so long as the general trend is toward improvement, then people's motivation and morale are likely to rise. Finally, it should be emphasized that writing agreements is a skill which may be learned.When writing agreements, it is important to go through the stages shown in Table 6.2. Sample agreements are shown as Appendix 6.3.

ASPIRE: Implementation of the plan

The key worker as coordinator of the plan

In any endeavour in which people with different backgrounds and from different agencies are required to collaborate, goodwill and mutual support are essential if things are to proceed smoothly. As demands on practitioners increase, and as public expectations of the standards which parents should attain rise, it becomes more and more important

Table 6.2: Steps in devising an agreement (after Sheldon, 1980)

1   Discuss whether using an agreement is socially acceptable to those involved. It may be familiar for business arrangements, but not for personal ones. If so, invite people to try the idea out.
2   Focus on actions or *behaviours,* rather than attitudes or feelings.
3   Select one or two behaviours initially. Avoid working with too many problems.
4   Start with a simple goal; early success is vital.
5   Describe those behaviours *in a very clear way.* Vagueness may seem to make the negotiation seem easier, but all the participants then interpret the agreement differently. This can lead to confusion and anger.
6   Write the agreement so that everyone understands it. Make the wording clear, brief and simple, and write in each person's first language.
7   The benefits for each person must be worth the costs as he or she perceive them.
8   The agreement should be written in positive language – specifying things which are to be done, rather than those which are not to be done.
9   Collect records. It is essential to know whether the situation is getting better or worse. Information can be collected on simple daily charts.
10 Renegotiate the agreement. A series of short-term agreements is generally more effective than one long-term one.
11 The artificiality and short-term nature of the agreement should be explained.
12 The penalty for failure to fulfil the agreement on each person's part should be clear.
13 Everyone concerned should sign the agreement, which should be dated.
14 If there are difficulties in meeting the clauses of the agreement, but one or more have been met, then emphasize those, not the areas of difficulty.
15 As soon as a stable position has been maintained for several months, begin to phase out the agreement.

to ensure that assessments are accurate, plans are realistic and goals are attainable. It is also crucial that the decisions arising from these assessments should be effectively implemented. As resources are diverted to support parents in the earliest years, and as more and more professionals become involved in the parent-training 'industry', so huge demands are made on a small number of appropriately trained professionals. We are expected to deal with highly complex situations and carry huge caseloads and responsibilities in situations of scarce resources.

In our example, a named social worker or his or her manager is authorized by the child protection case conference to hold practitioners accountable to complete undertakings which they or their agencies have entered into. It is the efficiency of such work which has protected thousands of children over past decades. These are not the few unhappy children for whom things have gone seriously wrong, and concerning whom social workers with limited training and poor resources are publicly pilloried, but the thousands of children who have been guarded against abuse, neglect or injury by teams of committed practitioners. I suggest that with the arrival of the new millennium, children with treatable difficulties require no less. Now that the information age is on us, and agencies demand that their practitioners use the tools of information technology as a routine skill, we have a rare opportunity for optimizing coordinated practice.

In any case, it is essential when entering into care plans for troubled children that these commitments are adhered to and that someone undertakes the coordination of the services provided. This is the role of the key worker. Because even people in the helping professions are sensitive to status, it will be important for that key worker to be someone of substantial seniority or someone endowed by the group with real power. He or she needs to be in a position to offer not only genuine support to those endeavouring to meet demanding deadlines, but also to monitor those lax in keeping to their undertakings and to insist that commitments are honoured. Such intervention must be carried out with a light touch! For most professionals working with troubled children seem to be highly conscientious people; they try not to promise more than they can deliver and often give time which belongs to themselves or their families to the children or parents who are looking to them for help.

Already, lead agencies such as social services departments have extensive experience of commissioning services from other agencies to provide specific services for families. For example, they commission specialist agencies to support parents with learning disabilities to work with family members towards *clear, specified and time-limited objectives*. Appendix 6.4 is a pro forma which may be used, for example, by social services departments to commission specific work with individuals or families. This may be useful as a model when contracting aspects of a child support plan to other agencies. In such circum-

stances it is the responsibility of the commissioning agency to negotiate the date for review and to ensure that the details of the contract
have been adhered to.

Monitoring the implementation of plans involving several agencies

Key workers are likely to develop 'critical paths' for the implementation of plans. For example, in respect of the Smith family, it was essential for the GP to provide a medical examination for John before the
health visitor could set in train her plan to give regular support to
John's parents. For children over the age of five or six, depending on
the assessment and the resulting formulation, work with parents and
direct work with children should proceed hand in hand (Webster-
Stratton, 1999a). Services offered to the parents might include the following:

- Direct work to raise self-esteem;
- Counselling for existing depression;
- Support within a women's group;
- Homestart visitor;
- Visit to a Well Woman clinic;
- Specific support for alcohol- or drug-related difficulties;
- Short-term nursery care;
- Play sessions for parent and child with specialized worker.

Table 6.3: Sample plan of services for Lisa, Don, Matthew and James Cox

Key worker: Janet Hall,
Rainham Road Health Centre, North Shields

Week beginning	Agency	Service	To whom	Dates
1 June	Friend in Need	Counselling	Lisa Cox	1 hour's counselling weekly 2–29 June
8 June	Acorn Lodge	Respite care	Matthew Cox	8–15 July
8 June	Health visiting (Janet Hall)	Parenting skills	Lisa and Don Cox	20 minutes per week, 2 June-14 July
1 July	Social Services (Diana Jackson Family Aide)	Play sessions With Lisa and James	Lisa and James	1 hour weekly 2 June -21 July

A simple outline, conveying the essence of the care plan, might be as shown in Table 6.3.

Support for parents

During the period of implementation parents need a great deal of support. Since, as already mentioned, we know that the parents of troubled children are usually reluctant to believe that they themselves have any part in the disturbed behaviour of those children (Sutton, 1999), it is often helpful to talk in terms of *skills* in managing their children which they can learn.

During this stage of implementation, other crises, great and small, will occur. During such times, attempts to help parents manage their children more positively are likely to be disregarded. However, rather than just letting things slide, it can be constructive to suggest that the plan should be 'put on hold' for the period that people are coping with a crisis. It can then be picked up again when people feel able to give their full attention

The key worker as 'trouble shooter' with and for parents

In any project to help children with emotional and behavioural difficulties, work planned with the parents is bound to run into problems. The best-laid plans do not always work; families encounter illness, crisis, complaints from neighbours and the breakdown of relationships. In my own work, I found that while some mothers were willing and able to cooperate with what I was suggesting to them, husbands or partners were less readily persuaded. Some of the objections I encountered are listed in Table 6.4.

ASPIRE: Review and evaluation of the plan

Review of the work

This corresponds to examining how the implementation of the plan is working at the multidisciplinary level (Sutton, 1999). It requires those involved, coordinated by the key worker, to reflect, together with the family members and the troubled child, on the areas of progress which have been made and what is the evidence for this progress (see Figure 5.2). This is the advantage of having clear goals: one can assess progress towards specific goals which have been identified at the out-

Table 6.4: Objections and possible responses in promoting Parenting Positively

Objection	Possible solution
1 We've tried what you said and it doesn't work.	Explore: • what have the parents tried? • for how long? • with what effect?
2 All this praise goes against our culture.	Explore specific grounds for this objection. The culture may be strict, but the evidence shows (Wilson, 1987) that firmness is helpful to children. Where specifically is the mismatch?
3 It's too soft.	Would you try it for a fortnight and see what effect it has?
1 My partner doesn't approve.	Try to enlist a male worker to explain what is being recommended.
5 It's too hard.	It *is* hard, but think of what is at stake.

set or which have been added in a considered way as the work moves forward. Evidence, both from what family members say and from the workers' impressions, will be available, but a more exact source of information comes from asking the parents and, if old enough, the child at least at every other meeting, what progress is being made in such a way that it can be measured. Herein lies the advantage of a simple scale which permits the parents to record either progress/improvement or deterioration. Week by week, or at some other regular interval, changes can be noted, and, as appropriate, strategies of helping can be developed, adapted or changed, according to discussion with the client.

Evaluation of the work

This is the point at which the work is concluded – preferably at a predetermined point – and the whole intervention evaluated. This can be done both quantitatively and qualitatively, using for example, both the Strengths and Difficulties Questionnaire (Appendix 5.3) and, if desired, some form of qualitative measure, such as a semi-structured interview. From a multidisciplinary perspective, each participating agency can identify the extent to which the child-within-his or her family has progressed towards agreed goals. So long as goals have been set in a coordinated way, it should be possible for each agency to evaluate how far a child and family has moved towards them. It should be possible to agree with family members which objectives have been fully, partly or not attained, to clarify the evidence of such full or partial attainment and then, if necessary, to identify any issues or evidence relevant to a new cycle.

In conclusion, I urge that *we use the theory to teach the theory*; that is to say, since we know that skills of, say, paying attention to their child's strengths rather than to their shortcomings may be both easily learned by parents and easily extinguished, then *it is essential that we provide families with booster contacts to maintain their skills*. So, after a sustained piece of work is finished, then either weekly or at the least fortnightly phone calls are required to maintain the improvements. I found no difficulty in arranging these; neighbours or friends were ready to assist families who had no phone. If we do not regularly reinforce these newly acquired skills we are likely to see that, just as the theory suggests, patterns of behaviour which are not regularly reinforced are likely to fade away.

Summary points

❐ Each agency participating in a multidisciplinary assessment has the responsibility for identifying its contribution to the overall plan for the child.

❐ This contribution is likely to be expressed in terms of specific objectives which the agency itself, or another agency, commissioned for the purpose, will seek to achieve.

❐ The overall plan should be written down and a copy given to parents and, if appropriate, to the child.

❐ The care plan should be supported by a written agreement.

❐ The key worker should act as coordinator of the plan and as 'trouble shooter' when things do not go according to plan.

PART IV

MULTIDISCIPLINARY APPROACHES TO PREVENTING CHILDREN'S DIFFICULTIES

7

Infants and their families: multidisciplinary approaches

As has been shown in earlier chapters, there is substantial evidence that, while a multifactorial formulation is always necessary, the children of very young mothers with a poor educational background, in poor housing and with little or no support, are particularly at risk of emotional and behavioural difficulties. Similarly, children in families in which there is much ongoing conflict are vulnerable. There are no great mysteries here; common sense might have pointed to the same conclusions; but now the data is in to support the common-sense view. In this chapter we shall first explore the research evidence for the contribution of specific variables to the overall picture and then go on to examine other evidence of effective multidisciplinary intervention with families when the infants are still very young. Finally we shall suggest a structure for such intervention.

The research background

Much research has focused on the earliest years and circumstances of a child's life, in an effort to determine both the particular factors which may lead to children developing emotional and behavioural difficulties and the numbers of those affected. In the last decade, postnatal depression has been investigated thoroughly. Although there has always been general interest in this disorder, the extent of the research has increased recently, partly as reliable scales developed for measuring its intensity, such as the Edinburgh Postnatal Depression Scale (EPDS), have become available (Cox et al., 1987). This Scale is included as Appendix 5.5. It is now available in a wide range of languages in *Perinatal Psychiatry: Use and Misuse of the Edinburgh Postnatal Depression Scale* (Cox and Holden, 1994).

The impact of postnatal depression

The experience of depression is known to most of us: it is marked by the following characteristics:

Affect (emotions): feelings of sadness, poor self-worth; low self-esteem. Behaviour: low levels of activity, including physical exercise and communication with others.

Cognition: negative and discouraging thoughts and beliefs, which the person thinks through again and again: 'I'm no good...'; 'I can't cope...' 'I've failed...'

Postnatal depression is a non-psychotic but major depressive disorder. Its effects seem to be serious and long-lasting. Cooper and Murray (1998) recently carried out a major review of the field; part of their evidence is summarized in Table 7.1.

As is commonly known, many vulnerable young mothers come from deeply disadvantaged backgrounds. A report in *The Times* (15 June, 1999) noted:

> There are nearly 90,000 teenage conceptions a year in Britain, resulting in 56,000 live births. About 7,700 conceptions are to under 16s.
>
> There is a striking correlation between countries with high rates of live births to teenagers and high levels of relative deprivation, dropping out of education and family breakdown.

Many of these young mothers become depressed either soon after the birth of their babies or later on, as the responsibilities of caring for dependent infants begin to have their effects. This is particularly so if

---

Table 7.1: Epidemiology, aetiology, prediction and detection of postnatal depression (Cooper and Murray, 1998)

- Postnatal depression affects about 10 per cent of women in the early weeks *post partum*, with episodes typically lasting two to six months.
- There is little evidence for a biological basis.
- Previous depression is a risk factor, especially when paired with obstetric complications.
- The main risk factors are ones indicative of social adversity.
- The only large-scale study of the predictive value of antenatal factors [Cooper *et al.*, 1996] produced an index of some use; its performance could be improved by including assessment of post-partum blues and infant temperament.
- Detection, while generally poor, presents no difficulty.

---

the biological father of the baby or another close relative or friend is not available to offer support (Farrington, 1995a).

Cunnington and Askew (1998) confirm from their ongoing work the oft-reported association between maternal depression and adverse social and economic circumstances. This depression can arise in both the antenatal and postnatal period, manifesting itself in low self-esteem and a low capacity to take initiatives. It is common in the absence of a confiding relationship with a husband, partner, mother or other supportive person (Brown and Harris (1978). Social isolation is a particularly damaging experience for vulnerable young mothers.

Domestic violence

The work of Dobash and Dobash (1978) and Gelles (1979) have highlighted the extent of domestic violence, almost entirely inflicted by men on women and children. In examining the variables affecting a woman's decision to stay with or leave a violent husband or partner, Gelles concluded:

> The less severe and the less frequent the violence, the greater the probability of staying and not seeking help ... The more the wife was hit by her parents as a child, the more inclined she was to stay.

It is clear that mothers being abused by their partners are more likely both to experience depression and be unable to obtain the social supports necessary for bringing about an improvement in their circumstances. The violence of itself leads to depression, which then contributes to adverse effects upon the child or children of the next generation.

The impact of postnatal depression on young children

Researchers have examined the impact of mothers' depression on emotional and cognitive development in the infant or toddler. For example, Murray (1998), reporting on prospective studies of samples of women with postnatal depression and their children, concludes that they suggest an association between postnatal depression in mothers and impaired infant cognitive development. She cites her own work in Cambridge, UK, (Murray, 1992; Murray *et al.*, 1996; Murray and Cooper, 1997), which found that:

> the children of mothers who had had postnatal depression were found to perform significantly less well on cognitive tasks at 18

months than did children of well mothers, especially the boys. Two London studies of more socioeconomically disadvantaged populations have found that this effect still obtained when the children were 4–5 years old.

And in respect of emotional development, she writes:

> Most studies that have systematically examined infant attachment in the context of postnatal depression have found a raised rate of insecure attachments... There is evidence that these emotional problems persist. A follow-up of the Cambridge cohort found that the 5-year-old children of mothers who had had postnatal depression were significantly more likely than controls to be rated by their teachers as behaviourally disturbed (Sinclair and Murray, 1998).

Cooper and Murray (1998) go on to suggest that the mechanism mediating the association between postnatal depression and adverse child developmental outcome is 'the impaired pattern of communication occurring between the mother and her infant'.

This impairment may mean that there is reduced emotional and cognitive interaction and satisfaction between mother and child. In practice, there is likely to be less of the 'talk, touch and gaze' behaviour which many mothers spontaneously engage in with their infants when they are feeling well, are not depressed and have adequate social supports. It is not surprising, then, that a mother who *has* experienced or is still experiencing postnatal depression, leading to reduced communication with her little child as a toddler, may find it almost impossible to gain the confidence and ability to manage him in a firm and consistent way, especially if she is isolated and unsupported. If this low level of confidence is compounded by difficulties during the period when her child is 2 and 3 – the stage in which he is establishing his independence – then she may totally lose confidence and manage him in an erratic and inconsistent way. This inconsistency is extremely unhelpful to the child, who benefits from firm, confident management with clear limits set to his behaviour and warm expressions of affection.

Cooper and Murray (1998) have summarized the impact of postnatal depression on the children of mothers coping with this disorder (see Table 7.2).

There has been a flood of research, mainly in the United States, concerning the interaction between variables affecting mothers and their young children. These studies have focused more upon attachment relationships than upon maternal depression, as in Britain. The picture which seems to emerge from the American studies is that infants who have an impaired attachment to the parent are at risk for the later development of aggressive and troubled behaviour in the child. Lyons-

---

Table 7.2: Impact of postnatal depression on child development (Cooper and Murray, 1998)

---

a) Cognitive development... is adversely affected, especially among male children and socioeconomically disadvantaged groups.
b) The children of postnatally depressed mothers tend to have insecure attachments at 18 months, and the boys show a high level of frank behavioural disturbance at 5 years.
c) The adverse child outcome in the context of postnatal depression is related to disturbances in the mother-infant interactions.

Ruth (1996) writes:

> Whereas most of the early longitudinal attachment studies focused on middle-income families, the Minnesota High Risk Study conducted by Egeland and Sroufe was unusual in following a large community sample of impoverished mothers and infants from birth into adolescence. The documented prediction from early maternal and infant behaviour to child maladaptation and aggressive behavior during the school years has been a major contribution of the study.

This work has, however, not been replicated by other researchers working with 'more economically advantaged families', for example, Fagot and Kavanagh (1990). It seems that it is the *interaction effects between impoverishment and impaired attachment relationships* which predispose to problems in childhood and adolescence.

Research on multidisciplinary interventions

A number of different types of intervention have been explored in attempts to find ways of ameliorating the discouraging situation reported above. There seems to be a consensus emerging from a range of studies.

The importance of social support

We are all aware of the importance of 'support' when we are feeling distressed or depressed; this importance has been demonstrated by a number of studies. In an early, influential example, Brown and Harris (1978) examined variables associated with depression in a large group of women in an inner London borough. This study provided evidence not only of the role of 'provoking agents' (that is, immediate stressors), but of psychosocial influences involving more fundamental aspects of a woman's life. The vulnerability factors are:

1 Loss of mother before the age of 11 years.
2 Three or more children in the family under 14 years of age.
3 The lack of a confiding partner.
4 The lack of paid employment.

The vital importance of support has been demonstrated by many studies. For example, Aneshensel and Stone (1982) have shown that not only does social support, such as that available from social networks or relationships, lessen the adverse effects of stress and depression but it may actively improve the depressive symptoms. More recently, Holden (1994) cites Cohen and Wills (1985) who suggest, on the basis of their work, that a single close and confiding relationship may be sufficient to offset the effects of stress. This is supported by Cutrona and Troutman (1986) who reported that at the three months' postnatal check, "social support" exerted a protective function against depression'.

Brown (1992) has described three essential elements of effective support for new, vulnerable mothers from a husband or other person who is emotionally close:

1 The availability of someone emotionally close whom the mother may confide in.
2 Ongoing support from that person.
3 The support-person making no or very few negative comments about the mother.

Holden reports an important study in this field:

> From a study of vulnerable women in Islington Brown (1992) reported that only 4 per cent of married women who expected and received such support from their partner became depressed. On the other hand, 26 per cent of those who did not confide and did not receive crisis support became depressed, while those who confided, and expected support but did not get it, were the most likely to become depressed.

Effective intervention by health visitors

A number of studies show the positive impact of health visitors counselling mothers with postnatal depression: Holden *et al.* (1989) examined the effects of an average of nine counselling sessions, based on client-centred approaches, over thirteen weeks. The mothers who received the counselling showed considerably greater improvements in their levels of depression than did those in the control group. This is supported by evidence from Sweden provided by Wickberg and Hwang (1996): here depressed mothers benefitted from as few as six counselling sessions by comparison with the control group.

A multidisciplinary study in Australia involving paediatricians, psychiatrists and community child health nursing staff was undertaken in an attempt to tease out the components of maternal depression more precisely. Armstrong *et al.* (1998) wanted to 'separate the chicken from the egg' – in other words, to distinguish the effects of sleep deprivation from those of postnatal depression. They worked with 114 families in Brisbane who had been referred to a children's sleep clinic and among whom 45 mothers, 40 per cent of the total, reached scores of higher than 12 on the Edinburgh Postnatal Depression Scale. By using well-tried behavioural strategies of establishing or re-establishing regular patterns of sleep, and by offering professional support, the researchers were able to reduce the number of mothers reaching greater than 12 on the EPDS to five, 4 per cent of the total. In other words, the mothers were suffering not so much from depression as from sleep deprivation. The authors make a plea for the holistic assessment of women with postnatal depression, so that contributory factors can be identified and dealt with.

In my own research, I worked by telephone with 23 mothers seeking help in managing their troubled pre-school children. Their mean score on the Beck Depression Inventory was just below 15 (a score indicating clinical depression). Teaching them skills in managing their children brought about scores indicating clear improvement in these children's behaviour, as measured by the Rutter Child Behaviour Scale. This improvement was mirrored by a marked reduction in the mothers' levels of depression.

Effective help for mothers as shown by its impact on their children

A few studies have gone beyond work with the mothers to explore the impact of strategies to improve postnatal depression on the infants of the mothers concerned. Cooper and Murray (1997) found that offering systematic counselling support to depressed mothers led to significant improvements in mothers' reports of their infants problems 'both immediately after treatment (four to five months *post partum*) and eighteen months later'. This was also related to a reduced rate of insecure attachment when the children were 18 months old. This result supports the findings of an earlier study (Seeley *et al.*, 1996). The convergence of this and other evidence has led many primary care groups in the United Kingdom to set up systematic support for mothers experiencing postnatal depression.

The effectiveness of this preventive approach has also been demonstrated in other countries. Olds *et al.* (1986a), in Canada, working with 400 mothers, arranged for home nurses to visit half the mothers (who had been randomly allocated to an experimental group and a control group) during pregnancy and the first two years of their babies' lives. These visits were shown to be helpful in that the postnatal home visits were associated with a decrease in recorded child physical abuse and neglect during the first two years of life. Commenting upon another similar study with over 100 disadvantaged expectant mothers in Montreal, Farrington (1996) reported:

> The home visits had beneficial effects since the babies of visited mothers sustained significantly fewer injuries in the first year of life compared with a control group who received no visits. But the best results were obtained with children whose mothers were visited both before and after their birth. These mothers were also rated by observers as the most skilled in taking care of the child.

Farrington (1996) is persuaded that intensive home visiting has been clearly demonstrated as having beneficial outcomes in both the short and long terms. He cited the work of Lally *et al.* (1988) who conducted a longitudinal study in which 120 children were followed up from infancy to the teenage years. Those whose mothers had received intensive early support both in terms of home visits and in terms of free day-care until age five, had had significantly lower rates of offending as measured by referral to the juvenile court.

In summary, then, we see that multidisciplinary support of vulnerable families, involving health-care workers, medical staff, family support workers and a range of other personnel can have extremely beneficial effects as measured both by reductions in depression on the part of the mothers and reductions in disordered behaviour by their children in the short and long term.

Multidisciplinary support to depressed mothers: an example

Shula is 18. She lives with her little son, James, aged 4 months, in a bedsit on a large estate in a Midlands town. Shula left home when her dad died in a car accident and her mother later began a new relationship with a man, Henry, whom Shula did not like and who did not like her. She met Paul, also 18, who, like her, had left home after family difficulties, and the two of them found a place together.

Things went well for a few months, but then they had a bad argument and Paul hit Shula and blacked her eye. Shula left him and went back to her mother and Henry, only to discover that she was pregnant. When Paul heard about this, he offered to marry Shula, but Shula didn't want this. She did go back to live with Paul, but they had further rows and although he was kind while she was pregnant and she could talk to him, after James was born he found it hard to put up with the crying and with Shula's being so wrapped up in the baby. He hit her twice more, but was immediately sorry afterwards. 'Something comes over me' he says; 'She says something I can't take, and I hit her'.

Because of the baby Shula asked to go back home and live with her mum, but after a week and a lot of rows and arguments, she decided once again that she was better off on her own, even if she got depressed. Shula says she loves James, but she wants some fun. She would like to get together with Paul again, but not if there is any chance of his hitting her.

Assessment

Step 1: Building supportive and empathic relationships

There is much evidence of the importance of the 'therapeutic alliance' between the worker and the person concerned, whether in a setting of counselling and psychotherapy or in work with parents. This positive and supportive relationship is the foundation of all the subsequent work, and supports the person concerned when all the efforts seem of no avail. So Jane, the health visitor, will spend as much time as she can building a strong and empathic relationship with Shula, but without encouraging dependency.

This is, of course, the stage of enabling people to get their feelings off their chests: to talk of their distress, resentment or unhappiness and to put into words thoughts and ideas that they have only half acknowledged to themselves. Shula, for example, will probably benefit from an opportunity to talk through her unhappiness and her loneliness with a supportive and empathic health visitor – someone who can give her time and support in talking of the overwhelming feelings of loss and sadness about the death of her dad, to whom she was emotionally very close; of anger and unhappiness towards the various people in her life; and of fear and uncertainty about the future.

Shula is at home when her health visitor, Jane, calls. She bursts into tears almost at once and says she wants some medication for her depression. Jane suspects that the GP will be reluctant to prescribe medication, but she cooperates with Shula's wishes and encourages her to go to her GP. Meanwhile she undertakes to call back two days later to hear more about Shula's circumstances. Jane duly visits Shula and spends more than an hour letting her put into words the confused feelings and anxieties which have built up for many months and years about the loss of her father, her ambivalence about her mother and her fears for the future.

Step 2: Information gathering

It is, of course, essential that any assessment of a parent's circumstances should be holistic – or as full as is possible in situations of limited resources. Jane, at the same time as listening to Shula, is able to gather relevant information about Shula's relationships, her support network, her feelings about the baby and about Paul, the baby's father.

Jane confirms that Shula is taking good physical care of James, but notes that he seems to be an unhappy baby, smiling seldom and spending a long time alone in his cot, sucking his dummy. His records show that he is still within his centile, but is not gaining weight as fast as he should. When Jane asks Shula whether she has ever felt that she might harm James, she says 'No' very emphatically. She explains that while she and her mum don't get on, she would always turn to her if she felt so low that she couldn't cope at all with the baby. But she really wants to manage on her own if she possibly can.

Formal assessment

Jane asks Shula to complete the Edinburgh Postnatal Depression Scale. She scores 10. This warrants contact with her GP, with whom she has already fixed an appointment. Shula is not so depressed, however, that she needs referral to a psychiatrist (score 12 or greater).

Step 3: Identifying the main areas of difficulty together

As Shula is pouring out her unhappiness, Jane, with her ear trained to discerning key areas of distress, makes a mental note of some of the main difficulties. She seeks Shula's permission to make notes and when Shula is calmer, talks gently with her to explore Shula's view of the main problems or needs. She asks Shula what *she* sees as the main difficulties. Shula identifies two particular factors, her loneliness and her fears for the future, and Jane has gently to add a third: her own professional concern about James. Shula immediately becomes defensive, but Jane's sincerity and the quality of her concern for Shula has gained Shula's trust. When she says that she has no intention at this stage of referring Shula and James to social services as James is still well within his weight centile, Shula believes her. Jane explains however, that they must work together to try to relieve Shula's depression, to improve James's weight and reduce his listlessness. The following list of areas of problem is therefore noted:

1 Shula's loneliness and unhappiness.
2 Her uncertainty what to do about Paul: have him back, and risk being hit again, or try to manage on her own.
3 Jane's concern about baby James: his lack of smiling and his failure to gain weight as fast as he should.

Step 4: Identifying the positive features of the situation

Shula is surprised when Jane, having been honest with her about her concerns, now tells her of her awareness of Shula's strengths and other positive features of the situation. Jane tells her that she has seen how Shula takes excellent physical care of James: he is clean and carefully dressed; his bedding is fresh; and although Shula doesn't find it easy to spend much time playing with and taking part in 'talk, touch, gaze', she obviously cares a lot about him.

Shula she says she doesn't know what Jane means about 'talk, touch, gaze', so Jane explains that interacting with babies by talking to them, stroking and cuddling them and smiling at them is very good for them. Shula says she would feel uncomfortable talking to a baby... she wouldn't know what to say.

Step 5: Identifying the desired outcomes of the work together

Jane explains that she can help Shula to learn to 'talk to' James. Together they work out what they would like to be the outcomes of their work together, to be assessed within one month's time.

- That Shula will feel less depressed, as shown by the EPDS (postnatal depression scale).
- That James will remain within his weight centile or will have moved up one.
- That James will smile/babble more than at present, which is 'very rarely'.
- That Shula will be clearer in her mind about what to do about her relationship with Paul.

Step 6: Attempt a formulation of/rationale for the difficulties

The formulation/rationale is an attempt to make sense of the difficulties which people experience. It is developed in close collaboration with them, and is explained as provisional, tentative and liable to change as more information comes to light. In Shula's circumstances there is no great mystery. It is entirely understandable that she is feeling depressed: she is having to cope with major responsibilities at a very young age, when many of her contemporaries are spending their evenings out and about and partying. Moreover, she has no close and supportive relationships among her own family and she is very uncertain about what to do concerning the baby's father, Paul. Her depression makes it understandable that, although she loves James and cares for his physical well-being excellently, she does not feel like spending a lot of time interacting with him. She didn't know that it was important that she should.

This rationale is suggested only tentatively to Shula, but it is suggested in a constructive and supportive way, and her own opinion is asked. Shula nods and says that it makes sense; she is quite glad, in a funny way, to know that she is 'depressed'. A number of women have reported this sense of relief at having their feelings validated by a diagnosis. (Holden, 1994, p. 69).

Step 7: Develop a baseline against which to measure progress

This is not difficult. The following ways of measuring developments are identified:

a) Jane's depression: this is already known. Her score on the EPDS is 10.
b) James's weight: this is already known. At 4 months, he weighs 14 lbs.
c) James's responsiveness: Jane asks Shula to go and smile and James. At first he does not seem to respond, but when she smiles at him again, calls his name and strokes him, he smiles beautifully at her. Jane and Shula agree that the length of time it takes for James to respond to one of Shula's smiles should be the baseline in this respect.

Planning

A provisional plan is drawn up by Shula and Jane. Shula is asked first to say what her wishes are. She says she would like James to go to a nursery for day-care, but Jane has to explain that although a brief time may be possible, it is unlikely that Shula would be seen as a high priority. Shula says she would also like to learn word-processing. So in the planning stage Shula and her worker consider:

1 Shula's need for day-to-day support.
2 The need for Shula to have help in interacting through 'talk, touch, gaze', with James. Shula says she has heard of 'baby massage' but she doesn't know how to do it. Jane says she doesn't know either, but she promises to enquire if there is anything available locally.
3 Help for Shula to get out of her flat more than she does at present.
4 Support in making a decision about whether to resume living with Dean. Jane tells Shula about 'anger-management' courses which a local psychologist is just starting.

The plan for Shula, James and Jane

A coordinated plan is devised with specific goals (Table 7.3).

Table 7.3: Agreement between Shula and Jane

Jane agrees to:

1 Visit Shula on six occasions, once weekly, to offer 'active listening'.
2 Teach Shula baby massage.
3 Contact the local parent and baby group to find someone to go there with Shula.

In return Shula agrees to:

1 Contact Paul and ask him to consider going to the anger management classes.
2 Give James massage twice daily.
3 Take James to the parent and baby group.

Implementing the plan

Jane, as the key worker,

- tracks down the nearest parent and baby group and finds that it meets in the community centre on Tuesday and Thursday mornings. The group has a policy that , wherever possible, it shall be run by the parents themselves, and, to Jane's pleasure, one of the young mothers who attends the group and who has herself moved from being a depressed mother to being on the committee, offers to call for Shula and to accompany her to the group.
- Jane also tracks downs the clinical psychologist who is running the anger-management group and discovers that Paul can join a new group starting within a month. She passes this information to Shula at her next visit.
- Jane goes to the nearby clinical library and does a literature search concerning 'baby massage'. She finds that there are several studies reporting the usefulness of interacting with babies in this way. Moreover, when she enquires among her colleagues, she discovers that there is an afternoon class at the local community college run by a physiotherapist. Shula would be very welcome to attend.
- Shula, for her part, goes to the local community college and finds, to her pleasure, that there is a class for beginnings in learning how to use computers, as well as a baby creche. She plans to start as soon as possible.
- To Shula's surprise, when she approaches Paul about attending the anger-management group, he agrees. He says he doesn't know what comes over him when he gets angry, and he wants to do something about it before it gets him into trouble. He can join the group starting in a month's time. Each course runs for 6 weeks, one evening a week.

Reviewing and evaluating the work

At the end of the appointed time, Jane and Shula meet to consider their work together.

Reviewing the work

Jane, as Shula's key worker, has liaised with the other practitioners: the GP, the Homestart worker, and the clinical psychologist who was running the anger-management courses. Shula herself says that she is enjoying the typing classes at the community college, where James is settling into the creche. Before the final meeting with Shula, Jane contacts each of these practitioners and hears that plans are working out well. Paul is doing particularly well with his anger-management work.

Evaluating the work

This is measured against the baselines that were taken at the outset of the work, some two months previously.

- Shula's score on the EPDS has now dropped to 6 – no longer a cause for concern.
- James has put on weight very satisfactorily. He has now crossed a centile into the next band.
- James is now far more responsive; he smiles and babbles immediately someone gazes at him, especially when he is enjoying his massage.
- Paul's scores on the anger-management scales are extremely encouraging.

In conclusion, while this example may seem to be too simple to illustrate all the principles of using the 'Assessment, Planning, Implementing the plan, Reviewing and Evaluating' approach in multidisciplinary work, it does provide a structure for key workers to use in liaising with and coordinating their work with other practitioners.

Summary points

❒ Postnatal depression in mothers has been identified by researchers as a major risk factor in contributing to impaired cognitive development, insecure attachment and behavioural disturbance in their children.

❐ These difficulties, which are more common in boys than in girls, seem to be linked to disturbances in mother–infant interactions.

❐ Social support to mothers is of the greatest importance. Research shows that health visitors have been particularly effective in providing this type of support to mothers coping with postnatal depression. This support has also been demonstrated to benefit the children.

8

Toddlers and pre-school children: multidisciplinary approaches

If, in the interests of preventing later difficulties, extensive efforts must be invested in supporting parents while their children are infants, then even greater ones must be invested in helping the parents of toddlers and pre-school children with emotional and behavioural difficulties. This is the time when the toddlers are still growing up within a relatively circumscribed group of people: the parent(s) and immediate family; perhaps a childminder or two; some nursery or playgroup workers. The number of settings within which the child moves is also fairly limited: the home, the nursery or playgroup, the shops and a few other people's homes. Furthermore, the numbers of people available to care for the child and oversee his or her behaviour is usually as high as it will ever be – certainly a far higher ratio of carers to children than the child will encounter in school.

Prevalence of emotional and behavioural difficulties in young children

We saw in Chapter 1 that a high proportion of young children display substantial emotional and behavioural difficulties (see Tables 1.3 and 1.4). Many difficulties will fade away given confident management, but confidence is one characteristic which many parents, especially those without strong supportive networks, lack. For example, while bedtime and sleeping difficulties do not constitute a mental disorder, the 13 per cent of London 3-year-olds who have persistent difficulty in settling at night, and the 14 per cent of the same age-group who wake persistently during the night, can put an intolerable strain upon their parents. We may note, too, the finding by Tizard *et al.* (1988) of the Thomas Coram Research Institute concerning children aged 4 to 7 in inner London infant schools; she reported 16 per cent as having definite behaviour problems in the eyes of their teachers and a further 17 per cent as having mild problems. The teachers' views were confirmed by independent researchers. To have almost a third of little children in inner London schools showing behaviour difficulties is extremely worrying.

Relevant research

Anxious little children

Herbert (1991), drawing upon international categorizations of children's disorders, has suggested the classification of young children's anxieties shown in Table 8.1.

Young children with serious behaviour difficulties/ conduct disorders

There have been a number of longitudinal studies to examine the links between behaviour difficulties in early childhood and those of later childhood, adolescence and adulthood. The seminal studies of Robins (1966; 1981) and Robins and Price (1991) have made a huge contribution to our understanding of continuity factors. Of Robins's work, Farrington writes:

Table 8.1: Forms of anxiety experienced by children. (Herbert, A. (1991) *Clinical Child Psychology: Social Learning, Development and Behaviour.* © John Wiley and Sons Limited. Reproduced with permission.)

- *Separation anxiety* is characterized by excessive anxiety concerning separation from those to whom the child is attached (American Psychiatric Association, 1987, p. 60). A child with separation anxiety may be reluctant to go to school in order to stay near his or her mother or with some other important attachment figure. Headaches or stomach aches or other physical symptoms are also common.

- *Avoidant disorder* is characterized by excessive shrinking from contact with unfamiliar people, of sufficient severity to interfere with social functioning in peer relationships. Such a child is likely to appear shy, socially withdrawn, embarrassed and timid when in the company of peers of adults. Of course, these behaviours may be appropriate at specific stages of development

- *Overanxious disorder* is characterized by 'excessive or unrealistic anxiety or worry' (American Psychiatric Association, 1987, p. 63). An over-anxious child tends to worry excessively about school work and future events and usually appears nervous or tense; he or she complains of a variety of physical complaints (e.g. nausea or dizziness) and shows frequent self-consciousness.

The view that a general syndrome of antisocial behavior arises in childhood and continues into adulthood has been argued most persuasively by Robins (1979, 1983, 1986). She has repeatedly shown that the *number* of types of conduct disorder shown in childhood predict the *number* of types of antisocial adult disorders, rather than one specific type of child conduct disorder (such as aggression) predicting one specific type of adult antisocial behaviour (such as violence).

Farrington (1991), p. 7.

In confirmation of Robins's views, the longitudinal studies of Olweus (1979) highlighted the stability of certain patterns of behaviour and in his review he concluded: 'marked individual differences in habitual aggression level manifest themselves early in life, certainly by the age of 3'.

It is now also known that there is a relationship between *early age of onset* of behaviour difficulties and subsequent disturbance. It is increasingly accepted that the more serious and the earlier the onset of behaviour difficulties, the greater the probability of their continuing into adolescence and beyond. In summarizing this area of research, Webster-Stratton and Herbert (1994) concluded that certain risk factors contribute to the continuation of disorders (Table 8.2).

Table 8.2: Risk factors which contribute to the continuation of disorders in young children (Webster-Stratton and Herbert, 1994)

- Early age of onset (pre-school years) of oppositional-defiant disorder and conduct disorder, Those children with conduct symptoms prior to age 6 are at greater risk for developing antisocial behaviour as adults than those whose problems start during adolescence.

- Breadth of deviance (across multiple settings, such as home and school). Those children most at risk of continuing antisocial behaviour as adults had conduct problems which occurred not only in the home but also at school and in other settings.

- Frequency and intensity of antisocial behaviour. The likelihood of becoming an antisocial adult increases in direct proportion to the number of different behaviour problems evidenced as a child.

- Diversity of antisocial behaviour (several versus few) and covert behaviours at early ages (stealing, lying, firesetting). The greater both the covert and overt behaviour problems, the greater is the likelihood of becoming an antisocial adult, although aggressive behaviour is probably the most stable over time.

- Family and parent characteristics (Kazdin, 1987). Children whose biological parent has an antisocial personality are at greater risk.

In the light of this evidence, great efforts are being made by researchers to pinpoint the particular points at which preventive strategies can be put in place. Unfortunately, there is still only a very limited body of research on successful interventions with pre-school children although, as discussed in the last chapter, researchers have begun to identify postnatal depression in mothers as a major predisposing factor.

Research into effective interventions with pre-school children

Interventions focused on 'intellectual enrichment'

A major longitudinal study, which has been extremely carefully evaluated, has shown pre-school programmes supported by home visits to have substantial and long-lasting positive effects. The Perry Preschool Program in Ypsilanti, Michigan focused on 3- and 4-year-old children in a very disadvantaged community. Children were allocated to either an experimental group or a comparison group; the children in the former attended a daily pre-school programme supported by weekly home visits to their parents for up to two years. Farrington (1996) clarified the aim of the 'plan–do–review' curriculum as 'to provide intellectual stimulation, to increase children's thinking and reasoning abilities and improve their subsequent school achievement'. The children in the comparison group were not offered these opportunities.

About 120 children in the two groups were followed up until they were 15 years old. It was found that the children in the experimental group, when compared with those in the control group:

- were better motivated in primary school
- were seen by their class teachers as better behaved at age 6–9
- were achieving academically to a higher standard at age 14
- had more positive self-reports at age 15
- had fewer self-reports of offending behaviour.

A further follow-up when the participants were age approximately 27 years showed that the experimental group had incurred only half as many arrests on average as the control group (Schweinhart *et al.*, 1993). They were receiving higher earnings and were more likely to be home owners.

Farrington (1996) comments:

Hence, it was seen that a pre-school intellectual enrichment programme had led to decreases in school failure, in offending and other undesirable outcomes. The Perry project is admittedly only one study based on relatively small numbers. However, its results become more compelling when viewed in the context of ten other pre-school programmes followed up in the United States by the Consortium for Longitudinal Studies and other high quality early years programmes... With quite impressive consistency, all studies show that pre-school intellectual enrichment has long term beneficial outcomes on school success, especially in increasing the rate of high school graduation and decreasing the rate of special educational placements. The Perry project was the only one to study offending, but the consistency of the school success results in all the projects suggests that the effects on offending might also be replicable.

This multidisciplinary project, involving social, community and educational workers, is discussed further in Chapter 11.

Research underpinning for the 'Sure Start' and other initiatives

It is because of research material such as the Perry project and the 'quite impressive consistency' with which all studies show that 'pre-school intellectual enrichment has long term beneficial outcomes on school success', as well as other advantages, that the present government has set in place huge innovations in the field of pre-school provision, such as the Sure Start initiatives and the Early Years development initiatives.

Multidisciplinary interventions with young, anxious children

In all cases, before help can be given to the child, support must be offered to the child's parents. Living with a very worried young child can be extremely stressful and, as Davis and Spurr (1998) have shown, it is essential to give families the ongoing help and reassurance necessary for their own tensions to subside before they can manage their children effectively.

Dealing with the common fears of little children

Table 8.3 shows fears characteristic of many little children, as reported by Ollendick and King (1991).

General principles for helping anxious children

- Show the child that you do not think he or she is silly to be fearful. Many children and many grown-ups have fears; it is natural to have fears.

Table 8.3: Common fears of little children (Ollendick and King, 1988)

Age	Common fear
Infants	Loss of support Loud noises Strangers Things which 'loom up'
1- to 2-year-olds	Separation from parents Strangers
3- to 4-year-olds	Darkness Being left alone Insects and small animals

- Reassure the child that you wish to understand and to be helpful. You will not laugh at anything that he says.
- Tell the child that unless his or her safety or that of someone else is at risk, you will not tell anyone else anything that the child confides in you unless you are told that you may.
- Provide a model of non-fearful behaviour to the child concerned, for example, of spiders or thunder. Many patterns of behaviour are learned simply by contagion or modelling.
- Do not attend too much to children's specific fears; there may be a danger of reinforcing them – so preventing them extinguishing naturally.
- Take steps to deal with things that are upsetting your child which are preventible, for example, name calling, racism or bullying. Work with teachers or other parents to ensure that these fear-provoking behaviours in children are stopped.

Principles drawn from cognitive-behavioural theory: desensitization

Since this body of theory (see Chapter 3) draws attention to the processes by which patterns of belief and behaviour are *learned*, so it throws light upon the processes by which fearful behaviours can be unlearned, or replaced by other learning. Just as the fear evoked by an unpleasant experience can *generalize* to other situations, so children who have been helped to relax can learn to tolerate tiny, but very gradually increasing, presentations of the object or item they have come to fear by the process of *desensitization*.

Table 8.4 shows a typical desensitization programme.

Table 8.4: A desensitization plan for a child very frightened by a car accident

1 Sitting on mother's lap just looking at a range of picture books.
2 Sitting on mother's lap looking at picture books with cars and trains in them.
3 Sitting on mother's lap looking at a video of Thomas the Tank Engine/ Noddy.
4 Going for ordinary walks to the park or shops, making no mention of cars.
5 Going for ordinary walks, past a bus or train station or garage. Low key.
6 Seeing someone wave Goodbye, drive round the block and reappear.
7 Helping mother or daddy clean the car.
8 Being allowed to sit in the driver's seat, door open, for a minute or two.
9 Being allowed to play in the car.
10 Going for a very short outing in the car to a special place.

Multidisciplinary interventions with young children with serious behaviour difficulties

The real test of the effectiveness of a given intervention is, of course, not just its short-term but its long-term impact. Because of the cost of such studies, there are few long-term evaluations available. One impressive American study, however, is reported by Lally *et al.* (1988) who, having begun their work with women in pregnancy, gave help to women on issues of child-rearing, health and nutrition. In addition, the child received free day-care, designed to develop their intellectual abilities up to age 5. When the children reached age 3 a matched control group was chosen. These children did not receive additional services. Twelve years later, about 120 children were followed up, and this showed that significantly fewer of the children in the experimental group (2 per cent as opposed to 17 per cent) had been referred to the juvenile court for offending behaviour.

My own work is also relevant here. I have referred elsewhere (Sutton, 1999) to the research study which I carried out with 44 families, using three active methods of educating and training parents to work with their pre-school children, and comparing the outcomes with these children with the outcomes of a waiting-list-control group. Briefly, this study showed that the three active methods of training – meeting parents in a group, visiting them at home and telephoning them – all achieved statistically significant results by comparison with the waiting-list control group, both immediately after the training and at 15–18 months follow-up. Here I wish to explore briefly the outcomes of a further group in which the work was done entirely by telephone.

A study carried out exclusively by telephone

This study was undertaken because of the evidence from the earlier study that parents could improve their young children's behaviour difficulties whether I met them face to face or merely weekly by telephone. At first I believed that this was a chance outcome. However, the evidence from other family-support services, notably the Ngala Family Resource Centre, in Perth, Western Australia, which in 1992–3 provided over 3,000 telephone consultations to families – of which 10 per cent concerned the behaviour problems of young children – led me to suspect that the telephone is seriously under-exploited. Accordingly, the study was designed to use the telephone exclusively.

As in the earlier study, my main collaborators were health visitors and social workers who undertook an initial assessment of the children to eliminate the possibility that the child's difficult behaviour was attributable either to an allergy or some other organic difficulty. Then, after taking initial measures of children's behaviour from all the families, I randomly allocated the referrals either to an immediate-intervention group or to a waiting-list control group. I then undertook the structured programme of intervention which had proved so successful in the earlier study. Thus, the intervention took the following format:

1 Eight weekly phone calls, one per week, of between 5 and 40 minutes. Calls became shorter at the end of the sequence as parents spent less time, 'relieving their feelings' and as they began to see the new strategies of parenting which I was teaching them by phone take effect.
2 One follow-up call two weeks after the final session.
3 One follow-up session two to three months after the final session.

The results of the study were very encouraging. As I reported:

1 It is possible to train parents of difficult pre-school children to manage them effectively by telephone. The 'package' of eight once-weekly phone calls and two follow-ups was an important core component, but further phone calls were requested by about half the participants.
2 Children whose parents received training became more manageable by comparison with the children of parents who did not receive training.
3 The effects of training persisted at 12–18 months, as reported to an independent evaluator.
4 The level of depression of mothers who had to wait for help increased during this time.
5 The levels of depression of the mothers, once they were all receiving help, fell significantly as their children's behaviour improved.

6 The mothers' levels of depression remained much improved at
   12–18 months following training.

Sutton, 1995, p. 13.

Figure 8.1 summarizes the results of this study.

There were a number of factors associated with outcomes. It became
apparent that it *is* possible to bring about marked improvements in the
behaviour of pre-school children by means of the telephone, if we can
obtain the collaboration of their parents. The following additional
points were demonstrated by my research:

1 It is important for parents who are trying to manage their children
   using strategies of Parenting Positively to have support from a partner or other family member.
2 Less successful families were characterized by a lack of consistency,
   or even active conflict, among parents or caregivers about how to
   handle problematic situations.
3 Some lone parents were extremely successful; this may be attributable to the fact that there was no-one in their household to question
   what they were doing or to interfere with their efforts to be consistent.
4 Persistence and competence in using Time Out emerged as of crucial importance. When the independent evaluator telephoned the
   families at follow-up one of her questions was 'Which way of handling difficulties did you find particularly helpful?' Ten of the eighteen parents specified Time Out as being particularly helpful.

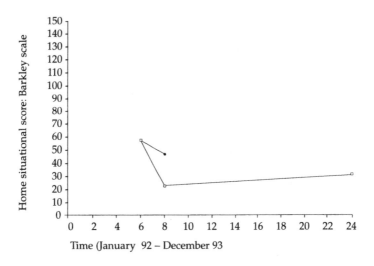

Figure 8.1. Effect of parent training by telephone at pre-training, post-training
and at follow-up, as measured by the Home Situations Scale (Barkley, 1981)
(reproduced by permission of the British Association for Behavioural and Cognitive Psychotherapy, from Sutton, 1995, *Behavioural Psychotherapy*, 23).

5 Those families who actively came back for further help after the conclusion of the standard 'package' were more successful at the evaluation.

Examples of multidisciplinary support to parents of pre-school children

There is abundant evidence that children of this age can be helped, and, as I indicated above, it is so much simpler to help now than later, when patterns of learned behaviour are entrenched. Let us consider some examples of children's difficulties and the way in which members of the helping professions can cooperate with parents to manage them.

Anxious little children

Shameem is the 3-year-old daughter of Muslim parents who came to Britain after turmoil in their own country, in which they were ostracized and threatened. She has a 3-year-old brother Aziz. Mrs Shah's parents are still in that country, and Mrs Shah does not know what has happened to them. Her husband is in a state of shock as he witnessed terrible things, including the death of his father from a heart attack following a confrontation with soldiers. He himself escaped because when the soldiers came he was out of the house, and, seeing their vehicles, he hid until they had gone.

The whole family are still frightened to the extent that they remain in the rooms which have been found for them on a council estate of a northern city, only going out at night to buy essentials at the nearby supermarket. They are found by a health visitor who has heard of the children from another Muslim family in the locality.

Mrs Shah is gaining some slight confidence as she acquires some English. Aziz wants to go out and play with the children whom he sees out of the window, but Mrs Shah is not sure whether to let him go or not. Shameem is still very frightened, not saying more than two or three words and staying as close as possible to her mother.

Assessment

Step 1: Building supportive and empathic relationships

A health visitor, Anne, is the primary care worker who establishes links with Mrs Shah. She has the double task of building an empathic and supportive relationship with Mrs Shah, her husband and her children, and of doing so via an interpreter. Mrs Shah may not have had contact with health visitors before but she is likely to recognize the kindness and concern of the worker demonstrated by Anne's smiles and gentleness. Through the interpreter Anne conveys the reason for her visit, namely the overall well-being of the family, and it is not until later that, reflecting on her visit, Anne realizes that Shameem was displaying not just ordinary shyness, or even the shyness of a little girl who has been through much, but sheer terror at the sight of a stranger. From long experience, Anne had simply smiled at the little girl, but Shameem, clearly still terrified, does not smile back.

Mrs Shah, realizing that Anne has come to help her, bursts into tears and through the interpreter explains that the family has been through a terrible time, being required by gunmen to leave their homes with only what they could carry in their hands. The children saw their parents' terror and both had been deeply affected by this and by the terrible journey which followed before they reached the northern city in Britain where they now found themselves. The story is translated by the interpreter in graphic and heartbreaking detail. Anne listens as long as she can but then, as Mrs Shah grows slightly calmer, she takes her leave explaining that she will come again in three days' time.

Step 2: Information gathering

On her return with the interpreter, Anne finds Mrs Shah still very distressed and tearful, and notices that Shameem is still terrified. While spending as much time as she can enabling Mrs Shah to weep again about her experiences and to pour out her distress and despair, Anne gives some time to finding out more about Shameem's experience.

Mrs Shah confirms that the little girl will not leave her side. She was terrified by the sight of the soldiers and the way they went round the house smashing windows and furniture. She still clings to her mother and will not let her out of her sight. The death of her grandfather was a further terror, as she had been accustomed to spending a lot of time with him. To find him lying still and unmoving had been confusing and upsetting for her. She is willing to play with Aziz for a few minutes, but if she sees one of her parents preparing to leave the house to go for food, she screams and screams. Mrs Shah, her own resilience put to a severe test, can do little more than try to reassure Shameem and let her follow her about every minute of the day.

Clinical assessment
It is inappropriate to try to measure Shameem's fear in any formal way, but it is apparent that she is showing all the signs of trauma. When Anne comes to the house, she becomes rigidly tense, hypervigilant, while holding on to her mother all the while. Anne recognizes her state as one of 'frozen awareness'.

Step 3: Identifying the main areas of difficulty together

While Anne is working with Mr and Mrs Shah to help them adjust to the strangeness of life in a northern town, and has found the elders at the nearby mosque very helpful in assisting them, she is also working to help relieve Shameem's fear. With the help of the interpreter, Mr and Mrs Shah are able to pinpoint some areas of change they would like to see in her:

- That she would allow her mother to go out of her sight for a few minutes without screaming to be with her.
- That she would play with another little Muslim girl who lives a few doors away.

Step 4: Identifying the positive features of the situation

Even with the help of the interpreter, Mrs Shah is surprised when Anne asks her to tell her about the things that Shameem likes to do. She finds it hard to identify anything until Aziz reminds her that she helps her mother in the house, taking items to and from the kitchen and assisting in preparing vegetables.

Step 5: Identifying the desired outcomes of the work together

Anne explains to Mrs Shah that she hopes that, as a result of some suggestions that Anne will discuss with her, it may be possible for Shameem both to:

- Allow her mother to leave the house for half an hour without screaming.
- Play with the little girl who lives in the adjoining house.

Step 6: Attempt a formulation of/rationale for the difficulties

Anne understands a great deal about how the situation may have come about. The following points seem to be important:

- Shameem has experienced situations which would have terrified anyone.
- Her grandfather, to whom she was very close, has died in her presence.
- Her parents, her main security, are still both deeply distressed and naturally show signs of that fear frequently.

Step 7: Develop a baseline against which to measure progress

In these circumstances formal measures would be totally inappropriate, but Anne asks Mrs Shah to take note of the intensity of Shameem's following her about at the present time, and of her unwillingness to play with the child nearby.

Planning

Mrs Shah's circumstances are so complex and difficult that she finds it difficult to focus on Shameem, but she is so in need of time free of being followed around that she agrees to do what Anne proposes. Anne undertakes to explore what support may be available to help Mrs Shah, who above all wants to be in touch with members of her own community.

Mrs Shah agrees:

a) That she will spend some time with Shameem after every meal, so that the little girl can learn to anticipate her mother's full attention.
b) That, having agreed that, 'following mother about' is the undesired behaviour, Mrs Shah will try to avoid even looking at Shameem or speaking to her when she does follow her.
c) Anne agrees to bring some toys from a store at the health centre for Shameem.
d) Anne says she will enquire from the community leaders at the mosque if there are opportunities for mothers and children to meet together nearby.

Implementing the plan

On Anne's next visit, Mrs Shah is still very unhappy and Shameem is still following her about. She is cheered to see the toys which Anne has brought, and the little girl sits down with them but does not play. Anne initially pays her no attention, and gradually Shameem begins to pick up the toys and play with them. Anne then sits down near her and gradually the little girl begins to interact with her, setting out the little family of dolls but saying nothing. After 10 minutes or so, Anne begins to pack the toys away and on this occasion takes them away with her.

On the next visit, Shameem looks pleased to see Anne, and is clearly hoping to play with the toys she has brought. Sure enough, as soon as the toys are set out, Shameem begins to play and reaches out for Anne's hand so that they can play together. Anne spends several minutes playing together with her, laughing and gaining her confidence.

Mrs Shah goes into the kitchen to make her first cup of tea unaccompanied by Shameem. However, as soon as she realizes that her mother is not in sight, Shameem screams and rushes into the kitchen. By now Mrs Shah has understood from Anne, via the interpreter, that she should pay very little attention to Shameem when she does this; rather, she should continue as though nothing has happened. She therefore deliberately goes into the kitchen several times during Anne's visit and sure enough, by the time that Anne has to leave, Mrs Shah is able to move easily in and out of the kitchen without complaint from Shameem.

Reviewing and evaluating the work

So things move forward, with Anne visiting the Shah family once a week and with Shameem gradually being able to spend longer and longer with her mother out of her sight. She begins to watch the other children out of the window, and as the better weather comes, her mother takes her to the nearby park where there are swings and a slide. A Homestart visitor has begun to spend an hour with the family each Wednesday.

When Mrs Shah and Anne review their work, Mrs Shah still finds it surprising that ignoring her little daughter's fears and demands for attention in a constructive way can reduce their frequency, but as she sees the suggestions made by Anne to be beneficial, she readily cooperates. Her own life is still deeply troubled, but she is happier that her little daughter is growing more confident, and that increasingly she is becoming accustomed to other children. There is even talk of introducing Shameem to the parent and children's group or the playgroup held in the nearby community centre.

When Anne attempts to evaluate her work, she is able to confirm to her manager that whereas Shameem at the outset would not leave her mother's side at all, she is now willing:

a) to amuse herself while her mother has a few minutes' rest in the middle of the day;
b) to allow her to move in and out of the various rooms of the flat without difficulty; and
c) to accompany her mother to the nearby playgroup and play with the children for up to an hour while her mother has a cup of tea with other parents.

Aggressive little children: a group-work approach

by Jane Askew, Joan Cunnington and Sharon Gregory, Health Visitors from North West Leicestershire

Having received a course of training by the author, Carole Sutton, we undertook group-work with families who had reported difficulties with the behaviour of their toddlers and pre-school children. Referrals were taken from a range of professionals and disciplines, including health visitors and general practitioners in the locality. A small number of participating parents referred themselves in response to notices advertising the group in libraries, playgroups, family centres, social services departments, Homestart and other voluntary services.

Assessment

Prior to the commencement of the group-work, a comprehensive assessment was undertaken in each child's home. It could be argued that the family home is the only place where an accurate holistic assessment can be made, as parents and children are more relaxed, enabling the nature of behavioural problems and the wider issues of family dynamics to be naturally revealed.

Behavioural problems were scored using the Rutter Child Behaviour Scale (Rutter *et al.*, 1970) although this was later discarded in favour of the Eyberg Scale (Eyberg and Johnson, 1974). Maternal depression, being a frequent factor in pre-school behavioural difficulties, was also measured using the Beck Depression Inventory (Beck, 1988). Scoring both behaviour and maternal depression prior to intervention provided a baseline against which to evaluate the outcomes.

Parents were given a weekly diary sheet and its use was explained. They were asked to record one week of a specified positive and negative behaviour before attending the group.

Planning and implementation of the plan

The course was based on a model of eight weekly meetings of two hours, with two follow-ups. Each two-hour session consisted of:

- Group feedback of experiences and progress made during the past week.
- A teaching component where parents were actively encouraged to participate in problem solving in an effort to raise and protect their feelings of self-esteem.
- One-to-one discussions, reviewing individualized programmes,

providing an opportunity to praise and encourage their efforts and to tackle any 'sticking points'

However, a flexible approach was imperative. Occasionally one member of the group would be unable to continue with the course on a particular week owing to relationship conflicts, or unresolved issues regarding their own experiences as a child or adolescent. On one occasion a mother disclosed details of sexual abuse by her father and her growing level of concen that he was now visiting her frequently and displaying a lot of interest in her pre-school daughter. Issues such as these had to be discussed in private and parents helped to determine the right solution for them before they were able to move on and focus on the child's behaviour.

Case example

Paula was attending the group because of her child's temper tantrums and soiling. She was having difficulty implementing the programme which had been planned with her because her own mother, who shared the child-care, was undermining her efforts by giving too much attention to the negative behaviour. Paula discussed this difficulty during group feedback and took up the offer to include her mother in future sessions. Her mother became an active participant, sharing her own parenting experiences, but she was willing to concede that in fact she had unwittingly been rewarding the undesirable behaviour.

Parents were given contact telephone numbers for support during the course if required, but this service was rarely taken up. Follow-up support was offered four weeks after the course. In practice, this meant initially meeting the group who had completed a course to assess their weekly diaries and to offer further encouragement, and then to introduce them to the new group, which gave them the opportunity to show off their newly acquired parenting skills. In turn, the new group felt reassured and optimistic about their own outcomes.

Some of the children had to be present during the sessions, as no other arrangements could be made for them. Although this meant that noise levels were sometimes high, their presence often provided valuable opportunities for putting aspects of social learning theory into demonstrable practice. In addition, a parent whose child was displaying aggression or tantrums gained immeasurable support and empathy from other group members. Members of the group took these events as opportunities to discuss and sometimes model positive play activities.

Case example

During one course a mother was attending because her child, Amy, aged 3, was abnormally clingy and under-confident. Progress was slow on the first two or three sessions and the child would not leave her mother's side. On the fourth session Amy's mother became very tearful during group feedback and expressed doubt about achieving any change. Other group members listened, offered encouragement and pointed out small changes that they had noticed. Following this incident the group members became actively involved in Amy's socialization. By the end of the course she was playing with the other children from the group and six weeks later she was attending a local playgroup.

Review and evaluation

Initially, all referrals were offered places in the groups, but it soon became apparent that preliminary discussion and screening of the referrals was imperative. This discussion sometimes led to a decision that a particular family's needs were too complex to be addressed at this level of intervention. Any referrals deemed to be inappropriate were discussed with the referrer and alternative sources of help were suggested.

In order to ensure that parents received maximum support and individual interventions from the three workers, the group size was limited to nine families. Thanks to the cohesive teamwork of the group leaders in offering clear messages and uniform advice, it was found that parents were able to carry out the programme successfully and relate to any of the group leaders during one-to-one discussion. This was helpful in preventing parents from becoming too dependent on one leader.

Parents unable to attend a session were expected to inform a health visitor in advance. Progress and advice could then be discussed by telephone. Failed attendance with no excuse usually indicated a lack of commitment, and no-shows were not always followed up, as it was considered that the responsibility lay with the parents to accept the help once it had been offered.

In the final session of the course, we reassessed the nature and severity of the children's behavioural problems and the mothers' levels of depression. Parents completed a course-evaluation questionnaire. Pre- and post-intervention scores could be compared, providing an indication of the success of the intervention. There was invariably a significant correlation between improvements in levels of child behaviour and reductions in maternal depression. We also gathered qualitative indicators and informative data including the views of parents who perceived that their children's behaviour was no longer a problem, even when quantitative scores, pre- and post-intervention, were not markedly changed. In addition, there was a noticeable and remarkable increase in spontaneous affection and a developing warmth between parent and child. An attempt was made to measure this by asking parents to complete a short retrospective questionnaire comparing their feelings towards their child before and after the course. Many parents reported an increase in positive feelings.

Summary points

❒ Many developmental, emotional and behavioural problems are short-lived, for example, fears in small children and temper tantrums in toddlers.

❒ However, the more serious and the earlier the onset of behaviour difficulties, the greater the probability of their continuing into adolescence and beyond.

❒ Many fears can be dealt with by a simple process of desensitization. Within the context of a calm and reassuring relationship, a child is helped to deal with frightening situations by encountering them in very small doses, gradually increasing as the child gains confidence in dealing with them.

❒ There is extensive evidence that children's behaviour problems can be effectively dealt with using principles of social learning/cognitive behavioural theory. It is sensible to make services available as early as possible in the child's life, in order to prevent difficulties becoming entrenched.

❒ There is evidence that this help can be successfully offered by trained personnel on an individual family basis, by telephone or to groups of parents coming together for a series of meetings once a week.

9

Children at their first schools:
multidisciplinary approaches

In this chapter we shall consider research into the emotional and behavioural difficulties of children when they are in their primary or first schools. They are likely to be aged about 5 through to about 9 or 10. Again, we shall examine first the nature and prevalence of the difficulties, then consider research into the problems of children of this age and finally, based on this research, we shall offer typical examples of the types of situations which may be encountered by practitioners, with some suggestions for how to proceed within a multidisciplinary framework.

This is an extremely important stage in the development of a young child. Although, as we saw in Chapter 8, there are large numbers of children with emotional and behavioural difficulties coming through into this age group there is less evidence from well evaluated studies of strategies for dealing with them. I shall consider such evidence as does exist.

Prevalence of emotional and behavioural difficulties of children at their first schools

We saw in Chapter 1 that emotional disorders, those based upon anxiety such as ritualistic behaviour, phobias and obsessions, together with depression, are very common. About one in twenty-two children in rural settings and almost one in ten children in urban settings are coping with troubling levels of fear and worry – enough to disturb their ability to make the best use of school opportunities. A rather higher number of children in both rural and inner-urban settings display conduct disorders, that is, serious behaviour difficulties: aggressiveness, disruptiveness and destructiveness. We have already considered some of the variables associated with different diagnostic categories, see Table 1.1, page 8.

Relevant research

Anxious children in their first schools

It is known that many children experience fear to such an extent that fearfulness is seen as normal. Ollendick and King (1991), writing of anxieties of children of this age, have noted the common fears shown in Table 9.1.

As I have written elsewhere (Sutton, 1999):

> Most developmental fears then, are transient. It appears that, under favourable circumstances, they fade away as a result of two main influences: first, children's naturally maturing cognitive processes, so that they come to understand that monsters, such as dinosaurs, are no threat to them; and, second, those who care for them avoid reinforcing their fears by giving simple explanations of upsetting noises like thunder and also by avoiding showing fear themselves.

Ways of helping anxious children

As suggested by Ollendick and King (1991), many of the approaches developed to help children with simple phobias are grounded in cognitive-behavioural approaches; for example, systematic desensitization, modelling, operant approaches and methods based upon cognitive strategies. Each will be considered briefly.

Table 9.1: Common fears of children aged 5 to 11 (Ollendick and King, 1988)

Age	Common fear
5- and 6-year-olds	Wild animals Ghosts Monsters
7- and 8-year olds	Aspects of school Supernatural events Physical danger
9- to 11-year olds	Fears about wars Health and bodily injury School performance Social fears

Systematic desensitization

This is a process whereby the fearful child (or adult) is supported, having been helped to become calm and relaxed, is introduced to very gradually increased presentations of the feared object or animal, moving from minimally frightening to the most frightening. Thus, a child with a terror of dogs, which is very common, might undergo the steps shown in Table 9.2 over a period of several weeks.

Modelling

Ollendick (1979) has distinguished three separate forms of modelling: by filming, with a live model who is simply observed, and with a model who gently coaches the child to take part in the feared activity. He then compared the effectiveness of these three forms of modelling which 'involves demonstrating non-fearful behaviour in the fear-producing situation *and* showing the child appropriate responses to use in the fearful situation' (see Table 9.3; Ollendick and King, 1991).

The principle of participant modelling is a valuable one. Many children can be helped to overcome fears of animals, of water, of social and similar situations by both being offered a model they can identify with and by being encouraged by a non-fearful child to achieve the desired goal.

Table 9.2: A desensitization programme for a little child very frightened of dogs

1   Sitting on her mother's lap, Janet looks at a book of nursery rhymes.
2   While on her mother's lap watching some very undisturbing scenes of small farm animals on television: lambs, calves, hens, etc.
3   Sitting on her mother's lap, Janet hears a story of the 'heroic money spider' who rescued a princess from a tower, or the Spot stories: the child's calmness and reaction guides the pace.
4   While on her mother's lap Janet watches scenes of the Dulux puppies: not much should be made of this; they are just there – like other creatures in the world.
5   When Janet and her Mum are out, they go past a pet shop with hamsters and gerbils in the window. Several trips are made but no particular comment is made.
6   When Janet and her Mum are out, they look in the window of the pet shop and see the small animals there.
7   When on an outing, they notice a young child, only a little older than Janet, taking a small dog for a walk on a lead.
8   They make several pre-arranged visits to a friend who has a sleepy dog guaranteed to take absolutely no notice of anyone.
9   They make further pre-arranged visits in which Janet watches a docile dog having a bath or a trim.
10   … and so on, with each step enabling Janet to feel less fear of and more confidence in managing a dog.

Table 9.3: Modelling as a means of helping fearful children (Ollendick, 1991)

Form of modelling	Procedure	Level of effectiveness
1 Filmed modelling	Child watches a film in which a model progressively interacts more closely with feared stimulus.	50–59 %
2 Live modelling	Child observes a live model engage in real-life interactions with the object or situation which is feared.	50–67 %
3 Participant modelling	Live modelling, plus contact with a fearless peer who actively guides the child through the feared situation.	80–92 %

Depressed children in their first schools

The cognitive abilities of children aged about 5 to 10 or 11 are developing fast. In Piagetian terms, they are passing through the 'preoperational' stage (around age 2 to 7) and the 'concrete operational' stage (around age 7 to 12). In the course of these developments they are increasingly able to move from an egocentric view to one in which they can understand the different perspectives of others, can anticipate the outcomes of different courses of action and can understand that events which occur to others, such as illnesses, accidents or family separations, might happen to them. Such abilities may make them more vulnerable to depression (see Table 9.4).

A number of other possible factors must also be considered in attempting to understand depression in young children. For example, Harrington (1994) has reported that:

Table 9.4: Circumstances which may predispose a young child to depression

1   Loss by separation from or bereavement of an emotionally important relationship, especially that of the mother or main carer.
2   Fears of loss, of family member, close friend, important pet.
3   Few or no friends.
4   Isolation, arising either from geographical factors or from unacceptable personal characteristics, such as shyness or smelliness.
5   Disability, both in terms of its direct effect and its indirect ones, such as difficulties in joining peer-group activities.
6   Being a lone child from a particular community, such as a lone African, Caribbean or Chinese child or a lone child from a travelling community.

Depressive symptoms have also been found in association with both physical abuse (Allen and Tarnowski, 1989) and sexual abuse (Goldston *et al.*, 1989). Depressive disorders have been said to occur in about 20 % of maltreated children.

Further, Rutter and Sandberg (1992) have drawn attention to the fact that when children lose their mother or main caregiver, the child not only has to cope with the loss per se, but also the 'associated reduction in parental care', which renders children vulnerable.

Aggressive children in their first schools

There is so much evidence of the continuities of aggression from the time when children are in their first schools through adolescence into adulthood that it is imperative to initiate preventive measures at this stage. Many longitudinal studies have shown that aggressiveness at this first-school age is a predictor of aggressiveness in adulthood. For example, in London, Farrington (1978) demonstrated that aggressiveness in boys, as rated by teachers when the children were aged 8, predicted self-reported violence at age 18; while in New York State Huesmann *et al.*(1984) followed up several hundred children and found that aggression as rated by peers at age 8 predicted self-reported aggression in men at age 30. Sadly, the indications are that many British schools, unable or unwilling to cope with disruptive and aggressive children, exclude them, with the effect that not only does their behaviour go uncurbed but their school-work suffers also (Gardiner, 1996).

This last report is particularly worrying in view of the evidence that 25.7 per cent of all exclusions are from minority groups and that two-thirds of those excluded are below average ability.

Gardiner also cited the large number of children in care being excluded – about two-thirds of all exclusions. Thus, the most needy of all children are those who experience greatest adversity.

Farrington (1991), in an impressive review of a huge field of research, reports the outcome of his own data analysis; it confirms other studies' reports that several factors emerge as precursors of aggression and violence: see Table 9.5.

Research into multidisciplinary interventions in the difficulties of children in their first schools

Preventive initiatives are, however, being taken. For example, a major initiative by the British central government, involving the Department of Health, the Home Office and the Social Exclusion Unit has made nearly £500 million available through the *Social Inclusion: Pupil Sup-*

Table 9.5: Factors associated with the development of subsequent aggressiveness in boys (Farrington, 1991)

1	Harsh attitude to and discipline by the boy's parents at age 8
2	Low family income
3	Parental criminality
4	Poor supervision of children by the parents
5	Separations from parents
6	High daring
7	Low intelligence

port Grant (Department for Education and Employment, 1999).

The objectives of this initiative include reducing the levels of truancy, bullying and levels of pupil disaffection by one-third within a three-year period. Such initiatives are intended to be multiagency, involving not only education, but also health, social services and the voluntary agencies. As a result of these initiatives, a number of projects are being set up across the country; we await their evaluated results with interest.

Helping anxious or depressed children across the home–school boundary

Many of the approaches which have been developed to help anxious children are grounded in cognitive-behavioural approaches; for example, systematic desensitization, modelling, operant approaches and methods based upon cognitive strategies. There is only the beginnings of a research literature concerning how best to help anxious or depressed children across the home–school divide (Ollendick, 1979; Harrington, 1994). Typically this is not because teachers are uninterested in children's personal difficulties or that they dismiss them as irrelevant, but because under the pressure of delivering a curriculum in extremely demanding school settings, they just do not have the *time* to attend to the detail of plans to support children in this matter. We shall consider an example later in this chapter (page 188).

Helping aggressive children across the home–school boundary

In an investigation of the effectiveness of different strategies in managing children with behavioural difficulties, Webster-Stratton (1999) undertook a review of the literature for this age group. She concluded that there are a number of effective strategies (see Table 9.6).

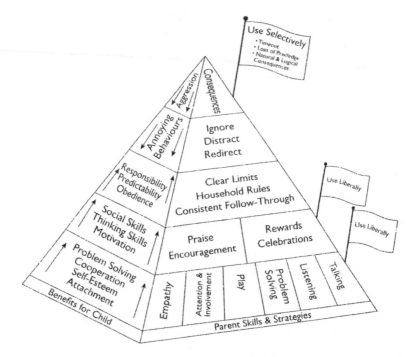

Figure 9.1. Parenting pyramid: principles of effective parenting. (From *The Incredible Years: Parents, Teachers and Children Training Series* developed by Carolyn Webster-Stratton Phd.)

As a way of illustrating the interlocking components of parenting and teaching, Webster-Stratton has devised the pyramid shown in Figure 9.1, illustrating how the various elements of parenting interact.

Figure 9.2 shows how the effective management of the child in the classroom echoes principles of effective parenting. In each case the approach is grounded in respect for the child, but it also uses principles which derive, whether people are aware of it or not, from social learning theory.

Helping hyperactive children across the home–school boundary

An area which is attracting a great deal of research attention at the present time is that of attention deficit/hyperactivity disorder (ADHD). It is a contentious field, as there is by no means a consensus about the extent to which this is a physiologically based difficulty and how far it is a learned behaviour. There is insufficient space here to discuss it in detail, but suffice it to say that a child with this condition typically dis-

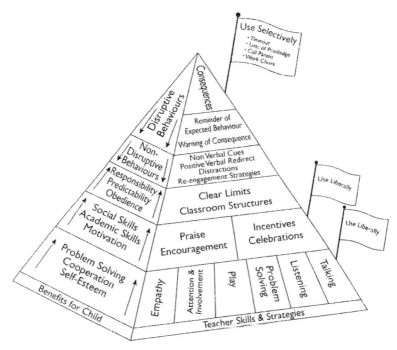

Figure 9.2. Teaching pyramid: principles of effective teaching and classroom managemnt. (From *The Incredible Years: Parents, Teachers and Children Training Series* developed by Carolyn Webster-Stratton Phd.)

plays three related behaviours: short attention span, over-activity and impulsiveness.

The condition needs extremely careful diagnosis against internationally established criteria. The assessment is usually carried out by at least two independent professionals, often a paediatrician and an educational psychologist, who will both take the views of the child's parents into account. I have discussed the condition more fully in my book, *Helping Families with Troubled Children: A Preventive Approach.* However, as researchers and practitioners devote time and effort to understanding ADHD, so guidelines to support teachers and others emerge.

Helping children with emotional and behavioural difficulties: 'Circles of Friends'

An approach which has been attracting increasing research attention and is included because of its promise in helping children with emotional and behavioural difficulties is the 'Circle of Friends'. Newton *et*

Table 9.6: Effective strategies for improving the behaviour of aggressive children (after Lloyd, 1999)

- There is evidence to show that parent-education programmes can be an effective way of improving the behaviour of pre-adolescent children who have behaviour problems. The effects last over time, although in a number of studies as many as 50 % of parents continue to experience difficulties.
- Overall, **behaviourally-oriented parent-education programmes** seem to produce the biggest subsequent changes in children's behaviour… .
- The results also indicate that **group-based programmes** may produce more changes in children's behaviour and be possibly more cost-effective and user-friendly than individual programmes.
- The most effective approach for the facilitator seems to be an **interactive model of learning** of teaching, leading and role playing which increases parents' confidence in their own ideas.
- Much of the research demonstrates the link between conduct disorders in early childhood and later delinquency, and consequently the importance of intervening early in a child's life…
- Being supported by **neighbours, friends and family living locally** are protective factors…
- Parents, teachers and mental health professionals need to work collaboratively to provide **comprehensive community-based services**.
- Programmes where **both parents** are involved seem to be more successful than those where only the mother takes part. As parenting education develops, greater efforts need to be made to engage fathers.
- Working with parents alone is not enough to achieve long-term change in children. Parenting programmes which include **direct work with the child** are more likely to be effective than those that do not.
- **Schools** are important influences in children's lives. Effective programmes help parents and teachers develop good working relationships and support children's learning.

---

al. (1996) have described a method of meeting the needs of children with major emotional and behavioural difficulties which derives from earlier work by Forest *et al.* (1996) to ensure the inclusion of children with special needs within their peer-group and neighbourhood school. Newton and colleagues adapted this approach to the mainstream classroom, where some children experience isolation as part of a vicious circle of unacceptable behaviour on their part, followed by rejection by other children, further unacceptable behaviour and so on.

Readers are referred to the original paper by Newton *et al.* (1996) but there is room here to say that the approach recognizes the dangers run by children with emotional and/or behavioural difficulties of being isolated and excluded. It involves staff in sharing responsibility for solving problems with pupils. Several essential stages are set out below.

A *Pre-requisites for the approach*

- A key member of staff must understand the approach and be committed to using it with the focus child.
- The child's parent or carer must have had the approach explained so that their consent and support is available.
- The approach must be properly explained to the child concerned, and he or she needs genuinely to accept what is about to happen.

B *Setting up circles*

The essence of the approach is that a professional worker who already knows the child, such as an educational psychologist or social worker, but who is not known to the class, meets all the children. He or she then goes through a series of steps in which first the strengths and then the difficulties experienced and caused by the focus child are identified by the children. The worker then discusses the place of friendship in their lives, using a set of four concentric circles to denote friendships (see Figure 9.3). The circles show:

Close family (intimate relatives)
Close friends ('whose lives enrich your own')
Acquaintances
Those in paid relationships: teachers, etc.

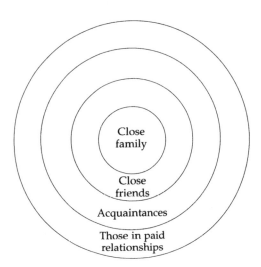

Figure 9.3. The concentric circles of relationships (Newton *et al.*, 1996).

Newton *et al.* write that the 'next stage is crucial':

> The group is asked to imagine how they would feel if their second and third circles were empty and that all they had in their lives was immediate family and paid people. This is a powerful part of the session, and a rich range of responses is always forthcoming. The following is a compilation of responses from pupils in primary and secondary schools: *'Lonely... Bored... Unhappy... Embarrassed... Sad... Angry... Like you didn't exist... Upset... Left out... Invisible... Unwanted... As if you had no control... Fed up with other people... Depressed... Like you're different... Scared...'* The depth of empathy in these responses shows how meaningful it is to the children we have worked with.
>
> The group leader then asks the class how they would act if they had these feelings. Again a rich range of responses is readily elicited. *'Be bad-tempered... Run away... Be angry and beat people up... Steal people's things... Swear... Try to get attention... Call people names... Try and be funny... Throw things at people... Cry... Day-dream... Go and hide... Break things...'* Pupils know how they would behave if they had no friendships. This is the turning point in the whole class meeting. (p. 43)

C *The overall process*

Space does not permit full details, but Table 9.7 shows the sequences of steps which is essential to move through in the process of establishing Circle of Friends groups and for running the initial session.

Table 9.7: The process for running an initial Circle of Friends session (Newton *et al.,* 1996)

1	Introduce self.
2	Agree the ground rules and explain confidentiality.
3	Agree the aims of the group, e.g. to help Craig make and keep friends and to help him get back on track with his behaviour.
4	Invite group members to tell the focus child why they volunteered to be in his or her group.
5	Elicit from the group, and list, positives and areas the child needs to work on.
6	Brainstorm strategies.
7	Agree which strategies can be tried and ensure commitment to these from the group. Be clear with the group about responsibilities, disclosures and boundaries. Let them know what is expected of them and the limits to this.
8	Agree a name for the group, avoiding the focus child's name. 'The listening group', 'the helpful group'.
9	Describe meeting and follow-up arrangements, and encourage mutual support in the group.

While, to the best of my knowledge, no controlled studies have been carried out comparing this strategy to others which cross the home–school boundary, I can confirm that one of the social work students I have worked with, Melanie Meggs, has successfully carried out the approach with a class of children in Derbyshire, UK, in respect of one little boy on the verge of being excluded from school.

Helping children with behaviour difficulties: work with parents

A centre of excellence has developed at the Oregon Social Learning Centre, deriving from the work of Patterson (1975) and Patterson *et al.* (1993). Forgatch (1991) writes of the work undertaken there:

> Our clinical experience has taught us that parents of antisocial youngsters have serious deficits in parenting practices (Patterson, 1982). The central hypothesis that has emerged from these efforts is that it is necessary to teach parents effective family management practices to effect lasting reductions in antisocial behavior problems.

Forgatch explains that the model of working with parents developed at the Oregon Social Learning Centre has three main components: family-management skills, skill in problem-solving and confidence in monitoring children. These components, however, focus exclusively upon the management of children's difficult behaviour while they are under the control of their parents. It neglects three areas which other analyses have shown to be of central importance (e.g. Webster-Stratton, 1999); accordingly, I shall include them, making six in all in Table 9.8.

Let us consider each of these components more closely:

Family-management skills
These have already been examined in some detail: see Chapter 5 for aspects of assessment and Chapter 6 for planning, implementation of the plan, review and evaluation. The whole approach has been explored in detail in a number of recent texts, including Webster-Stratton and Herbert (1994) and Sutton (1999). Figure 5.1 summarizes the overall approach from the point of view of workers trying to help families.

In my own work, for example, I was in touch with a family who asked to take part in the study I was undertaking to discover whether the cognitive-behavioural strategies offered to parents within a supportive relationship could be successfully passed on by telephone. Their boy, Neil, aged 8 years, was older than I usually felt suitable to accept into the telephone mode of intervention, but the parents were so pressing that I finally agreed.

Table 9.8: Core skills identified by researchers for helping parents with children showing emotional or behavioural difficulties (after Forgatch, 1991)

1 Family-management skills:
  * Tracking or pinpointing and recording specific child behaviour difficulties, e.g. compliance with a request versus non-compliance
  * Giving praise contingent upon good behaviour
  * Administering mild penalties or sanctions: e.g. Time Out; reduction of TV
2 Confidence in monitoring children: providing close supervision for children, especially when they are out of the house. Forgatch (1991).
3 Skill in problem-solving strategies: ability to identify problems which might arise, e.g. travel home after a late event at school or at a friend's house.
4 Direct work with children, as found to be so important in the analysis of key variables by Webster-Stratton (1999).
5 Constructive communication among family members.
6 The contribution of mentors to support young school children.

Neil had already been excluded from one school and was in danger of being excluded from another because of aggressiveness; he was rude and cheeky to his father and stepmother, and was bed-wetting most nights. After Neil had been screened for organic difficulties, a number of specific behaviours were identified and these were the focus of specific behaviour-management approaches. His parents were exemplary in carrying out the various procedures of the eight-week programme, and things soon began to improve. After the follow-up his parents sent me an unsolicited letter indicating that Neil was settled in school, that his behaviour was improving day by day and that his bed-wetting had completely stopped.

Monitoring children's activities and providing close supervision
A number of studies, notably those of Wilson (1980), addressed the extent to which parents knew the whereabouts of their children and provided supervision of their activities, especially when they were out of the house. As I have written elsewhere:

> The studies of Harriet Wilson (1980, 1987) are instructive here. She compared the delinquency rates of children living in either the inner city or the suburbs according to whether the degree of parental supervision exercised over them was 'strict', 'intermediate' or 'lax'. She found that, after controlling for other variables, 'strictness' as defined by parents' knowing where their sons were and exercising control over their activities, conferred protection against delinquency; within the inner city, for example, the delinquency rate of 'lax' families was over two and a half times that of 'strict' families.

Clearly, this sort of monitoring has to begin *before children go to school* and continue throughout the years in which the child is in first and secondary school. There is no point in beginning to attempt to impose supervision of this kind when a child is entering the teenage years.

Skill in problem-solving strategies.
These also have been addressed in Chapter 3. To recapitulate, the process involves:

- specifying the problem-to-be-solved very closely
- brainstorming a large number of possible solutions
- withholding criticism of any of those suggested
- exploring the potential effectiveness of all the solutions
- selecting the one which seems the best
- testing out that solution and, if it is indeed effective, monitoring this
- if it is not effective, testing out another solution from the list.

This approach can be applied to a wide range of difficulties in bringing up children, particularly those in which conflict often arises, such as who is responsible for domestic chores, the care of animals, hours of coming home, doing homework and bed-times.

Direct work with children
There are several bodies of evidence to draw on here. In Chapter 10 we shall consider a broader spectrum of work with children, but there is only enough space here to report briefly on the work of Harrington *et al.* (1998). These authors reviewed the psychological treatment of depression in children and adolescents and in their consideration of treatment research concluded that:

> the most promising psychological treatment interventions for depression in children are individual rather than family therapies. Cognitive-behavioural therapy seems to be an effective treatment for depressive symptoms and mild depressive disorders.

These authors make it clear that typically the cognitive-behavioural therapy consisted of ten group sessions which emphasized training in self-monitoring, problem-solving and self-reinforcement.

Constructive communication among family members
This is the counterpart to the 'confiding' found by Brown and Harris (1978) to be an essential component of relationships which protected mothers from depression. If it is essential for an adult to have someone to confide in, how much more important is it for a child attempting to cope with the demands and difficulties of home, school and playground? To be able to share fears and worries, to be able to talk about

difficulties of relationships with teachers, school-friends, relatives and neighbours, can provide an invaluable release from stress for children. This talking and sharing may well be the child's equivalent of the experience of counselling.

The contribution of mentors to support young school children

In both the UK and the USA, considerable work has been undertaken in the field of mentoring. In essence, the mentor is an adult outside the family who has volunteered to receive specialist training to befriend and support vulnerable children and young people.

A recent Home Office Report (Roberts and Singh, 1999) provides an evaluation at the two-year stage of a three-year community-based development project based in Islington, London, which offers early intervention for young children who are 'at risk' of long-term behaviour problems, school failure or exclusion, and criminality. The project, entitled CHANCE (Challenging but Enabling), focuses upon children aged 5–11, who are in primary school, and known to be vulnerable to risk factors associated with offending behaviour: antisocial behaviour, family problems, school failure/problems, health problems or poverty.

Children were screened using the Strengths and Difficulties Questionnaire (SDQ) developed by Goodman (1997) (see Appendix 5.3). In addition, however, selection criteria included family, demographic, educational and social indices. Details of the forty children are shown in Tables 9.9 and 9.10.

It will be noted that this initiative does not have a control group, and that the project is still in its initial stages. Further, there do not seem to be plans for *maintaining* any positive outcomes, the necessity for which has been noted by many researchers, including myself (Sutton, 1992; 1995). With these important caveats, however, Roberts and Singh (1999) conclude:

Table 9.9: Children assigned mentors by CHANCE: proportion with problems reported by teachers (Roberts and Singh, 1999)

	%
Above UK 80th centile for behaviour problems	100
Hyperactive	91
Conduct problems	82
Social problems	62
Peer problems	59
Emotional problems	44

Table 9.10 Other characteristics of the children (Roberts and Singh, 1999)

Age at referral	6–10 years
Proportion of boys	97 %
Ethnicity	
White	50 %
Black	21 %
Asian	10 %
Mixed/other	19 %
Proportion:	
Excluded from school	50 %
Having free school meals	82 %
With single mothers	50 %

- CHANCE is successfully recruiting, vetting, training, supporting and retaining mentors and matching them with vulnerable young children. About forty mentors and children are involved each year.
- The project has built good relationships with schools and other agencies which regard the CHANCE team positively, i.e. professional, highly organized and committed.
- It has established effective criteria which focus on known risk factors and targets its referrals carefully and accurately.
- Strong, affectionate and trusting relationships have been built between mentor and child. Such relationships make possible solution-focused measures designed to change problem behaviour by teaching life skills, promoting active learning, personal responsibility and self discipline, and encouraging independence.
- Initial indicators suggest these measures are improving children's behaviour – their mothers, teachers and mentors all report some positive changes.

With these reports of effective interventions with primary school children in mind, let us consider some examples of multidisciplinary work with children with emotional and behavioural difficulties.

Examples of multidisciplinary support to children and their families

Some evidence is becoming available that children of this age can be helped – and that this is a good time to offer help. If matters are left until the child reaches secondary school, the greater number of situations, and the greater number of people concerned, make it far more difficult to make an effective intervention. Let us consider some examples of children's difficulties and the way in which members of the helping professions can cooperate with parents to manage them.

An anxious child at primary school

Henry is 5, the long-awaited and only child of older parents. He grew up with little contact with other children and finds them noisy and frightening. He is a very intellectual little boy who finds the rough and tumble of the playground too much to cope with. If he could be allowed to stay in the classroom working on the computer, he would choose to do this most of the time.

He did not look forward to going to school and found it extremely difficult to settle in. There are few children who could be called his friends, partly because he does not know how to make friends, and partly because other children do not find him a very rewarding companion. He does not enjoy football or other physical activities and finds the enthusiasms of his peers dull and boring. He tends to retreat to the computer on every possible occasion, as here he can display his competence without threat or challenge. His teachers recognize his anxiety and try to reassure him, but although Henry responds well to them, he is still finding the classroom a frightening place. It may be that he is in danger of becoming school phobic.

Assessment

Step 1: Building supportive and empathic relationships

This school does not have the services of a home–school liaison worker but it can call upon the help of a very sensitive and understanding volunteer, a grandfather, Mr Potter, who used to be a teacher and who misses contact with young children. Mr Potter recognizes the dilemma of Henry, the intellectually able child, but one who lacks confidence in himself and who therefore retreats into a narrow but lonely world.

Mr Potter comes to the classroom on Tuesday and Friday mornings. On one of these mornings, he is introduced to Henry's mother and gains her agreement that he should work with the boy. Henry looks terrified; his mother, Mrs Hamilton, however, is very relieved.

Step 2: Information gathering

One particular Tuesday, Mr Potter sets aside some time to talk with Mrs Hamilton. His natural warmth of personality and his evident years of experience reassure her that Henry's difficulties can be managed constructively, but her anxiety leads her to pour out her fears, the difficulties she has had since she gave up her very satisfying job as a nurse manager in order to care for Henry full-time, and her fears that he is 'odd'. She tells him of the disappointment that she and her husband feel that their child has not the happy, friendly personality which they had anticipated, and of how on occasion they shout at him out of sheer frustration. This makes him all the more fearful and he often shakes and 'twitches' for an hour or more afterwards. In fact, Mrs Hamilton, confides, he is sometimes so odd, preferring his own company to playing with other children and setting out all his computing equipment in ways which must not be interfered with, that she and her husband have wondered if he may be becoming autistic.

Referral for assessment by an educational psychologist

Mr Potter listens calmly to Mrs Hamilton's fears and then says that, on the basis of his own years of experience, he does not believe that Henry is becoming autistic but that he is acutely anxious. It is this which leads him to twitch and to behave in rather obsessive ways at times. At Mrs Hamilton's request, however, he promises to give her details of an educational psychologist who works privately, as he knows that it is unlikely that Henry would be seen by the local authority educational psychologist for many months.

Step 3: Identifying the main areas of difficulty together

On the following Tuesday, Mr Potter and Mrs Hamilton meet to clarify the areas of difficulty together. Since this is an arrangement to cross the home–school boundary, it would have been desirable for Mr Hamilton to attend but, as a senior officer at the nearby air force base it is difficult for him to take time for the meeting. He promises that he will try to cooperate with any suggestions made by the school. Mr Potter and Mrs Hamilton identify the following changes which they themselves would like to see, with the understanding that these would be explored with Henry later:

- That Henry will get ready for school each morning without tears or throwing things about.
- That he will spend three spells of 10 minutes daily playing with another child in the classroom.
- That he will regain the ability to be dry at night.

Step 4: Identifying the positive features of the situation

With the help of Mr Potter, Mrs Hamilton is able to identify a number of Henry's positive features. Using the Strengths and Difficulties Questionnaire (Appendix 5.3) as the basis for discussion, Mrs Hamilton and Mr Potter are able to identify several positive features of Henry's behaviour. For example, Mr Potter reports how he had seen Henry go up to another child, a little girl, who had just arrived in the school, and hold out a teddy he had found to her. Mrs Hamilton nods, saying that Henry was devoted to his teddy and always wanted it when he was unhappy; she was so pleased to know that Henry had been thoughtful towards another child. She herself is then able to volunteer that sometimes when she has a headache and just wants to put her feet up, Henry will say, 'You have a rest, Mum. I'll play by myself until you feel better.' Finally, Mrs Hamilton was able to report that both she and her husband agreed that Henry was able to concentrate for very long periods. This was often on the computer, but he also enjoyed puzzles and jigsaws.

So, on the basis of this discussion, Mr Potter and Mrs Hamilton are able to note Henry's strengths:

1 He is kind to younger children.
2 He is helpful if someone is upset or feeling ill.
3 He sees tasks through to the end.

Step 5: Identify the desired outcomes of the work together, in discussion with the child

Mr Potter and Henry's mother agree, after discussion, that Mr Potter will tell Henry and the class teacher of their talk and will also fully involve Henry in planning. When Henry asks what he would like to happen in the future, he replies and he says, 'I would like a friend'. The class teacher is kept informed. The agreed goals for the collaborative work together are that Henry,

• Will leave home for school in the mornings, calmly and quietly.
• Will play with at least two other children daily for at least 10 minutes.
• Will take part once weekly in group activities, such as singing and drama.

Step 6: Attempt a formulation of/rationale for the difficulties

Mrs Hamilton understands a good deal about how the situation may have come about. The following points seem to be important.

• Henry is an only child, who has had little contact with other children in part because the family home is so isolated.
• The family has moved around the world a lot because Henry's father is an air force officer
• He has developed absorbing interests which centre round the computer.

Table 9.11: Record of Henry's interactions with other children for a period of 10 minutes daily: the baseline

	Monday	Tuesday	Wednesday	Thursday	Friday	Total
Responds to another child			1	1		2
Approaches another child				1		1
Plays with another child for 2 minutes						0
Shows another child how to use the computer	1	1				2

Step 7: Develop a baseline against which to measure progress

Mr Potter is very familiar with the idea of making a record against which to measure possible changes in Henry's behaviour. He devises a chart on which he agrees to record Henry's play and other activities. By recording Henry's interactions with other children for 10 minutes each morning over one week, the picture shown on Table 9.11 emerges.

Planning

There is clearly a need for a plan to cross the home–school boundary in this setting, since it would be all too easy for the strategy adopted by Henry's mother to be different from that adopted by Henry's teacher. In this instance, there are three different sets of participants all working together to help Henry: his parents, Mrs Fraser, the class teacher and Mr Potter, the classroom support worker, and, of course, there is Henry himself.

He is a bright little boy, who understands that if he wants to play with other children, he needs to learn how to do it. After initial fearfulness, he participates in working out a plan as follows:

a) Henry will watch what Keith, a very confident boy, does when he wants to play with another child.
b) Henry agrees, with his teacher, that he will only use the computer at the times specified for the rest of the class. He understands that he

may not play on it at break or in the dinner hour. [This is because when he is engaged in solitary activity, he is missing opportunities to interact with other children and to watch how they cope with difficulties.]

c) He will help other children who do not know how to use the computer by having them sit by him for two periods of 5 minutes in each computer session.

Implementing the plan

After a difficult two days when Mr Potter had a cold and could not come to the classroom, the plan begins to work well. Tables 9.12 and 9.13 show the gradual changes in Henry's behaviour, first after two weeks and then after a further four.

Reviewing and evaluating the work

A review of the work shows Henry has made consistent progress. He is visibly happier and interacts readily with other children.

In terms of the evaluation of the work, the quantitative data is very clear. The little graphs in Figure 9.4 show Henry's progress.

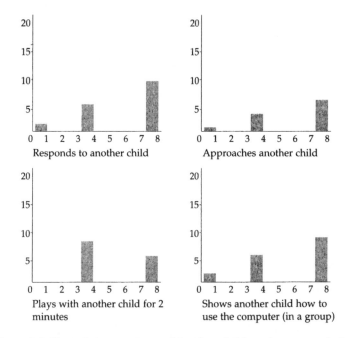

Figure 9.4. Henry's interactions with other children for two periods of 10 minutes daily at baseline, after two weeks and a further month

Table 9.12: Record of Henry's interactions with other children for a period of 10 minutes daily after two weeks

	Monday	Tuesday	Wednesday	Thursday	Friday	Total
Responds to another child	1		2	2	1	6
Approaches another child	1		1		2	4
Plays with another child for 2 minutes	2		2	1	3	8
Shows another child how to use the computer	1	3			2	6

Table 9.13: Record of Henry's interactions with other children for a period of 10 minutes daily after a further month

	Monday	Tuesday	Wednesday	Thursday	Friday	Total
Responds to another child	2		2	3	3	10
Approaches another child	2		3		2	7
Plays with another child for 2 minutes	1			2	3	6
Shows another child how to use the computer	2	1	3	2	1	9

A child with behaviour difficulties at primary school

Paul Bentley is 8 years old. He is of dual heritage, having a white mother and a black father. He is the fifth child of a family of six children, who live in cramped accommodation on a big housing estate in Sheffield. He is restless, constantly on the go, impulsive and with a short attention span. His mother, Shirley, was depressed after his birth, as her husband, John, had to return to Jamaica because of the illness of his father who lives there. While John was away he was killed in a road accident. Paul often asks why he hasn't got a dad. He is increasingly staying out of the house and spending more and more time with older boys.

Paul's teacher is increasingly losing patience with him. Whereas she was initially sympathetic to his difficulties in settling to work and showing concentration, she is now finding that he is becoming increasingly cheeky and rude. She is getting into more and more confrontations with him. Shirley has been up to the school twice but as the only thing that happened was that the teacher, Mrs Miller, gave her a long account of Paul's misbehaviour, she has refused to go again.

Assessment

Step 1: Building supportive and empathic relationships

This primary school does not have a home–school liaison worker. It does have the occasional services of an educational welfare officer, who is based at County Hall, some eight miles away. Mr Davidson is extremely hard-working but Paul has been on his waiting list for some three months. When he is able to visit, however, he suggests that, on the basis of Paul's circumstances, he could be accepted on the local mentoring scheme which is similar to the CHANCE project, except that it has more male mentors.

A black male volunteer, Colin Harris, offers, via the mentoring organization and after due training, to be Paul's mentor. He explains to Shirley, Paul's mother, that his own partner is white and that they therefore know something of the difficulties which children of dual heritage sometimes experience. They have two grown-up children, who have now left home to go to college, and who both experienced name calling and having their possessions tampered with. Shirley is initially apprehensive and says that she feels her child may be stigmatized in having to have a mentor, but Colin is able to reassure her that unless Paul wished it, no one would need to know about him. Other children have aunts, uncles and cousins; Paul could look at him in this way. So Shirley is won over, and after some initial uncertainty on Paul's part, so is he.

Step 2: Information gathering

This way of working has less need for information gathering in a formal sense, but over the course of time Paul confides in Colin that he does not like school, that he has few friends and that he wishes he had a dad like other children. He tells Colin that he likes modelling ships and aircraft and he likes football. Paul says he has heard people using the word 'hyperactive' about him, and he thinks it means that he can't do his school work for a long time at a stretch. He doesn't like sitting still and his teachers all get cross with him because he keeps getting out of his place.

Clinical assessment

The class teacher explains to Shirley, Paul's mother, that it would be helpful if she filled in the Strengths and Difficulties Questionnaire (SDQ) (Appendix 5.3) to see how she sees Paul's qualities and problematic behaviour. Mrs Miller explains that she will fill in a version of the form showing how she, as his teacher, sees him. This is done, and there is much similarity between the two separate ratings; the *average* scores are therefore recorded (see Table 9.14).

Mrs Miller explains to Paul that both she and his mother agree that Paul seems to be coping with a number of difficulties, and they and Colin Harris all want to help.

Step 3: Identifying the main areas of difficulty together

Colin and Paul arrange to meet twice a week after school, on Tuesdays and Thursdays. Paul says that on one day he'd like to go swimming and they will do whatever they feel like on the other. Over the course of these meetings, Paul gradually confides in Colin the main things which are making him unhappy.

- He feels he is getting picked on at home. He loves his Mum, but he feels she is always on at him.
- He used to like school, but this teacher is cross, and gets on at him when he keeps getting up from his place.
- He doesn't have any friends.
- He hits people when they call him names; that gets him into trouble.

Table 9.14: Paul's scores from two SDQ appraisals

	Mother	Teacher	Average
Strengths:			
Notices when other children are upset	3	3	3
Difficulties			
Hyperactivity	4	4	4
Conduct problems	4	4	4
Peer problems	3	5	4
Emotional problems	2	2	2
Overall difficulties score	13	15	14

Colin makes a mental note of these difficulties, and realizes that Paul is probably getting involved in name-calling arguments in the playground which have elements of bullying and racism. He decides, in line with the policy of the mentoring service, to report this back to the Educational Welfare Officer (EWO). Meanwhile Colin and Paul discuss some goals to work towards together over the next month:

- That Paul will have at least one friend to spend time with at breaks.
- That he and his Mum will have fewer arguments together.
- That he will not get so many tellings-off at school; he had five this last week.

Step 4: Identifying the positive features of the situation

Colin asks Paul to tell him all the things that he enjoys doing and that he is good at. At first Paul cannot think of anything, but then with encouragement he says he is quite good at swimming. He also says that when Miss Johnson was the teacher, he used to be good at maths, but because someone called him 'swot/teacher's pet', he has started playing around in maths lessons. Colin notes these things, and together they make a list of things Paul is good at, as well as things he is really interested in and which he would like to find out more about.

Things Paul is good at:

- He is a good swimmer; he can swim four lengths of the local swimming pool.
- He is good at maths, but at present he is not doing his best.

Things Paul would like to find out more about:

- Using the computer.
- Wild animals.

Step 5: Identify the desired outcomes of the work together, in discussion with the child

Colin and Paul talk together about how they might enjoy themselves during their times together and what they might try to achieve as well. Over the next month or so, they work out the following goals together:

That within four weeks Paul, with Colin's help:

- Will have joined the nearby library where he can borrow books about animals.
- Will have put his name down for practising the computer.
- Will find his old sums/maths book and go through some of the sums to check that he understands them.

That Colin, with Paul's help:

- Will also have put his name down for learning to use a computer.
- Will have learned to swim a width of the swimming pool.
- Will have learned the names of Leeds United's team (Paul is a Leeds supporter).

Step 6: Attempt a formulation of/rationale for the difficulties

Colin does not spend too much time looking for reasons for Paul's difficulties. Instead he gets on with the job of befriending Paul. He knows that Paul will look at his situation in terms of other people's unfairness, rather than in terms of 'vulnerability factors', but he also knows that Paul himself can, with help, take steps which will improve his chances of staying in the school and thus getting a sound education.

Colin explores with Paul the idea that although he has real difficulty in settling to his school work, Paul can, with help, learn to manage his restlessness. He promises to see if he can sit in his seat in school without getting up out of it for four spells each of 10 minutes, two in the morning and two in the afternoon. Paul will put a mark on a paper each minute that he stays in his desk, and will say 'Well done, Paul! Colin will be very pleased!'

Step 7: Develop a baseline against which to measure progress

Paul and Colin discuss how things are at the present time (see Table 9.15).

Planning

Here there is a need for a plan to involve five people, which, although it need not be extremely detailed, does require the involvement of four separate adults, or at least that they should be kept informed. These people are: Paul himself, his mum, Mrs Miller, the class teacher, Colin Harris, the mentor, and Mr Jackson, the Educational Welfare Officer.

Paul enters into the spirit of the plan very readily. He knows he has been called hyperactive, and wants to know what this means. He is afraid of being tested, however, and at first doesn't want anything to do with this. (See Table 9.16.)

Table 9.15: Goals for Paul – and some for Colin

Present situation	Within one month
1 Paul can swim four lengths	Paul will swim eight lengths
2 Paul does not belong to the library	Paul will have joined the library and chosen two books about animals to look at.
3 Paul does not use the computer at all	Paul will join the computer tutor class.
4 Paul does not help his Mum at all	Paul will make his bed every day
1 Colin cannot swim	Colin will join a Learn to Swim class.
2 Colin does not know much about	Colin will know all the Leeds United players' names.
3 Colin does not use the computer at all	Colin will have another go to learn.

Implementing the plan

Paul and Colin have had four weeks of meetings by the time the plan is agreed, explained to Paul's mum and teacher, and their approval obtained. Mrs Miller is still concerned about whether Paul may be hyperactive, so she adds a clause to her part of the agreement confirming that she will follow up her referral of Paul to have the possibility of hyperactivity considered.

Paul and Colin begin their visits to the swimming pool and they prove very enjoyable for both of them. Paul practises his swimming hard and Colin cheers him on. They also begin to save up to go to a match between Arsenal and Leeds, although they know they will have to save a long time. Colin listens as Paul tells him all about the players one week, and the next week Paul tests him on what he has learned.

Over the course of the first month, a boy calls Paul a 'black bastard'. In line with what had been agreed, Paul tells Mrs Miller, who passes the information to the head teacher. The boy concerned and his parents are sent for, and Paul and his mother later are informed that the boy has been transferred to another school.

Table 9.16: Goals of the plan made by Colin and Paul

1 To help Paul develop his swimming and sporting skills
2 To help Paul get on better with his mum
3 To help Paul settle better into school
4 To help Paul calm his active behaviour
5 To help Paul learn more about aspects of his black heritage
6 To ensure that Paul is not being bullied or called racist names

Goal	Paul	Colin	Mrs Bentley	Mrs Miller
1 To help Paul develop his swimming and sporting skills.	Will practise his swimming each week.	Will go with Paul to the baths.		
	Will tell Colin about the Premier League.	Will try to learn the names of the Leeds team.		
2 To help Paul get on better with his mum.	Will make his bed every day.		a) Will thank Paul for making his bed daily. b) Will spend 10 mins daily with Paul doing whatever he asks: e.g. looking at a football magazine.	
3 To help Paul settle at school	Will do his daily reading and maths.	Will ask Ms Miller for advice on how to help Paul.	Will listen to Paul's reading 10 mins daily.	Will mark Paul's reading book daily.
4 To help Paul calm his behaviour.	Will practise saying, 'Be calm, well done...'	Will provide Paul with a chart to mark calmness.	Will commend Paul when he behaves calmly.	a) Will commend Paul when he behaves calmly.

Table 9.16: (continued)

Goal	Paul	Colin	Mrs Bentley	Mrs Miller
				b) Will speak again to the EWO about the referral to the educational psychologist.
5 To help Paul learn more about aspects of his black heritage.	Will look at books and videos with Colin about black heroes, heroines and traditions.	Will find books and videos about black heroes, heroines and traditions.	Will support Paul in learning about this important aspect of his dual heritage	Will include stories and pictures of black heroes, heroines and traditions in the class curriculum.
6 To see that Paul is not bullied or called racist names.	Will, in line with school policy, inform Mrs Miller if he is called racist names or is bullied.	Will encourage Paul to take this step, and to deal with what may result from this.	Will help Paul if he is called names; will help him to learn about both aspects of his heritage.	Will listen to Paul if he says he is being bullied, and will take the matter to the headmaster.

Reviewing and evaluating the work

After three months, Colin, Paul and his mum go out to McDonalds together to talk about what has been achieved.

Goal 1 This has been achieved very well; the swimming is going well for both Paul and Colin, and both of them know a lot more about the footballers. They have saved up about half of the cost of ticket to see a match.

Goal 2 Paul made his bed for all the first week, but his mum only thanked him three times and grumbled at him once for leaving the rest of his room in a mess. They all agree to try again to achieve this goal.

Goal 3 Paul's school work is definitely improving. Mrs Miller is giving him positive messages about his reading each day, and because Paul is enjoying going to the library with Colin, his reading ability is nearly up to par for his age.

Goal 4 Paul is still behaving very actively, however, and Mrs Miller thinks he may well meet the criteria for hyperactivity. Nothing has been heard from the educational psychologist, so Mrs Miller will pursue this further. Colin wonders if she might work with Paul to help him control his behaviour further.

Goal 5 This is going well. Colin has tracked down a number of story-books about black history and traditions and both he and Paul say they like looking at the books together.

Goal 6 The incident of bullying was dealt with very effectively by Paul, and it is confirmed that the name-caller has been moved from the school.

Overall, everyone is very pleased with the mentoring arrangement so far, and it is agreed to update the goals and work towards the next three months' achievements!

Summary points

❏ At this age, many children show fears which, if handled construc-tively, fade away under three main influences: adults giving simple and truthful explanations of upsetting noises like thunder; adults avoiding showing fear themselves; and children gradually coming to understand that some things they fear, like dinosaurs, are no real threat to them.

❏ Many fears can be effectively reduced by 'modelling', that is, pro-viding a fearful child with a model of someone encountering the feared object or dealing effectively with the feared situation. Filmed modelling helps about half of fearful children; live model-ling helps rather more, but the most effective strategy is participant modelling, in which a fearless child guides the fearful child through the encounter with the feared object or situation.

❏ Factors associated with the development of subsequent aggressive behaviour in boys include a harsh attitude and discipline by the boy's parents at age 8, low family income, parental criminality, poor supervision of children by the parents, separations from the parents, and on the part of the boy, high daring and low intelli-gence.

❏ Both British and American studies have shown that aggressive behaviour in boys aged 8, as judged by teachers in Britain and by peers in America, predicted aggression in adulthood in Britain at age 18 and in America at age 30.

❐ There is evidence to show that parent-education programmes can be an effective way of improving the behaviour of pre-adolescent children who have behaviour problems. However, as many as 50 per cent of parents continue to experience difficulties.

❐ Overall, behaviourally oriented parent-education programmes seem to produce the biggest subsequent changes in children's behaviour.

❐ Group-based programmes may produce more changes in children's behaviour and may be more cost-effective and user friendly than individual programmes.

❐ Direct work with children is highly desirable, and so is work which spans the home–school boundary.

10

Children at secondary schools:
multidisciplinary approaches

This chapter will examine the well-being of young people of secondary school age, from about age 11 through to about age 18. Because a great deal of public attention focuses upon young offenders and their circumstances, there seems to be less knowledge and concern about the wide range of mental health issues concerning young people. The sections below will attempt to redress that balance.

Prevalence of emotional and behavioural difficulties in young people

Early research (Rutter, 1979) examined the prevalence of emotional and behavioural difficulties of 2,000 14-year-olds in the Isle of Wight, UK, and noted that parents and teachers reported 10–15 per cent as experiencing problems of these kinds. A further group of teenagers reported marked distress which had not been recognized by either parents or teenagers. This raised the prevalence rate to 21 per cent. Of this 21 per cent, the types of disorder experienced were as follows:

Emotional difficulties: anxiety, depression	40 %
Conduct disorder: aggressive and destructive behaviour	40 %
Mixed emotional and conduct disorders	20 %

Rutter (1986) has noted the increased levels of depression during adolescence by comparison with pre-puberty. He surveyed children at age 14–15 who had been already assessed at age 10 and reported

> The same children were reassessed at 14–15 years with very different findings... depressive feelings being considerably more prevalent. Over 40 per cent of the adolescents reported considerable feelings of misery and depression during a psychiatric inter-

view, 20 per cent reported feelings of self-depreciation, 7–8 per cent reported that they had suicidal feelings...

Indicators of depression

Herbert (1991) has indicated the main signs of depression in young people:

- A demeanour of unhappiness and misery (more persistent and intense than 'the blues', which we all suffer from now and again).
- A marked change in eating and/or sleeping patterns.
- A feeling of helplessness, hopeless and self-dislike.
- An inability to concentrate and apply oneself to anything.
- Everything (even talking and dressing) seen as an effort.
- Irritating or aggressive behaviour.
- A sudden change in school-work.
- A constant search for distractions and new activities.
- Dangerous risk-taking (e.g. with drugs/alcohol); dangerous driving; delinquent actions.
- Friends being dropped or ignored.

The seriousness of the difficulties experienced by a proportion of young people is attested to by national data. Between 2 and 4 per cent of adolescents attempt suicide and seven people in 100,000 aged between 15 and 19 complete that suicide. The greater proportion are young men (Department of Health, 1995b).

Origins of young people's difficulties

Rutter (1986) has suggested that one or more of the following factors may be implicated in the increase of depression in puberty:

- Hormonal changes associated with puberty; including increased sexual drive.
- Genetic factors: there is evidence of their involvement in emotional disorders.
- An increase in the number of environmental stressors at puberty: for example, a growing awareness of the world of work, and the importance of the young person's finding a place within it.
- Families may be supportive or may constitute a stress.
- Differing opportunities to express or discharge emotion.

Protective factors

Because so many young people are so vulnerable to difficulties, researchers have explored which variables may act to protect them. There seems to be a convergence of evidence from studies in a diversity of settings, all of which focus upon the same three variables:

a) Features of the child's temperament and disposition (likely to be attributable to genetic factors).
b) Family cohesion and warmth.
c) Supportive figures in the school or local environment.

As we saw in Chapter 9, a number of agencies are trying to take account of this last factor by engaging 'mentors' to support vulnerable young people.

Two major studies by Katz and colleagues (1997, 1999) have examined, among many issues, the circumstances which protect young people from major difficulties in adolescence. The first, on young women, examined the responses of approximately 3,000 young women to a questionnaire carried out by Express newspapers and made widely available through the UK. From these responses 638 (21 per cent) were chosen who seemed particularly positive. The authors report:

> Criteria of confidence, optimism and motivation were chosen and 638 girls confirmed to this composite concept. They are called 'Can-do' girls. Another group of 241 girls at the opposite end of the spectrum – 'Low Can-do' girls – was identified. The remaining 2121 girls in the middle group affect the majority of girls and create the main trends.
>
> Katz *et al.*, 1999, p. 5.

Table 10.1 shows some key characteristics of the two end-spectrum groups.

In respect of young men, Katz *et al.* (1999) report that the study shows that young men with high self-esteem (with a 'Can-do attitude') are linked with:

- Positive parenting style – listening to problems and views, emotionally supportive.
- High family togetherness: doing things together and going places together.
- Highly involved fathering – by a father or father figure who spends time with the young person and shows interest in him.
- School ethos: which values and protects the individual both emotionally and physically.

Table 10: 1 Some characteristics of two groups of girls (Katz, 1997)

Characteristic	High 'Can-Do' (%)	Low 'Can-Do' (%)
Turn to their mother for support	81	58
Say parents listen to their problems and views	66	33
Volunteer to help charities or give other help in the community	31	18

Research on approaches to working with young people

A great deal of research is needed to establish the most effective forms of intervention with young people with emotional and behavioural difficulties. As shown in Chapter 2, four tiers of services are likely to be available. Despite acute need, there is as yet only the beginnings of a research literature to inform practice. We shall examine some of the key areas below.

Work with anxious young people

Kendall and colleagues (1991) have considered the needs of anxious young people and the research background for helping them. Here too the conclusion is that a range of cognitive-behavioural strategies produce the best outcomes. They recommend the following groupings of approaches:

1 *Relaxation*: This is a form of the progressive relaxation developed by Jacobson (1938) and adapted in various formats for children and young people.

2 *Building a cognitive coping routine*: This refers to the strategy of identifying and modifying maladaptive self-talk, similar to that described above. For example, an anxious but lonely young person, frightened by social situations, may shun meetings or parties where he might have to talk informally to other young men and women. On talking his beliefs through with a supportive worker, it may emerge that when, on a recent occasion, he entered the room where a gathering was to be held, he interpreted the fact that no-one greeted him as evidence that he 'looked strange'. He immediately decided that no-one would talk to him all evening, left the gathering and went home.

The practitioner can help him examine this conclusion, and explore other interpretations, such as:

- The other people were also nervous and uncertain what to do.
- The other people too did not know anyone else, but had eventually found someone to talk to.
- The other people were hoping that someone would come and talk to them.

3 *Problem-solving*: This strategy has been examined before, (page 69) so will only be recapitulated here. In essence, the difficulty is formulated in terms of the goal to be achieved: for example, that the young man discussed above will be able to attend gatherings of between ten and twenty people and to stay for half an hour or more at them.
- Step 1: the precise identifying of the difficulty.
- Step 2: alternative solutions are described.
- Step 3: the best apparent solution is selected.
- Step 4: this solution is tried out.
- Step 5: in the light of the feedback that strategy is confirmed as successful, and a new goal is identified, or that strategy is confirmed as unsuccessful and another strategy is tried out, until the best strategy for that difficulty is pinpointed.

4 *Contingent reinforcement*: This, in the form of praise or encouragement, is offered by the therapist whenever the young person takes a step in the direction which has been agreed: for example, practising relaxation, keeping records of agreed tasks undertaken, such as positive self-talk, etc.

5 *Modelling*: As already described, non-fearful behaviour can be demonstrated in actual situations, so providing the young person with an actual example to follow.

6 *Exposure*: This approach too enables fearful young people to be exposed in a gradual away to the frightening situation, for example, a shopping expedition. The approach used is desensitization, where a gradual hierarchy of difficulties from the least difficult to the most difficult is developed. For example, for a young person, Kevin, with an uncomplicated school phobia, an educational psychologist might work in cooperation with a home–school liaison worker and a teacher to use the approach shown in Table 10.2.

Table 10.2: A desensitization process for an uncomplicated school phobia involving an educational psychologist, a school counsellor or educational welfare officer and a young person

---

1 Kevin is helped to relax and goes with the worker for a short walk in the direction of the school. He repeats this daily for a week.
2 As above; he goes for a short walk past the school gates. He comes home.
3 As above; he goes for a walk into the school grounds when no young people are about; coming home.
4 As above; Kevin goes to the school at, say, 4.30 when few people are about; and enters that part of the school where he feels reasonably safe. He and the worker meet the teacher for five minutes and then go home. Repeat for a week.
5 He goes alone to the school at the end of a day and with the support of the teacher/school pastoral worker join a class he enjoys for half an hour at the end of the day. He comes home.
6 As above, Kevin goes to the school at midday and joins his own class for half an hour The teacher who has been involved in the exercise and welcomes him but then pays him no further attention. He comes home at lunch-time.
7 Kevin goes to school alone at lunch-time and meets with a supportive person of his choice from his year group for a snack lunch. He comes home.
8 Kevin goes to the school at 11.00 or 2.30, spending the rest of that half-day in a lesson which he enjoys and which has an understanding teacher. He comes home. This is repeated until Kevin feels able to move to the next step.
9 Kevin goes to the school for a full half-day and then comes home.
10 With quiet encouragement from his family members, Kevin extends the pattern of attendance to a full day. He recognizes that there will be days when he has to slip back to a lower step in the hierarchy before moving back up again.

Developing a repertoire of approaches

Kendall and colleagues (1991) have devised an integrated approach to helping anxious children and young people. They write:

> The overall goal is to teach children and teenagers to recognize signs of unwanted anxious arousal and to let these signs serve as cues for anxiety-management strategies. Identifying the cognitive processes associated with excessive anxious arousal, training in cognitive strategies for anxiety management, and behavioral relaxation and performance-based practice opportunities are sequenced within the treatment program to build skill upon skill.

They describe a range of available strategies, shown in Table 10.3.

Table 10.3: Key steps in dealing with anxiety (Kendall *et al.*, 1991)

- awareness of bodily reactions and cognitive activities when anxious
- identification and modification of anxious self-talk
- modeling of coping strategies
- exposure to anxiety-provoking situations
- role playing and contingent reward procedures
- homework tasks
- affective education
- relaxation procedures
- graduated sequence of training tasks and assignments
- application and practice of newly acquired skills in increasingly anxiety-provoking situations.

Working with depressed young people

Depression is best understood in terms of interacting variables, rather than as a result of a single event or factor. Akiskal and McKinney (1975) have brought together the many variables which research has identified as being involved into a multifactorial model. The emphasis is upon interacting variables which converge into a 'final common pathway', reflecting changes in brain chemistry and experienced by the person as depression. Within this model, depression can be either very severe or less severe, with major depression a one end of a continuum and mild depression, compounded by anxiety, at the other.

Concerning ways of helping depressed young people, Herbert (1998) writes:

> The need for a broad-based intervention with depressive problems seems to be the conclusion of recent studies. Tricyclic medication, counselling, psychotherapy, behaviour therapy, cognitive therapy and group therapy are the main options... Depression in older children (and adolescents) lends itself to a cognitive-behavioural approach. Most depressed clients manifest a high rate of intrusive negative thoughts, including selective ruminations about past negative attempts and thoughts about the hopeless of the future and their helplessness in the face of their perceived dilemma.

Herbert continues by describing how Reynolds and Coats (1986) randomly assigned thirty moderately depressed adolescents to one of three conditions: cognitive-behavioural therapy, relaxation training or waiting-list control. Students on medication were excluded. The cognitive-behavioural programme stressed self-monitoring of thought patterns, self-evaluation and self-reinforcement ('I am doing well in keeping going with these exercises'); the relaxation approach involved practise in relaxing muscle groups in tension-provoking situations.

Both these types of intervention resulted in a significant reduction in depression by comparison with the experience of those in the waiting-list control.

Such psychological approaches can and should be supplemented by strategies to help young people in other aspects of their lives: for example, Burke (1986) has shown how racism and discrimination have been major factors in triggering depression in black people. This is often compounded by poverty, poor housing and a lack of jobs and opportunities.

An approach to helping mildly to moderately depressed adults by means of three main strategies clearly has relevance for mildly to moderately depressed young people.

1 Strategies focusing on interpersonal factors.
2 Strategies focusing on cognitive factors.
3 Strategies focusing on behaviour.

It will be seen that these three groupings are essentially components of a holistic approach. It is commonly, and truthfully, said 'You climb out of depression step by step', and that an array of approaches and strategies is helpful. Let us consider each of the above in turn.

Strategies focusing on interpersonal factors

These take into account the absolute need which we all have for close, supportive human contact, for friendship and for someone to confide in. They will include, therefore, discussion of the human needs of the person concerned, and how, even if the young person shrinks from interpersonal contact, he or she may be encouraged to participate, even at a minimal level, in social activities.

The strategies, therefore, include stimulating the person concerned in ways which involve other people. The worker may help the young person identify the things he or she enjoyed doing before he became depressed: sport, as player or as spectator, playing an instrument, walking or climbing, acting as volunteer helper, and so on. She may then encourage the young person to resume these activities, in the company of people whom he trusts and likes and who are likely to be understanding. This is important even if the person concerned is initially reluctant or complains that he or she does not enjoy the activity. Social contact with a supportive companion seems to have stimulating effects upon the central and autonomic nervous system.

Strategies focusing on cognitive factors

Here the emphasis is on the actual patterns of thinking of the person concerned (see Herbert (1998) above). Depressed people are known

(Beck *et al.*, 1979) to rehearse self-critical and self-damaging patterns of thinking: 'I'll never be able to cope'; 'It's like my dad said, I'm a total failure'; 'Living is too difficult for me '. Inevitably, such ruminations induce serious pessimism in the young person, inducing a vicious circle of self-defeating thoughts and actions.

There is abundant evidence, some of which has been discussed in Chapter 3, that educating people in understanding these self defeating patterns and teaching them strategies for checking the thoughts, exploring whether there really is evidence to justify them, and substituting a range of alternative cognitions, can, with support, bring about a realization of the destructive power of negative thinking and the means of controlling it. Then, again with support, young people can be helped to substitute effective coping patterns of thinking and behaviour.

For example, when young people have found themselves in situations where they are in conflict with significant people in their lives – their parents, their teachers or other people of influence – the use of a problem-solving approach (see page 69 and below) can be extremely constructive.

Strategies focusing on behaviour

These encompass a cluster of strategies for which there is evidence of a positive effect on depression. There is an array of approaches which have the effect of stimulating the physical resources and coping strategies of the person or young person concerned. They include those shown in Table 10.4.

Improving relations between parents and young people

Because of the mounting concern about the numbers of troubled and troublesome young people, a great deal of research has been directed towards means of helping them. One focus has been on activities which parents can take part in with their children which seem to build family cohesiveness. Blair *et al.* (1999) have identified ways which seem to achieve this for young women as well as for young men. They include:

- Actively planning and participating in family outings and activities, such as visits to motor shows, computer fairs, and the like.
- Playing or watching sport together; swimming, cycling, walking, climbing.
- Taking an active interest in hobbies: model building, music, camping.
- Sharing a new interest together: learning to play an instrument, tracing family history, amateur dramatics, and so on.

Table 10.4: Strategies for enhancing coping skills

Physical exercise: walking, jogging, swimming, table tennis, cycling, forms of participant sport

Monitoring diet

Gaining skills in self assertion

Problem-solving approaches (see page 69).

Practising relaxation

These authors have also distilled from their research specific parenting skills which have been shown to lead to reductions in negative interactions between parent and young person and to improved teachers' reports on young people (see Table 10.5).

Direct work with aggressive young people

There has been an increasing amount of research directed towards the perceptions, biases and beliefs of aggressive children and adolescents, since it has been persuasively shown that many aggressive young people have 'cognitive distortions'; that is, they have a low threshold for dealing with potentially threatening stimuli and tend to respond aggressively to cues which others might ignore (Feindler, 1991). Following this understanding, there has been extensive research into the management of aggression and anger control.

Table 10.6 lists some important components of anger-control training. It is item b) in the table, cognitive change, which has attracted extensive research attention recently. For example, work by researchers such as Lochman, White and Wayland has focused upon the specific cognitive characteristics of aggressive children: see Table 10.7.

Table 10.5: Specific parenting skills identified as improving interactions between parent and young person (Blair *et al.* 1991

1   Making neutral (i.e. not threatening) requests for help (e.g., John, please help me tidy up).
2   Making simple, rewarding comments (e.g., Thanks for helping me John).
3   Monitoring young people's whereabouts: who they're with; where they are; when they're due back ...
4   Working out family rules about letting people know where you are when the children are still young; parents and young people all follow the rules.
5   Providing reasonable, predictable consequences for breaking family rules.
6   Enforcing these rules, without threat or argument.
7   Helping young people solve problems: see page 69.
8   Active listening; letting young people talk about their concerns.

Table 10.6: Key components of anger-control training (after Feindler, 1991)

---

a) arousal reduction
b) cognitive change
c) behavioural skills development
d) moral reasoning development
e) appropriate anger expression

Table 10.7: Cognitive characteristics of aggressive children (From Lochman, J. E,. White, K, and Wyland, K. (1991) In P. Kendall (Ed.) *Child and Adolescent Therapy: Cognitive–Behavioural Procedures*. London: Guilford Press

---

1 Social-cognitive products
      Social-cognitive appraisals
            Overly sensitive to hostile cues
            Bias in attributing hostile intention to others
            Underestimating own aggressiveness
      Social problem-solving
            Limited repertoire of solutions for the most aggressive
            For pre-adolescent aggressive children: few verbal-assertion
              solutions and excess direct-action solutions
            Aggressive-backup solutions
      Appraisal of internal arousal
            Over-labelling of affective arousal as anger
            Low levels of empathy

2 Cognitive operations
            Difficulty in sustaining attention
            Commission errors in short-term memory
            Retrieval of salient solutions when automatically retrieving
              solutions from long-term memory

3 Schematic propositions
            Higher value on social goals of dominance and revenge rather than
              affiliation
            Less value placed on outcomes such as victim suffering, victim retal-
              iation, or peer rejection
            Expectation that aggressive behaviour will produce tangible
              rewards and reduce aversive reactions
            Low self-esteem

Cognitive interventions with aggressive young people

In an attempt to see whether these young people can be helped to inhibit their aggressive responses, Feindler (1991) developed a programme to help young people who tended to react with aggression gain some control over these tendencies by teaching them strategies for reappraising the situations in which they found themselves. Table 10.8 illustrates the components of the programme.

Table 10.8: Self-statements designed to counter cognitive distortions (Feindler, 1991)

1 Hostile attributions bias
  'I'll try to stay calm and *listen* to what they say.'
  'Are there good intentions behind what they are saying?'
  'Not all adults are out to nail me.'
  'Some people (i.e. father, therapist, teacher, tutor) do care about what happens to me.'

2 Legitimization of aggression and retaliation
  'He or she may have started with me, but I don't have to respond in kind.'
  'Is there another way to respond/solve the problem?'
  'It doesn't have to be an eye for an eye; I'm better than that.'
  'Ignoring them takes their power away, and may be the best retaliation.'

3 Immunity from consequences
  'Getting kicked out of school means I can't control whether I graduate.'
  'I have lost privileges and possessions as a result of my behavior.'
  'If there is a possibility of negative consequence, I don't want to take a chance.'
  'Maybe there are consequences I haven't considered.'

Feindler (1991) found that this cognitive approach led to the young people themselves reporting lower numbers of aggressive encounters and a greater ability to control themselves. However, these changes were not of sufficient extent or magnitude to be perceived by others. Feindler, in an admirable critique of her own work, comments upon the absolute necessity for further efforts to help maintain and extend the improved sense of self-control which she was able to bring about, with and within the young people concerned, and for the inclusion of training in self-control approaches within a broader multisystemic approach.

School-based work to prevent bullying

Farrington (1996) has reported on school-based programmes to reduce bullying, and concludes that the approach adopted in Norway has provided the best evidence for its effectiveness. He reports that the following measures were undertaken in all Norwegian schools:

- The distribution of a 30-page booklet describing what is known about bullying, and recommending steps to reduce it.

- A 25-minute video was also provided.
- All parents were sent a four-page folder containing information and advice.
- Self-report questionnaires were completed anonymously by all children.

Additional interventions were made by teachers, who were encouraged to develop explicit rules about bullying, to discuss the issue in class and to undertake role-play exercises. They were also asked to improve the supervision of the children, especially in the playground.

For evaluation purposes, 42 schools in Bergen provided information to the team and post-intervention data showed that the strategy had reduced the prevalence of bullying by half.

Examples of multidisciplinary support for young people

As children move into adolescence, it is obvious that it becomes a greater rather than a lesser undertaking to help them cope with emotional and behavioural difficulties. As they mature physically, cognitively and sexually, so they become affected by more and more influences – not least those of the peer-group, in association with commercial interests. As we have seen, the suffering of adolescents coping with emotional and behavioural distress is intense, with high rates of suicide, particularly among boys, while the impact on others, not least their families, is difficult to exaggerate. For some young people, the teenage years may offer the last real opportunity of gaining help. In this section we shall examine some examples of help offered by practitioners from different disciplines to troubled young people.

Young people coping with anxiety

Beth is 14. She is extremely shy and painfully thin. She is an only child and grew up on a farm where she encountered few children, so found the rough and tumble of the playground and the bustle of the classroom difficult to deal with. She is an extremely sensitive young woman, fearful of the nickname 'Stick insect' which she has attracted, but kind to others and particularly considerate of others like herself who do not readily fit in. She has been referred to the school counsellor because she has been missing school and there are fears that she is not eating enough. Her attendance at school is generally good, but there have been an increasing number of absences recently.

Beth's mother has epilepsy. She has had several epileptic attacks when Beth has been at school. There is some evidence that she drinks heavily on occasion, but this is not generally known. Her father has given up the farm and is working in Britain and overseas as a representative of a firm of agricultural engineers; this keeps him away from home for long periods of time. Beth feels increasingly responsible for and acutely anxious about her mother. This anxiety is generalizing into a range of settings beyond the original one, and she has told a teacher that she has wondered about taking an overdose...

Assessment

Step 1: Building supportive and empathic relationships

Beth's school is fortunate to have the services of a part-time counsellor, Mrs Williams, who is in school two and a half days a week. There is a waiting list for her help, but, in view of the concern in the school for preventive help to be offered to young people, Mrs Williams is asked to see Beth as a matter of urgency.

Mrs Williams is liked and trusted by the young people of the school and, as the mother of two teenagers herself, she has no difficulty in putting Beth at her ease. They agree to meet weekly for a month.

Step 2: Information gathering

With this support, Beth pours out her distress and fears. She says that she hates herself and, were it not for the anguish this would cause her parents, she would like to put an end to her life. She is worried about everything, her mother, her father, what she looks like, her loneliness, her difficulties with school-work. She cannot bear coming to school any more, so she has been leaving home at the usual time in the morning but wandering round the town, going into the public library to look at schoolbooks and sometimes going on a bus to the nearby town so that no-one will see her and ask why she isn't in school.

Initially, Beth is unwilling for her mother to be informed of her difficulties, saying that this will just make her epilepsy worse, but when the realities of the situation are explored and the necessity of informing her mother is discussed, she says, 'Well, at least it would be out in the open...'

Clinical assessment
Beth agrees to fill in the Strengths and Difficulties Questionnaire (Table 10.9).

Beth falls within the normal range in respect of her difficulties score and has a very high strengths score. This is encouraging for her. She is amazed that Mrs Williams sees her so positively. This cheers her up a lot.

Table 10.9: Beth's scores from two Strengths and Difficulties appraisals

	Beth	Mrs Williams	Average
Strengths:	6	10	8
Difficulties			
Hyperactivity	0	0	0
Conduct problems	0	0	0
Peer problems	4	4	4
Emotional problems	7	5	6
Overall difficulties score	11	9	10

Step 3: Identifying the main areas of difficulty together

By the end of their first talk, Beth says that she is already feeling better for having got so many things off her chest. She agrees to tell her mother that she is meeting the counsellor. Mrs Williams then asks Beth during the following week to make a list of the areas of her difficulties.

Next week, Beth brings her list:

- She is lonely. She has no friends, either at home or at school.
- She is worried about her mum. The epileptic attacks are really worrying, for both of them, and Beth is afraid that if her mother has one when she is alone, she may die. Beth does not say anything about her mother's difficulties with alcohol at this stage.
- She has not started her periods yet.
- She is called 'Sticks', short for 'Stick insect', which she hates.

Mrs Williams notes these difficulties. She has already, with Beth's agreement, spoken to her class teacher, Ms French. Meanwhile she and Beth discuss some goals to work towards together over the next month:

- That they work out an arrangement so that, if Beth's mum does have an epileptic attack and needs help, a firm plan can be in place.
- That Beth will have at least one friend to spend time with at breaks.
- That Beth should have a medical check when the school nurse next comes, to see if there is any reason why her periods have not started.
- That people will stop calling her 'Sticks'.

Step 4: Identifying the positive features of the situation

Mrs Williams next asks Beth to tell her all the things that she really enjoys doing or which other people might appreciate in her. Beth cannot think of anything. She is genuinely amazed when Mrs Williams says that the class teacher, Ms French, has said that Beth has great sensitivity to literature as well as a talent for writing. Beth smiles and acknowledges that she does love poetry, especially the Lakes Poets. It is one of her ambitions is to go to the Lake District and see the countryside which so inspired Wordsworth and Coleridge. She also says that she tries to write poetry herself, and wants to be a writer when she is older.

Mrs Williams, with Beth's reluctant agreement, notes down her strengths both from what Beth has confided and from drawing upon the Strengths and Difficulties Questionnaire:

- Beth is very talented at English, particularly in poetry.
- She is considerate of other people's feelings.
- She shares readily, helping other class members with homework.

Beth is pleased but embarrassed that these qualities have been identified by her class teacher. She tends to dismiss these strengths, but Mrs Williams insists upon their reality and importance.

Step 5: Identify the desired outcomes of the work together, in discussion with the young person

Mrs Williams and Beth talk about what they might try to achieve during the course of their meetings. They agree that over the next month or so, they will work towards the following goals.

That within four weeks:
- Beth can be confident that should her mother feel an epileptic attack coming on, there will be a plan in place.
- In view of Beth's interest in English, Mrs Williams will explore with Ms French how this interest could be developed.
- On any occasion when Beth is finding it difficult to come into school, she will phone the school and ask to speak to Mrs Williams.

Step 6: Attempt a formulation of/rationale for the difficulties

Beth wonders why she is so tense and unhappy. She believes that she is 'different', not like other young people because she doesn't enjoy partying and the teenage scene. Ms Williams suggests that even from what Beth has already told her, she can see that she is coping with very real stresses which make it hard for her to settle into school. She mentions the difficulties which they have already talked of and, wisely, adds, 'And there may be things happening which you haven't felt able to talk about yet…'

Step 7: Develop a baseline against which to measure progress

Ms Williams asks Beth if she will complete the young person's self-esteem scale, which she does. She gains a score indicating low self-esteem.

Goals which Beth says she want to work towards:

1 To have a meeting with the school nurse in connection with her low weight and her not having started her periods yet.
2 To have made at least one friend with whom she can spend at least two hours a week.
3 To know that an action-plan is in place in the event of her mother having an epileptic attack.
4 To have taken active steps towards furthering her interest in English.

Planning

Here there is a need for a plan to involve several people which, although it need not be extremely detailed, does require the involvement of four separate people, or at least that they should be kept informed. These people are: Beth herself, her mother, Ms French, the class teacher, and Mrs Williams, the school counsellor. The plan is outlined in Table 10.10.

Implementing the plan

Over the next few days the plan is put into effect. Each person carries out her undertakings and Beth meets with Mrs Williams each week to talk about her ongoing successes and difficulties. She makes the appointment with the school nurse and Mrs Williams keeps the promises she made to Beth.

It is in the course of the third weekly meeting between Beth and Mrs Williams that Beth seems to feel confident enough to tell Mrs Williams that she realizes her mother, in addition to her difficulties with epilepsy, also seems to have a drinking problem. Beth tells Mrs Williams how, increasingly, her mother finds it hard to wake in the morning; how each evening she explains to Beth that she needs a good drink to help her keep going; and how Beth realizes that this is to do with her father's spending so much time overseas, apparently deliberately, away from the family. Mrs Williams, who has felt that Beth had not yet been ready to tell her of such intimate family difficulties, listens empathically to her account and avoids over-reassurance. Beth says that there is nothing to be done; she just feels better to have talked to

Table 10.10: Coordinated plan to support Beth

Goal	Beth	Mrs Williams, counsellor
1 To have had a meeting with the school nurse within two weeks	Agrees to fix the appointment within the next week.	
2 To have at least one friend with whom she can spend at least two hours each week.	Agrees to pluck up her courage and attend the school poetry group, which is run by a sensitive teacher. There is an older girl there whom she likes.	Agrees to talk to the teacher who runs the group and draw his attention to Beth's love of poetry. She will find out the time of the next meeting.
3 To know that an action plan is in place should her mother have an asthma attack.	Agrees to talk to her mother about her worrying constantly about her asthma.	Agrees to talk to Beth's mother, should she ask to be in touch with Mrs Williams.
4 To take forward her love of English.	Agrees to go to the meetings of the poetry group for at least two meetings and agrees to send off a poem she has written to a competition for young poets.	Agrees to explore whether Beth could be included on the school visit to the Royal Shakespeare Company at Stratford. This is an all-school initiative.

someone in a confidential setting about the situation. She says she would like to go on meeting occasionally with Mrs Williams to explore other ideas she has had: she has wondered about contacting her father about her worries.

Reviewing and evaluating the work

After two months, Bath and Mrs Williams agree to review how far the goals which Beth set have been achieved:

1   *To have had a meeting with the school nurse.*
    This has been achieved fully. Beth has been to see the school nurse, who has encouraged her to eat more. Her diet has been inadequate and Beth is considerably under-weight for her age. Beth has explained that she has been so worried that she has almost forgotten she needed to eat regularly, but now that the probable effect of low weight delaying the onset of her periods has been explained,

she has undertaken to eat three balanced meals a day. She has started to do this, and feels better for it.

2 *To have at least one friend with whom she can spend at least two hours a week.*
This is within sight. Beth has joined the Poetry Society and in the company of others who also enjoy poetry, she is feeling more confident about talking to other students. There is another girl who attends whom she has begun to talk to and who seemed as glad as Beth to meet a friendly person.

3 *To know that an action-plan is in place should her mother have an epileptic attack.*
Beth has told her mother how frightened she is that she will have an epileptic attack while she is in school, and that this has stopped her going to school some days. Her mother is upset on her daughter's behalf, and there and then bought an alarm which she can use to summon help should she be alone. Nothing has been said about the drinking behaviour for the time being.

4 *To take forward her love of English.*
Joining the Poetry Society has met this objective also. Beth is now convinced that her future lies in writing, and possibly the writing of poetry.

When Beth and Mrs Williams evaluate their work together again using the Strengths and Difficulties Questionnaire, Beth has moved to an overall lower score of 8. Despite the continuing concerns, she says she feels very much better.

Young people behaving aggressively

Sean is 14. He has lived in a children's home ever since his parents placed him in the care of the local authority because of his violent and unmanageable behaviour. Sean hates living in a children's home and disguises his circumstances from other young people in his class.

Sean has never learned self-control. If anyone displeases him, he tends to lash out both verbally and physically. He knows that this gets him into deeper trouble, but he doesn't know what to do about this pattern of behaviour.

Assessment

Step 1: Building supportive and empathic relationships

The member of staff who finds herself with responsibility for helping Sean is his field social worker, Jackie Barton, who has teenager children herself and who understands something of Sean's difficulties. There are potential difficulties between Jackie, as the field worker who has statutory responsibility for Sean, and Philip, the residential worker who is Sean's key worker in the children's home. However, both Phil and Jackie are mature practitioners well aware that they need to act in a consistent way in order to help Sean and to avoid him playing them off one against the other.

Both of them have developed firm and friendly relationships with Sean, who seems to trust them. It is accepted that while there is some information which both have in relation to Sean, there are other matters which Sean has confided only to one or the other – for example, how he is getting on with friends at school. This is regarded as confidential to the person to whom it was entrusted; it is never discussed between workers.

Step 2: Information gathering

Normally, it would be Jackie, Sean's field worker, who would undertake much of the work with Sean, but because she is unable to devote as much time as she would wish to meeting Sean, it is agreed at senior management level that Sean's key worker in the children's home will undertake the greater part of the work with him. Philip has already a good deal of knowledge about Sean, which is represented in Sean's file, but he is also concerned to hear Sean's view of events.

Sean tells Philip that 'he has always been able to run rings round his mum – and his dad too, whenever he was around'. Philip gathers that Sean's mum has become afraid of her son, because of his size and strength, and that this has been so for as long as Sean can remember. Sean tells Philip that he was excluded from two schools before he was six because 'he was always hitting the teacher'. He says, 'When someone tells me to do something I don't want to, or if someone upsets me, I just thump them.'

Quantitative assessment

Sean initially objects to filling in the Strengths and Difficulties Questionnaire but eventually agrees. Philip explains that with Sean's permission, he would like to fill in the relevant sheet himself and get Sean's teacher, Ms Ball, to fill it in as well. The average scores are recorded (see Table 10.11).

When Sean meets Philip and Jackie to discuss these scores, he becomes unusually silent. They perceive this and wait for him to speak. 'I'm a bad case, aren't I?', he says eventually. 'Does it mean there's no hope for me?' This is the first time that Sean has spoken in this reflective way. Jackie simply reflects back Sean's words to him, opening the way for him to say more. 'No hope?' she repeats. Sean is almost in tears and says, 'It means I'm a bad person: everyone thinks

Table 10.11: Scores for Sean from three Strengths and Difficulties appraisals

Ms Ball	Philip	Sean	Average	Average
Strengths	6	5	6	6
Difficulties				
Hyperactivity	4	2	0	3
Conduct problems	9	8	7	8
Peer problems	6	6	6	6
Emotional problems	5	4	3	4
Overall difficulties score	24	20	16	21

so... and I think so, too... I'll go to prison, won't I?'

This is a very different Sean from the brash and noisy young man who hits people who upset him in any way. Jackie has to leave before long, but Philip spends a long time with Sean, and sees a frightened and vulnerable youngster who says, to Philip's surprise, that he just wants to go home. 'How can I stop hitting people?' he asks.

Step 3: Identifying the main areas of difficulty together

In a long, very important meeting, Sean and Philip identify the following main areas of difficulty:

1 Sean's tendency to lose his temper whenever anyone threatens or provokes him.
2 His inability to back down once he finds himself in a confrontational situation.
3 His difficulty in recognizing situations where it is vital that he controls himself, such as the classroom.

Step 4: Identifying the positive features of the situation

When asked to say what he likes about himself, what are his strengths, Sean can think of nothing. He remains silent and looks extremely distressed. Philip is able to return to the Strengths and Difficulties Questionnaire, where he notes that 'Helpful if someone is hurt, upset or feeling ill' has been marked positively both by Jackie and Phil. Sean looks almost embarrassed when this is pointed out. Jackie is able to ask Sean what, in an ideal world, he would like to do with his life – and he replies 'I wouldn't mind doing what you do, Phil, looking after people like me who have to go into hospital, but men don't do things like that, do they?'

Phil and Jackie are able to reassure him that men can and do go into jobs where they help people, and they talk about *Casualty* and the sort of jobs that male nurses do there. They wait for Sean to think this through and then are amazed to hear him say, 'Then that's what I want to do – like that guy in *Casualty*'.

Step 5: Identify the desired outcomes of the work together, in discussion with the young person

A few days later Jackie and Philip meet Sean again. They are very clear with him. It is essential that he gains control of his behaviour. Whatever he does, if he uses violence in difficult situations he will find himself in trouble. It is essential that he should learn to control his aggressiveness.

Sean looks hopeless. 'I don't know how to' he says. 'If someone calls me, I hit them. It's as simple as that.' Jackie and Philip explain that there are people who specialize in helping people, teenagers and adults, to control their temper. Sean looks doubtful. 'Let's turn this into a set of goals'. says Jackie. So they work out the following goals for their work together.

1   To work towards Sean learning to control his aggressive behaviour.
2   To work towards Sean and his mum getting on better.
3   To work towards Sean's calming his behaviour.
4   To enable Sean to improve his school work.

Step 6: Attempt a formulation of/rationale for the difficulties

'How has it come about that you thump people, Sean?', asks Jackie. 'I only do what was done to me', replies Sean. 'My dad used to belt us for the slightest thing – it didn't do me any harm…'.

Jackie does not reply for a moment. 'Tell us a bit about that', she says. There is a long pause. Then Sean says, 'For the slightest thing, he used to hit us… I remember being knocked across the room because I dropped a can of beer and a bit was spilled – only a drop or two, but across the room he knocked me… He hit my mum about too…'. 'We should talk about this some more Sean' says Jackie,' but it's not too difficult to understand where you learned your violent behaviour from, is it?' 'I never thought of that', says Sean. 'You mean, it's not a deep-down part of me?' 'Not necessarily', says Jackie, 'you've learned this pattern of behaving, but it is possible to learn another pattern instead.' Sean looks amazed… 'I know it gets me into trouble', he says, 'but I don't know how to control it…'.

Step 7: Develop a baseline against which to measure progress

Sean and Jackie discuss how things are at the present time. They use the scores on the Strengths and Difficulties Questionnaire (Appendix 5.3).

Planning

Here there is a need for a plan to involve several people which, although it need not be extremely detailed, does require the involvement of four separate people, or at least that they should be kept informed. These people are: Sean himself, his mother, Jackie and Phil. The plan is outlined in Table 10.12.

Implementing the plan

Jackie undertakes her commitment. She discovers that an anger-management class for teenagers is beginning in a fortnight and that Sean will be welcome to join. It is agreed that Jackie will accompany Sean for the first three sessions, both to learn what she herself can of this way of working, but also to help Sean to settle in.

Sean's mother is very pleased with the progress that Sean is making, both his learning a practical way of coping with his losing his temper and in his commitment to schoolwork. She has kept to her word to have Sean home each Saturday and they have been together to a football match to support Arsenal – they won! She is still cautious about considering Sean's coming home on a full-time basis, but says 'It's up to him; if he can behave himself, then I'll think about it, but he's got to show us he can control his temper before I'll consider it.'

There are some inevitable setbacks. One day, out of the blue, another resident at Speedwell Lodge, named Mac, accidentally bumped into Sean. He, thinking it was deliberate, turned and before anyone could restrain him, punched Mac so hard that it sent him flying against the wall, breaking his glasses and producing a huge bruise to the left side of his face. Once Sean realized what he had done, and that the bumping into him had been accidental, he was shamefaced; although he brazened it out, he was visibly embarrassed. His penalty was to contribute £2.00 a week out of his allowance over the next six months towards the new glasses and to write a letter of explanation to go in the Unit records to explain how Mac came by his bruised face, a penalty which he accepted with a minimum of grumbling.

Thereafter, Sean progresses fast. He seems to begin to trust Phil and the other care staff, and takes steps to follow up all the exercises which his trainer requested.

Table 10.12: Coordinated plan to support Sean

Goal	Jackie	Sean	Phil	Sean's mum
1 To work towards Sean learning to control his aggressive behaviour.	a) Will find out if there are classes in anger management available locally. **b)** Will attend the first session with Sean in part to find out what the classes involve.	If there are, he will attend the anger-management class locally.	Will notice when Sean tries to control his temper	Will tell Sean that she is very pleased he has agreed to go to anger-management class.
2 To work towards Sean and his mum getting on better.	Will talk to Sean's mum about the possibility of Sean coming home for an occasional weekend.	Will practise the anger-management exercises.	Will develop a chart/graph with Sean to help him monitor his mood at Speedwell Lodge.	Will resume visiting Sean at Speedwell Lodge each Saturday following the Friday anger-management class.
3 To work towards Sean calming his behaviour overall.	Will purchase a relaxation tape for Sean.	Will practise using the relaxation tape.	Will help Sean to set up a time for using the tape. Will commend Sean for using the tape.	
4 To help Sean to improve his schoolwork.	Will explain the plan to the two teachers who work with Sean.	Will do his reading and writing homework each day.	Will listen to Sean reading 10 mins. Daily.	Will tell Sean that she is pleased with any improvements in schoolwork.

4.7 *Reviewing and evaluating the work*

This is undertaken against the agreed goals, as follows:

1 *To work towards Sean controlling his angry behaviour*
   Sean has attended the anger-management class regularly over the last month. He is finding the experience very surprising but also very enjoyable. The worker there, Carl, an African-Caribbean young man, is very pleased with Sean's progress and is particularly helpful to Sean as he has told him that he used to be ready for a fight at any time of the day or night, but he decided there must be another way. Sean finds Carl a very helpful person to talk to.

2 *To work towards Sean and his Mum getting on better*
   Sean's mum has been as good as her word. Each Saturday, following Sean's visit to the anger-management class on the Friday, she has come to visit him. They have been out together to McDonalds, to buy some new clothes and to the cemetery where Sean's grandpa, whom Sean just remembers, is buried. This was at Sean's request. During these outings, Sean and his mum have talked together in a way which they never have before. These meetings have become important to them both.

3 *To work towards Sean calming his overall behaviour*
   This is going well. Sean practises his relaxation tape in the mornings, when he wakes up, and at night to get himself to sleep. Other young people at Speedwell Lodge are beginning to use it too, as well as the residential social workers.

4 *To enable Sean to improve his schoolwork*
   This too is going well. As Sean's overall level of tension subsides and as the other young people also become calmer, so in general schoolwork improves. His teachers, who use a positive style of teaching anyway, are able to give him genuine warm encouragement and Sean begins to enjoy learning for the first time ever.

Final evaluation on SDQ showed a calmer and far more settled young man. It is hoped that he will be going home soon, with continuing support from Speedwell Lodge staff.

Summary points

❐ There is evidence of increased levels of depression during adolescence by comparison with levels pre-puberty.

❏ These increases may be linked with hormonal changes during puberty, as well as an increase in the number of environmental stressors, such as growing awareness of the world of work, and social and peer-group pressures.

❏ High self-esteem among young women seems to be linked with being able to turn to their mothers for support and having their views and problems listened to.

❏ High self-esteem among young men seems to be linked with similar emotional support, but also with high family togetherness, doing things and going places as a family, having a father or father-figure who spend time with the young person and takes a genuine interest in him, and a school ethos which values the young person.

❏ Anxious young people can be helped through a range of cognitive-behavioural approaches, including relaxation, developing coping strategies, problem-solving, contingent reinforcement, modelling and desensitization.

❏ Strategies which help improve parent/young person relationships include: making neutral requests, thanking young people for cooperation, monitoring young people's whereabouts, negotiating family rules about coming-home times and enforcing these calmly.

❏ Aggressive young people can also be helped through a range of cognitive behavioural approaches, including arousal-reduction, social skills training, making positive self-statements and appropriate anger expression.

11

Young offenders: multidisciplinary approaches

Prevalence of youth offending

David Farrington, one of the most widely respected researchers in the field of youth offending in Britain, after reminding us that official crime statistics distinguish between 'indictable' offences – which can be tried by a jury – and less serious 'summary' offences, begins his important text *Understanding and Preventing Youth Crime* (1996) as follows,

> Since October 1992 juvenile delinquency in England and Wales (dealt with in the Youth Court) has applied to the years 10 to 17 inclusive... Officially recorded juvenile offenders have either been found guilty in court or cautioned. Although the minimum age of criminal responsibility is 10, few offenders under the age of 14 are found guilty in the Youth Court.

Table 11.1 provides some salient facts.

Farrington reports that 'Ninety per cent or more of both boys and girls were cautioned. The most common offences committed by juveniles were burglary, vehicle theft and shoplifting.' He highlights the importance of early 'onset' (the first conviction) as his and other evidence suggest that this 'foreshadows a long criminal career and many offences'. He continues:

> The males first convicted at the earliest ages (10–13) tended to become the most persistent offenders, committing an average of 8.1 offences leading to convictions in an average criminal career lasting almost exactly 10 years. Those first convicted at age 10–11 had an average career length of 11.5 years. However, the average duration of criminal careers declined precipitously from onset at age 16 (7.9 years) to age 17 (2.9 years), suggesting that those males first convicted as juveniles were much more persistent offenders than those first convicted as adults. (Farrington, 1996, p. 3)

Table 11.1: Number of offenders found guilty of indictable offences (1997)

1997	Age 10–13	Age 14–17
Boys/Young men	17,000	78,700
Girls/Young women	5,700	18,700

Origins of youth offending

This book has emphasized throughout the risks incurred by children as they, through no fault of their own, are subjected to experiences which leave them vulnerable to falling into patterns of offending. The flow chart devised by Clarke (1977) shows the many risks to which young people may be exposed. (See Figure 11.1.)

Loeber and his collaborators (1987) undertook extensive work to pinpoint the crucial *predictors* of a pattern of offending by young males. They identified the five specific risk factors shown in Table 11.2.

It should be emphasized that these variables have been identified by means of *prospective* not just retrospective studies, and that these same patterns have been found in international research, not just that relating to the United States.

Research into the prevention of offending

David Farrington has made an immensely important contribution to understanding both the origins of youth offending and how it may be prevented. I have already made reference to his book, *Understanding and Preventing Youth Crime*. In addition, a further publication written with an American colleague (Farrington and Welsh, 1999) reviews the field of the prevention of delinquency using family-based interventions. Table 11.3 is drawn from that review.

Table 11.2: Predictors of patterns of offending by young males (Loeber and Stouthamer-Loeber, 1987. In Quay, H. C. (Ed.) *Handbook of Juvenile Delinquency*. © John Wiley and Sons Limited. Reprinted with permission)

1 Poor parental child-management techniques
2 Childhood anti-social behaviour
3 Offending by parents and siblings
4 Low intelligence and low educational attainment
5 Separation from parents

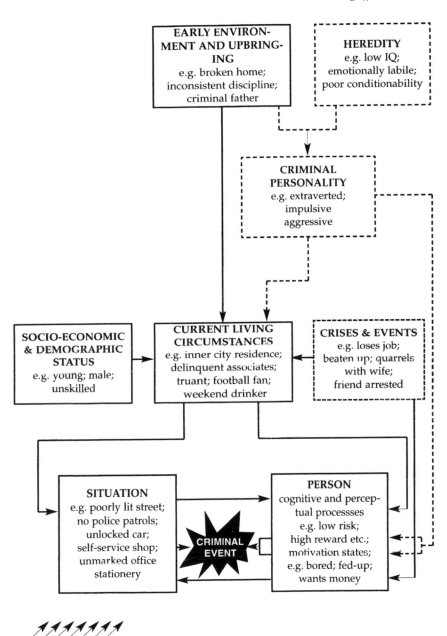

Note: The examples given within each box will have significance only in respect of types of a particular crime.
The dotted line represents the author's view that the evidence in these areas is not fullypersuasive

Figure 11.1. Elements contributing to the occurence of a criminal event. (Clarke, 1977)

Table 11.3: Summary of prevention programmes (Farrington and Welsh, 1999)

Author	Initial sample	Main intervention	Main results[1]
Home visiting			
Olds (1998)	400 mothers	Parent education	Child arrests at 15(+)
Kitzman (1997)	1139 mothers	Parent education	Child injuries (+)
Larson (1980)	115 mothers	Parent education	Child injuries (+)
Stone (1988)	131 mothers	Parent education	Child behaviour problems at 5–8 (0)
Day care			
Johnson (1987)	458 children age 1	Parent education	Aggression at 8–11 (+)
Lally (1988)	182 children age 0	Parent education	Delinquency at 15 (+)
McCarton (1997)	985 children age 0	Parent education	Child behaviour problems at 8 (0)
Preschool			
Schweinhart (1993	123 children age 3	Skills training	Arrests at 27 (+)
Webster-Stratton (1998)	426 children age 4	Parent training	Child behaviour problems at 5 (+)
Pagani (1998)	404 boys age 4	Skills training	Delinquency at 12 (+)
School			
Hawkins (1999)	643 children age 10	Parent/teacher training	Violence at 18 (+)
Tremblay (1995)	319 boys age 6	Parent/skills training	Delinquency at 15 (+)
Reid (1999)	671 children 7–11	Parent/skills training	Aggression (+)
Kolvin (1981)	592 children 7–12	Skills training	Antisocial behaviour at 10–15 (+)
Clinic			
Webster-Stratton (1988)	114 children age 4	Parent training	Behaviour problems (+)
Webster-Stratton (1997)	97 children age 5	Parent/skills training	Behaviour problems at 6 (+)
Kazdin (1992)	97 children age 10	Parent/skills training	Conduct problem at 11 (+)
Strayhorn (1991)	105 children age 3	Parent training	Aggression at 5 (+)

Table 11.3: (continued)

Author	Initial sample	Main intervention	Main results[1]
Community			
McCord (1978)	650 boys age 10	Counselling	Criminal behaviour at 45(−)
Dishion (1992)	119 children age 12	Parent/skills training	Behaviour problems at 13 (0)
Harrell (1997)	671 youths age 12	Risk focused	Delinquency (0)
Multisystemic			
Borduin (1995)	176 youths age 14	MST	Arrests at 18 (+)
Schoenwald (1996)	118 youths age 15	MST	Time in institution at 16 (+)
Henggeler (1997)	115 youths age 15	MST	Delinquency at 17 (+)

Key:
(0)   No significant difference between outcomes for groups receiving service and comparison group
(+)   Desirable effect of intervention
(−)   Undesirable effect of intervention
MST   Multi-Systemic Therapy
Immediate follow-up unless otherwise stated

Effective longitudinal studies

The studies which Farrington and Welsh regard as particularly successful and important in preventing delinquency are the home visiting programme of Olds *et al.* (1998); the pre-school programme of Schweinhart *et al.* (1993); the parent-skills training programme of Tremblay *et al.* (1995); and the teacher-skills training programme of Hawkins *et al.* (1991, 1992). Let us consider each of these in greater detail.

Home visiting programme of Olds et al. (1998)

This concerned 400 mothers in New York State who had been allocated to one of three regimes of visits by nurses:

- fortnightly home visits from nurses during pregnancy, or,
- fortnightly home visits both during pregnancy and during the first two years of life; the visits lasted about an hour and a quarter, or,
- a comparison group who received no visits.

It was found in this study that, by contrast with mothers in the comparison group, those mothers who were visited gave evidence of the following outcomes:

- teenage mothers had heavier babies;
- mothers who had previously smoked decreased their smoking and had fewer premature deliveries;
- there was a reduction in recorded child abuse and neglect during the first two years of life (4 per cent among visited mothers by contrast with 19 per cent in unvisited).

The follow-up study fifteen years later found that children of the mothers who received prenatal and/or postnatal home visits had less than half as many arrests as children of mothers in the control group.

The pre-school programme of Schweinhart et al. (1993)

This well-known programme showed both short- and long-term beneficial effects. It was part of the Head Start initiative and targeted disadvantaged African-American children who were allocated to one of two groups. One group attended a daily pre-school programme where intellectual stimulation was provided: this was supported by weekly home visits (to involve the mother in the programme) covering the third and fourth years of the children's lives. The control group had no access to the pre-school programme or home visits.

Farrington and Welsh (1999) reported that about 120 children were followed up at a number of stages. By comparison with the control group children, those in the study who had received the interventions showed the characteristics reported in Table 11.4.

Table 11.4: Characteristics of children who received enhanced educational and social support by comparison with control group children (Schweinhart *et al.* 1993, Farrington and Welsh, 1999)

At age 15
- showed higher motivation in their first schools
- reached higher standards at age 14
- reported lower rates of offending at age 15

At age 19
- were more likely to be employed
- were more likely to have graduated from high school
- were more likely to have received college or vocational training
- were less likely to have been arrested

At age 27
- had been arrested only half the number of times on average as the controls
- had significantly higher earnings
- were more likely to be home owners
- more of the women were married

School-based prevention programme (Tremblay et al., 1995)

This team of researchers worked with over 300 aggressive and or hyperactive boys at age 6, using a multidisciplinary approach. Between the years of 7 and 9 the experimental group were trained in small groups in skills of social interaction and self-control. Meanwhile, their parents were trained in skills of managing their sons' behaviour by positive attention and praise for desirable behaviour. The control group boys and parents received no training.

By age 12, the boys who had received training committed fewer offences, were less likely to get drunk and reported being involved in fewer fights; they also reached higher levels of achievement in school. They reported fewer involvements in offending behaviour.

Teacher-skills training programme (Hawkins et al., 1991; 1992)

This multidisciplinary study with almost 500 children aged 6 in twenty-one classes in eight schools divided children randomly into an experimental or control group. The children in the former received the following:
- programmes designed to increase their attachment to parents and school
- training in interpersonal cognitive problem-solving.
- their parents were trained to notice and reinforce socially desirable behaviour.

- their teachers were trained in classroom management: e.g. to provide clear instructions and expectations to children, to reward children for taking part in desired behaviour and to teach children socially desirable methods of solving problems.

Table 11.5 summarizes the effects of the programme.

Table 11.5: Impact of early multidisciplinary intervention upon offending and other behaviours (Hawkins *et al.* 1991, 1992)

Eighteen months after the end of the study:

The boys who had received the experimental programme were significantly less aggressive than the control boys, according to teacher ratings.
The girls were not significantly less aggressive, but they were less self-destructive, anxious and depressed.

By age 11:
The children who had taken part in the experimental programme were less likely to have initiated offending behaviour or drug use.

By age 18:
Working with 643 children, the researchers found that at age 18, the full intervention group reported using less violence, less alcohol and having fewer sexual partners than members of the control groups.

Studies using multiple strategies of intervention

Farrington and Welsh also identify successful interventions for young offenders which were carried out in families, schools and communities; in other words, in which a multidisciplinary intervention is tailored to the specific needs of the young person. Thus, a given youngster might receive individual counselling and anger-management training; his parents might receive training in managing his difficult behaviour, and his teachers also might receive complementary help in dealing with him in school.

Farrington (1996), for example, reports the beginnings of a body of research upon 'peer influence strategies'. He cites work in St Louis in the United States in which 400 boys, aged about 11, who were referred for antisocial behaviour were randomly assigned to two types of activity group, one containing referred young people only and the other containing ten young people without antisocial patterns of behaviour and just one or two of the antisocial young people. The behaviour of the antisocial young people in the second type of group improved (Feldman *et al.*, 1983).

A number of studies applying an integrated and coordinated model of support for troublesome young people and their families has demonstrated substantial reductions in the numbers of arrests incurred by the youngsters in the experimental groups by comparison with those in the control groups. Studies by Borduin (1995), by Schoenwald (1996) and by Henggeler (1997) all showed that so-called 'multisystemic therapy' brought about significant improvement in terms of reduction in number of arrests at age 18, time in an institution at age 16 and delinquency at age 17, respectively.

Strategies which can reduce reoffending: cognitive-behavioural approaches

In the above section, reference has been made to some specific approaches employed by practitioners with young people which have had demonstrable effects in diverting young people from a career in crime. This section is devoted to examining a range of these strategies all of which fall under the cognitive behavioural 'umbrella', the core of which was considered in Chapter 3 (see Table 11.6). Some examples are then given.

Table 11.6: Cognitive-behavioural approaches for use with offenders, and common elements of these approaches (NACRO, 1998)

Cognitive-behavioural approaches:

- Coping skills.
- Problem-solving approaches.
- Cognitive restructuring.
- Structural cognitive therapy.
- Solution focused approaches.
- Social skills training, via modelling, rehearsal and positive feedback.
- Short-term behavioural interventions with young offenders and their families.

Common elements exist across these approaches:

- Begin with a well-planned rationale.
- Include training in skills to be used to deal with daily life more effectively.
- Place emphasis upon independent use of the skills.
- Encourage attribution of improvement to the participant's own changes in thinking, habits and behaviour (self-efficacy).

Problem solving approaches

This is essentially a cognitive-behavioural approach, with strong emphasis upon exploring a range of possible solutions to difficult problems. It derives from the work of Spivack *et al.* (1976). The approach can be adapted to an extremely wide range of situations which cause problems, and notably have been employed by Falloon *et al.* (1984) in the context of supporting families in which there is a schizophrenically ill member. The steps, within a context of dealing with offending behaviour, are these:

In the context of an assessment,

1 *Pinpoint the problem.* For example, Mark is constantly stealing cars.

2 *Formulate this problem in terms of a goal to be achieved* – with those involved. For example, Mark says he would like to limit his stealing to only one car during the next month. He just does not think it realistic to try to stop stealing cars altogether.

3 *Brainstorm possible solutions*: no suggestion must be criticized; the aim is to be as creative as possible.
   a) Mark will stay indoors and not go out, so he will not be tempted to steal cars.
   b) Mark will save up to buy his own car.
   c) Mark will get a Saturday job, so that he can pay for driving lessons.
   d) Mark will practise walking by cars and not trying their doors, first with a 'coach' and then unaccompanied.
   e) Mark will take up another sport which gives him thrills, like climbing.
   f) Mark will agree to link up with a mentor.

4 *Evaluate potential of each solution*: Mark and his family/ worker consider the possibilities of each suggestion and the advantages and disadvantages of each one. Mark had not considered several of these possibilities.

5 *Agree on best strategy*: b) and c) both appeal to Mark, together with f). All are achievable.

6 *Plan clear objectives*:
   b) c) Within two months, Mark will have found a Saturday job, with the help of the youth worker.
   f) The youth worker will have identified a male mentor for Mark.

7 *Implement the objectives*: These plans are put into effect.
8 *Review the plan*: In two weeks time, the plan is reviewed. It took nearly 10 weeks before a Saturday job was found for Mark, but a job and a mentor have been found – and a bank account has been opened!

Solution-focused therapy

This is also in essence a 'cognitive-behavioural' approach; that is, it employs, whether its practitioners claim to or not, a range of principles which derive from learning theory and from research into the effects of cognitive processes such as patterns of perception and habits of thinking. Its name derives from the emphasis upon negotiating potential solutions to problems, as distinct from focusing upon the problems themselves, but this is also a feature of much cognitive-behavioural therapy (see Herbert, 1987; Sutton, 1992, 1995; Sutton and Herbert, 1992). Indeed, there are a great many features of the therapy which it shares with other approaches: for example:

1 Offering people a respecting and supportive relationship.
2 Showing empathy and understanding concerning areas of difficulty in the lives of the persons concerned.
3 Goal-setting: supporting the person(s) in working towards goals which he/she/they want.
4 Focused positive feedback.

The authors of *Diverting People from Crime* (NACRO, 1998) suggest:

> More than anything else, solution-focused work involves individuals' [receiving] positive feedback about their goals and their successes. It may be necessary to check out this feedback, looking for non-verbal agreement before progressing, or use feedback to strengthen or clarify either goals or progress. Compliments and praise will increase the person's self-image, strengthen both commitment and confidence and communicate an acceptance of the person's unique strengths and abilities.
>
> Additional features, however, which solution-focused practitioners use include:
>
> 1 Engaging in problem-free talk: the practitioner attempts to work with the whole person, not just one who has a problem.
> 2 Scaling questions: using a 0–10 scale for breaking change into small steps. For example, on a scale of 1 to 10, where 10 is the perfect miracle and 1 is the absolute worst things have ever been, where are you now?

3 Identifying exceptions; that is, circumstance when the difficulties do or did not exist. Then attempting to find opportunities of replicating those circumstances.
4 Recognizing that searching for 'causes' is not vital to finding a solution.

Many cognitive-behavioural practitioners would claim, as I do, that to pick out any one of these approaches, such as problem-solving or solution-focused therapy, as a distinct theoretical approach can cause confusion to beginning practitioners. These and other approaches under the cognitive-behavioural umbrella take, or should take, account of well-established principles of learning theory, such as contingencies of reinforcement, generalization of a behaviour from one situation into others, as well as the impact of individual patterns of thinking and habits of behaviour.

Short-term behavioural intervention with young offenders and their families

An early but still extremely important piece of research was carried out by Alexander and Parsons (1973). Focused upon young people aged 13 to 16 years and their families, this compared three different strategies for reducing offending: client-centred family groups; a psychodynamic family programme and a short-term behavioural intervention. The offences included shoplifting, habitual truancy, possessing banned substances and having 'been declared ungovernable'. Alexander and Parsons write that earlier research by Patterson and Reid (1970) had:

> demonstrated that when the amount and balance of mutual positive reinforcement has been altered (i.e. made more equitable by therapeutic intervention) families have moved from 'bedlam' to relatively low rates of disruptive behaviour.

Building upon this conclusion, Alexander and Parsons reported that they developed a specific, short-term (lasting a few months only) programme of work which was designed to:

a) increase the extent of positive interactions among family members;
b) make communications among family members clear; and
c) establish a pattern of 'contingency contracting' or focused agreements among family members. This required active negotiation among family members, with each one receiving some specific reward for each responsibility which he or she accepted.

In practice, these researchers helped families very practically in the following ways:

a) by separating out background 'family rules' from requests to do things. Alexander and Parsons comment that parents often set too many rules and are inconsistent in their punishment when these rules are broken. By helping families negotiate a few clear rules, for example, about coming-in time, and being firm about following-through on sanctions for breaking the agreed rules, they helped parents clarify and simplify family life.
b) helping family members interact in a clearer, more attentive way, so that each could really understand what the others were trying to say.
c) actively praising verbally or non-verbally efforts made by family members to interact in this clearer, more rewarding way.
d) helping family members to say how they would like other family members to respond to them, for example, by actively taking time to talk about the day with them, or by spending time in a simple activity, e.g. playing cards, or making a cake together.
e) helping family members to offer more 'social reinforcement' (positive comments, thanks, appreciation) to each other.

Alexander and Parsons report that while many families initially resisted this active style of intervention, they found that by starting with small goals and devising very modest agreements about small issues, (for example, the young person agrees to wash up in return for the parent agreeing to do the young person's laundry) the improvements in family life which resulted enabled them to persist and to use the approach for dealing with larger issues.

The patterns of reoffending of the young people who had taken part in these various intervention programmes were compared. It was found that this structured approach, which we would now call a cognitive-behavioural approach, was associated with a markedly lower rate of reoffending than that shown by young people who had taken part in client-centred or psychodynamic approaches (see Table 11.7).

Table 11.7: Outcome measures: reoffending rates for treatment and comparison groups (groups compared statistically) (Alexander and Parsons, 1973)

Treatment	Reoffending rate (%)
Short-term family behavioural treatment	26
Client-centred family groups treatment	47
Eclectic psychodynamic treatment	73
No treatment controls	50

Reflecting on the above data, it seems to me that, in essence, the researchers were systematically teaching the families who received short-term behavioural intervention to communicate better, to be more attentive to each other and to be more rewarding to, as against threatening or ignoring, each other. In these circumstances, the young people who had formerly found their sources of satisfaction outside the home in patterns of offending behaviour, found it more rewarding to be at home – the family members were now actively listening to them, appreciating them and responding positively to their requests for time and attention.

Multidisciplinary interventions with young offenders

In Britain one of the best-known and most effective of the agencies concerned with the reduction of offending is the Northamptonshire Diversion Unit, as it was known when it was first established in 1993. The work of the Unit is described in *Diverting People from Crime* as follows:

> The Diversion Unit serves the public by contributing to a reduction in crime and the harm created by it. It helps to 'resolve' offences by, for example, helping individual victims and offenders to reach an understanding of why the offence was committed and what sort of settlement in relation to it would be satisfactory to both parties. It also tackles significant personal and structural factors associated with offending behaviour.
>
> Personal factors include alcohol and drug misuse, personal relationships, controlling anger and roles in groups. Structural factors include unemployment, poor housing, poverty and leisure facilities...
>
> Its inter-agency service is funded by the local education, police, probation, social, youth and health services, who each provide staff on secondment to work alongside permanent staff...

I shall use this agency as an example of what can be achieved in respect of inter-agency and multidisciplinary working both because its youth offending team is long established, and because it has been chosen by the Home Office in Britain as a model for the rest of the country. This choice is based upon the evidence arising from an evaluation by independent researchers of the high degree of satisfaction the community expresses with the work of the unit, and also upon the indications that 'the re-offending rate of 34.8%... is consistent with the view that the Diversion Unit has played a significant role in reducing re-offending'.

This evidence is, of course, weak by comparison with that derived from the sophisticated longitudinal studies such as those we have considered above. It is encouraging to note, however, that it is the multidisciplinary and multisystemic approach adopted in the American studies which achieved the greatest reduction in offending and that it is the convergence of evidence from both sides of the Atlantic, which has led to the setting up of these multidisciplinary youth offending teams throughout Britain.

Multidisciplinary work with a young offender

As youth offending teams are established, so the range of knowledge and skills which multidisciplinary teams can offer will become a resource not just for one profession, such as probation or education, but for other members of the team. This dissemination of knowledge and skills seems highly desirable. Let us consider how such a team might cooperate to help Jon, a young person already in trouble with the law.

Jon Harvey, aged 12, has been referred by the police to the youth offending team for three instances of shoplifting and one of breaking into a dwelling house, all committed within a two-month period. The offences were carried out in the company of a group of young people from Jon's school. He has been truanting from school increasingly during the two-month period.

Assessment

Step 1: Building supportive and empathic relationships

Jon Harvey's parents are very angry. Jon's dad is an executive in a security company and he is acutely embarrassed by his son's behaviour. His mum tries to defend Jon, but overall there is a high level of conflict within the family. The worker, who on this occasion is an educational welfare officer, Steve, has managed to develop a supportive relationship with them, and they have been able to vent their frustration with, and disappointment in, their son in privacy.

Steve has agreed to make the first contact with the family, but is able to make considered use of the resources of the youth offending team.

Step 2: Information gathering

Steve hears that Jon's difficulties appear to have begun when the family moved house following his dad's promotion. This meant he changed school and lost contact with his friends who live on the other side of the city. Jon had seemed to settle down, but now the teachers at Jon's school are concerned that his truancy has been increasing. All the offences have occurred at times when he should have been in school. He has never been easy to manage, but he has become more difficult with the move of school, since when he began getting in with a crowd of youngsters who were 'disaffected' from school.

Quantitative assessment

After establishing constructive and supportive relationships with family members, Steve asks if they will all agree to complete the Strengths and Difficulties Questionnaire. Jon's parents agree, as does Jon, though in his case reluctantly. The results are shown in Table 11.8.

Comparing these figures with the scales provided by Goodman (1997) it is evident that Jon falls within the normal range for his strengths and within the borderline range for his conduct problems score. Jon's mum and Jon are relieved by these results, as they had thought he was 'a bad case'; Jon's dad, however, is not. All, however, are very pleased to have Jon's strengths highlighted, especially as the phrases 'Considerate of other people's feelings', 'Kind to younger children', and 'Helpful if someone is hurt, upset or feeling ill' have all been ticked. Steve points out that these are extremely positive clauses and ones which can be built upon in the future.

Step 3: Identifying the main areas of difficulty together

The workers agree with Jon's parents, and with Jon himself, that the main areas of difficulty are:

- The number of rows between Jon and his parents, especially his dad.
- Jon's truanting from school.
- His going into town at night with a group only concerned to shoplift.

Table 11.8: Jon's score on the Strengths and Difficulties Questionnaire (Goodman, 1997) before intervention

	Mother	Father	Jon	Average
Strengths	6	6	6	6
Difficulties				
Hyperactivity	0	0	0	0
Conduct problems	7	9	5	7
Peer problems	6	6	6	6
Emotional problems	0	0	0	0
Overall difficulties score	13	15	11	13

Step 4: Identifying the positive features of the situation

Steve asks Jon's parents and Jon himself to tell him about some of the other aspects of Jon's life. He gets them to sit down together, guides the conversation into positive channels and is soon hearing about Jon's success at sport in school, his interest in aircraft and how he has built up a large collection of model planes in his bedroom. Steve enquires how he had become so interested in planes, and hears that Jon's dad, Mr Harvey, had been in the Royal Air Force as a young man and has passed on his interest to Jon.

It becomes apparent that Jon has real talent in model-building; he used to belong to a modellers' club but that this has all been neglected since the friend with whom he went to the club had moved away. Out of all this, however, Steve was able pinpoint a number of Jon's positive features:

- Jon did well at his primary school.
- He has a talent for model building, learned from his dad.
- He is kind to younger children – and when a neighbour's child was ill in bed for several weeks, he had gone to see him and had played board games and listened to records with him.
- His teachers want him back at school, etc.

Using a solution-focused approach, Steve asks Jon's parents 'When are the good times? When do the difficulties with Jon not occur?' They agree that this is when Jon and his dad tackle a job together, clearing out the garage, helping a neighbour lay the foundation for an extension, putting insulation in the loft... Jon agrees, saying that he used to like doing things with his dad, but Mr Harvey seems to have been too busy recently

At this point, Steve writes the Pre-Sentencing Report, (PSR), which he presents to the magistrates' court. Jon behaves well in court, expresses regret for his actions, and Steve's positive report impresses the magistrates. Jon is given a supervision order for six months. Steve as a social worker will continue as the key worker.

Step 5: Identifying the desired outcomes of the work together

A short period after the court hearing, Steve meets with first Jon and then with Jon's parents to discuss the way forward. The family are dismayed by the supervision order, but agree things could be worse. Using great tact and patience, Steve asks the family what are the outcomes they would like to work towards. After listening to dad's threats to 'throw Jon out if he ever does anything like this again', and managing to prevent another row between Jon and his dad, the following goals for the work together are negotiated:

1 That Jon and his dad will spend at least two hours' leisure time weekly together over the next month.
2 That Jon will attend school each morning without fail.
3 That Jon will spend at least four evenings at home each week.
4 That Jon will resist pressure to take part in any further criminal activities.

Step 6: Attempt a formulation of/rationale for the difficulties

Steve asks Jon's mum and dad why they think the situation has come about. To his surprise, they do not completely blame Jon. His dad says that he has been reading in the papers about how youngsters of Jon's age need to have a 'father figure' to take an interest in them, and since he got promotion in the company he works for, he hasn't had the time to give to Jon that a teenager needs.

His mum takes part in the discussion too, and says that she's been noticing a difference in Jon since his dad got so busy. The family used to be close and Jon used to love family days out, but these had stopped since his dad's promotion.

Step 7: Develop a baseline against which to measure progress

The baseline is taken as being the most recent available data for each of the agreed goals:

1 Time spent undertaking an activity together in the previous week – 0 hours
2 Number of sessions (out of a possible 10) spent in school in the previous week – 5
3 Number of evenings spent at home in the previous week – 1
4 Number of petty offences which Jon has been involved in previous week – 2
   (Jon tells Steve about these when they are alone.)

Planning

Since Jon's parents seem willing to do what they can to help him, and since Steve's tact is enabling them to see, without losing their dignity, that their difficulties have contributed towards Jon's distress, it is possible to move forward smoothly to planning with the family. Jon's dad is surprised, and quietly pleased, that Jon actively wants to spend time with him, and he agrees to take part in a plan. Steve explains that it is likely that he will remain as key worker, but that he will speak to his colleagues at the youth offending team and enlist the education worker in particular. This he does, and education worker liaises with the headmaster of Jon's school, the education department and Jon's class teacher.

All the practitioners work closely together, and in the light of the goals which have been agreed, the plan shown in Table 11.9 is developed. It will be reviewed weekly.

Implementing the plan

The plan gets off to a difficult start. Jon and his dad are both embarrassed to find that to spend two hours together all in one go is too long. During the first week they go out for a 'walk and talk' but they do not find it easy to talk... They discover that taking it in turn to choose things to do is a good plan. One of their best experiences is to go together to an air show, where both become engrossed in the latest aeronautical developments.

Jon reports that he has attended school each day, but his parents keep checking up on him, phoning the school and cross-questioning him when he gets in. This makes him very angry and he complains bitterly when the family meet at the pre-arranged Tuesday evening meeting. Steve has to work hard with Mr and Mrs Harvey, acknowledging that it is their anxiety which is driving them to keep checking up on Jon, but showing them how counter-productive this checking is. Steve's skill, experience and firmness is sufficient to bring them to promise not to phone the school and to greet Jon positively when he gets home.

The agreement to spend at least four evenings at home each week has also proved problematic. Jon has been at home, as promised, but he confides in Steve that he has been bored stiff after the third evening. Accordingly, a sub-agreement is developed. In return for Jon's giving his mum and dad a phone number where he can be contacted on the evenings when he is out, Jon can invite a friend home for the evening once a week. The choice of friend is his.

The plan of rehearsing how to resist pressure to take part in shoplifting is going better than Steve had expected. They have had only one session, but Jon can see how he has got drawn into activities which he doesn't enjoy and which only cause him grief at home. He likes seeing more of Steve. His class teacher is being OK with him too, no longer threatening him with exclusion, and instead taking more of an interest in Jon's abilities and strengths.

The weeks go by, with Steve meeting with the family and Jon on a weekly basis. His role is to 'trouble-shoot', to emphasize what is being achieved rather than areas of failure, and to encourage the family, with generous positive feedback, to work towards the goals it agreed.

Table 11.9: Agreement devised among Jon, his family and others

Goal	Steve	Jon	Jon's dad	Jon's mum	Teacher
1 That Jon and his dad will spend 2 hours each week in leisure time together.	Will help them plan what to do each week in a calm way. After, he will hear how it went and try to solve difficulties.	Will make a list of three things he would like to do each week: e.g., football, swimming or out for a meal.	Will choose one of the three things which Jon has selected.	Will encourage Jon and his dad to keep to the plan agreed.	
2 Jon will attend school each day.	Will talk with the EWO and get him to greet Jon daily.	Will go to school. If he has difficulties e.g. with maths he will tell his class teacher.	Will *not* ask Jon whether he has been to school. Will trust Jon to keep his word.	Will invite Jon's friends to tea once-weekly.	Will spend 10 min twice a week with Jon, taking an interest in his work.
3 Jon will spend at least four evenings at home each week.		Will choose what to do two of the four evenings, e.g. modelling, TV, board games, or cards in winter; outings in summer.	Will choose what to do two of the four evenings, e.g. modelling, TV, board games, or cards in winter; outings in summer.	Will choose what to do one of the four evenings, e.g. modelling, TV, board games, or cards in winter; outings in summer.	
4 Jon will resist getting drawn into petty offending activities.	Will rehearse with Jon how to resist group pressure to take part in shop-lifting and breaking into cars.	Will rehearse with Steve how to resist group pressure to take part in shop-lifting and breaking into cars.	Will not ask Jon whether he has taken part in shop-lifting. He will trust him.	Will not ask Jon whether he has taken part in shop-lifting. She will trust him.	Will involve Jon in class activities with young people who are not dis-affected.

Reviewing and evaluating the plan

Eight weeks later, as negotiated, all the family members meet together again. They examine the evidence relating to each of the goals they agreed two months before:

1 *That Jon and his dad will spend two hours each week in leisure time together.*

 Overall, after a very difficult start, this has gone really well. Both Jon and his dad now take it in turns to choose their way of spending their time together, and they have been to football matches, have played pool, have been swimming regularly and have watched videos with the rest of the family. The best outing was the visit to the air show. This spurred Jon to resume his model-building and his dad has gone out of his way to work on this with him.

2 *That Jon will attend school each day.*

 This has gone fairly well. Jon says he has been at school almost every day, apart from two instances when the leader of the group he used to go shoplifting with called him 'Chicken' and 'Boff' when he said he didn't want to go with them. To prove them wrong he had gone out with them in the second week of the period of the agreement, but the store where they had shoplifted compact discs before had installed CCTV so they had given it a miss.

 When Jon's parents hear that Jon had nearly been in trouble again, they are very angry. Fortunately, it happened just before a meeting with Steve, so he is able to remind them that that he had warned them that there might be some backsliding while everyone adjusted to doing what they had undertaken. He emphasizes that he had checked with the school and had established that Jon had been present virtually every day since the agreement began, and that his parents must attend to Jon's strengths rather than his shortcomings if they want him to go on keeping to his part of the agreement.

3 *That Jon will spend at least four evenings at home each week.*

 This part of the plan is working well. Jon's mum says she really enjoys these evenings. Jon gets his homework done and then they all say a bit about what they have been doing during the day. Afterwards they play a lot of games, especially Monopoly and Cluedo, as well as lots of cards and end up with Jon's favourite tapes and CDs.

 After initial dislike of the friends whom Jon brought home in the evening, Jon's mum begins to see herself in the role of confidante to some of the youngsters. Many of them see very little of their parents, and they all seem to enjoy coming to Jon for a good meal and some ordinary family life. Steve tells Mrs Harvey that this was how he had begun being a youth worker; seeing how many youngsters lacked adult companionship. Why didn't she think of doing the same thing? Jon's mum is amazed, but says she will think it over…

4 *Jon will resist getting drawn into shoplifting activities.*
This has only gone reasonably well: see the second goal, above. He has enjoyed the role-plays with Steve, however, and now says he understands better what Steve is trying to achieve. He has had a success recently: when under pressure from group members to go out shoplifting with them, he walked away, saying, 'Get lost; I've got better things to do', and ignored their name calling.

Using data to evaluate the effectiveness of the plan

Steve discusses with the family the three separate ways in which they can evaluate how effective the plan has been: gathering data against the baselines established two months earlier, completing the Strengths and Difficulties Questionnaire again and reporting back their own individual views of the work undertaken together.

1 *Gathering data against earlier baselines.*
The baseline is taken as being the most recent available data for each of the agreed goals:

   1 Time spent undertaking an activity together in the previous week – 4 hours
   2 Number of sessions (out of a possible 10) spent in school the previous week – 10
   3 Number of evenings spent at home in the previous week – 4
   4 Number of petty offences which Jon has been involved in previous week – 0

2 *Completing the Strengths and Difficulties Questionnaire again.*
When the family use the Strengths and Difficulties Questionnaire as a means of evaluating the effect of their work over the last two months, there are not many changes, but what there are are all in the desired direction (see Table 11.10).
   His new average score, 11, brings Jon within the range of *normal* for the Total Difficulties score. His parents and Jon are all very pleased.

3 *Reporting their individual views by family members.*
All the family members, including Jon, say they can look back and see that there has been an improvement of relationships among family members over the past two months.

Table 11.10: Jon's score on the Strengths and Difficulties Questionnaire (Goodman, 1997) after intervention.

	Mother	Father	Jon	Average
Strengths	6	6	6	6
Difficulties				
Hyperactivity	0	0	0	0
Conduct problems	6	7	5	6
Peer problems	5	6	4	5
Emotional problems	0	0	0	0
Overall difficulties score	11	13	9	11

They all feel less tense and unhappy, less stressed about what rows or complaints the next day will bring and more confident of good experiences in the next weeks and months. As Steve had warned them, there have been some really difficult times, but they have learned that just as Steve focuses upon the positive features of the situation, so they must focus on Jon's strengths, not his shortcomings. They want to draw up another agreement for the next two months.

In view of the success of the work, which is reported to the youth offending team, a decision is made to confirm 'Informal Action' by the police. That is, a record will be kept by the police to assist with the future decision-making should Jon reoffend.

Summary points

❐ The timing of the first offence is an important predictor of later patterns of offending. Males first convicted at the earliest ages (10–13) tend to become the most persistent offenders.

❐ Patterns of offending have a multifactorial explanation.

❐ Predictors of future offending seem to include poor parental child-management strategies; antisocial behaviour in childhood; offending by parents and siblings; low intelligence and low educational attainment; and separation from parents.

❐ Several specific approaches have been shown to be successful and important in preventing delinquency:

a) fortnightly home visits by nurses during pregnancy and during the first two years of life;

b) pre-school programmes for children, with weekly home visits to support their parents;

c) for aggressive and hyperactive 6-year-olds, a multidisciplinary programme training them in skills of social interaction and self-control, accompanied by training for their parents in giving their children positive attention and praise for desirable behaviour;

d) training parents of 6-year-olds to notice and reinforce socially desirable behaviour; accompanied by training their teachers in firm classroom management and in providing clear expectations for children's behaviour and in commending them when they behaved as expected; as well as direct work with the children, involving training them in interpersonal problem-solving.

❐ A wide range of cognitive-behavioural strategies are available to help reduce offending; these include teaching children and young people coping skills, problem-solving approaches, solution-focused approaches, social skills training and cognitive restructuring. These essentially form a repertoire of approaches which the practitioner can discuss with the young person, so that a shared decision is made about which skills to learn and in what order.

❐ There is evidence that intervention using short-term cognitive-behavioural approaches, in which families are trained to communicate clearly and parents are trained not only to make clear rules with young people and to follow through when they are broken, but also to notice and commend a child's positive behaviours, are more effective than either client-centred or psychodynamic approaches in reducing reoffending.

12

Summary of key ideas, and ways forward

We have seen in the previous chapters something of the seriousness of the situation confronting both policy-makers and practitioners in respect of children's emotional and behavioural difficulties. In this chapter I wish briefly to summarize key information and concepts explored in this book and to suggest some ways forward.

Summary of key ideas

The seriousness of the situation

We have seen the seriousness of the situation which confronts Britain, with about one in twenty children in rural areas and about one in ten in inner-urban areas afflicted by distressing emotional difficulties, and similar numbers displaying serious behavioural difficulties. These data, however, only represent the distress of the young people themselves: they do not represent the distress caused to their families, their schools and their communities. The cost to society of a young person who displays serious conduct disorders as a young child and goes through the welfare and juvenile justice system into a pattern of adult offending may be around £1,000 000 – and even then the young person may be in prison, still with no assurance that he can participate in society in a constructive and settled way.

We can take some comfort in the fact that central government has accepted the evidence and the common-sense view that the way forward is via prevention. We welcome its attempts to mobilize and extend the resources of not only the voluntary sector, but also all three major departments which have direct responsibility for work with children and young people – health, education and social services. An attempt is being made to put in place and coordinate a structure of resources and services both to prevent children's difficulties from occurring in the first place and to help them once they have occurred.

The Home Office, too, is closely involved in supporting community initiatives to the same end.

We have noted how socioeconomic deprivation has been shown by, for example Blanz *et al.* (1991), to be closely associated with, if not the direct cause of, children's emotional and behavioural difficulties; and it may be that until poverty is eradicated or markedly reduced then children will continue to suffer. We know also, however, that families from all backgrounds, rich and poor, seek help for their children and, as Farrington (1996) has shown in a discussion of cumulative risk factors, not only socioeconomic difficulties but also poor parental child-rearing techniques, especially harsh or erratic discipline, inadequate supervision and separation from a biological parent, place immense stresses on children's well-being and pose threats to that well-being in adulthood. In other words, we need not just sit and wait for poverty to be eliminated; other steps can be taken. This book is about some of those steps.

Early intervention: learning from American research

The case for a preventive approach has now been made. It is acknowledged in publications of the Department of Health such as *Transforming Children's Lives: the Importance of Early Intervention* (1999), that this is the way forward. The quality of some of the longitudinal studies from the United States as well as those of some British researchers, such as Kolvin (1981), persuades us that not only does early intervention protect children from entering into criminality but it also enhances their educational prospects and overall well being.

In considering the picture at the end of the twentieth century, Webster-Stratton (1999) summarizes her view thus:

> Research suggests that certain family characteristics put some children at higher risks of developing conduct problems: family poverty, single parenthood, teenage parenthood, parental psychotic illness, and parental history of drug taking and criminality... Children whose parents are inconsistent in their discipline, or physically abusive or highly critical also are at greater risk, as are children whose parents are disengaged from their children's school experience and provide little cognitive stimulation in the home... there are also some biological factors in these children which place them at higher risk, namely learning disabilities, language and reading delays, attention deficit disorder and hyperactivity. Children with two of these risk factors are four times more likely to have a mental health problem, compared to children exposed to one or no risk factors. Children with four risk factors are ten times more likely to have a mental health problem.

In emphasizing a multidisciplinary approach, Webster-Stratton goes on to pinpoint key features of effective parenting programmes and also key features of programmes which work directly with children. These are shown in Tables 12.1 and 12.2.

Webster-Stratton (1999) shares her excitement about the extension of her work from a focus exclusively upon parents to direct work with children and teachers together. She writes:

> We are involved in an exciting study now where we're randomly assigning families to interventions where there is teacher training, child training and parent training and various combinations of each. Our preliminary results suggest that the combination of par-

---

Table 12.1: The most effective parent programmes (Webster-Stratton, 1999)

Have these features:

- Are broader-based, i.e. multisystemic, dealing with marital problems and mental illness.
- Combine cognitive, behavioural and emotional components.
- Are longer than twenty hours in duration.
- Are collaborative with parents, learning from them and sharing ideas with them.
- Focus on parents' strengths, not their deficits.
- Involve partners (fathers, grandparents).
- Are culturally sensitive.
- Are based on performance-training approaches: actually doing the job.
- Use multiple learning methods: video, discussion, role-play, etc.
- Involve teachers and parents in partnerships.
- Are sensitive to barriers for low socioeconomic class families.

Table 12.2: The most effective child-training programmes (Webster-Stratton, 1999)

Have these features:

- Are developmentally based.
- Include affective, behavioural and cognitive components.
- Provide lots of practice activities in a variety of settings.
- Utilize role-plays and videotape modelling.
- Utilize fantasy and games (child-friendly).
- Are collaborative – using group problem solving.
- Involve teachers and parents in reinforcing newly acquired skills.
- Provide memory clues.
- Are offered in small groups.
- Utilize incentives and consequences.
- Give homework.

---

ent training, child training and teacher training produces the most sustained reductions in conflict problems, both at home and at school and in peer relationships.

In support of her claim that interventions in family difficulties must be multisystemic, Webster-Stratton sets out frameworks for direct work with children (see Table 12.2).

Approaches with older children and young offenders

We saw in the later chapters of this book that the most effective strategies for working with troubled young people and potential or actual offenders are, in effect, an extrapolation of those found helpful for young children: they are multisystemic and, hence, multidisciplinary. Thus they involve the child or young person, his or her parents and his or her teachers. They are collaborative and address the difficulties which families have in respect of mental ill-health or substance abuse as well as offering ongoing support when the formal training is over.

Emerging research in the field of parenting orders is showing that the fear and hostility shown by parents who are required to attend for compulsory training can be not only reduced but actively eliminated (*Guardian*, 29 September, 1999). The work going on in Sunderland under the leadership of Helen Watson is leading to parents asking to be allowed to attend the group, only to be told that they have to have an offending child to qualify! Clearly talented practitioners, using theoretical ideas in a natural and spontaneous way, can achieve outstanding results. The next task is to discover how this talent can be acquired by others via training.

Ways forward

At the primary level

At this level, universal parenting programmes should be available in a non-stigmatizing way to all parents. These must be based on sound research, that is, on evidence of what parents want and the best means of providing it: in short, evidence-based practice. Without having to go through the fifteen years of research described by Webster-Stratton and her team, we can begin to set in place the structures and practices which she recommends and establish the training courses and supervisory support necessary to take them forward.

Indeed the huge Sure Start initiative in Britain, for which £540 million has been set aside, is itself a recognition of the central role of early intervention in preventing children's emotional and behavioural difficulties. Further, although we may not have huge financial resources, we do have a magnificent service of health visitors, highly qualified women and men who are specifically trained to work with all families with young children – so that everyone in the community is entitled to receive their services.

At this primary level the aim should be to inculcate the attitude that it is a responsible action to attend parent-education programmes, just as it is to take a course in learning to drive. Quite as much is at stake. Such education programmes could readily be run by community colleges, health centres, libraries and GP's surgeries, coordinated by appropriately trained group facilitators. They would avoid a focus on pathology, but would build instead on the strengths and competencies of people as parents and grandparents; they would take a positive view of the capacity of mothers and fathers to solve problems and deal with difficulties. An active campaign to promote the view of responsible parenting is called for; as Webster-Stratton says, 'We should do as good a job marketing parenting as we do marketing Frosted Flakes'.

Policy-makers are the key people at this level. It is they who, because of their command of resources, and because of their regular contact with departmental heads of major agencies and leaders of the voluntary sector, are able to set in place coordinated policies for supporting parents. It is, as I have argued in Chapter 2, essential that integrated plans to support parents, resourced in part by integrated funding, should be in place as soon as is possible.

At the secondary level

Here we need to identify parents belonging to vulnerable groups and offer support of a kind and frequency that is acceptable to them. We have discussed above who some of those vulnerable groups are; here my purpose is to identify how they may be engaged. Again, to quote Webster-Stratton:

> High risk children, those with a parent who is mentally ill, or abusive, or at risk because of their own developmental difficulties such as attention deficit disorder or reading delays, need additional support in strengthening their social competence through small group training that includes social skills and problem-solving.

Some services are already in place in a number of localities. Table 12.3 illustrates some existing provision of early-support intervention.

Adequately trained practitioners for these groups are few. Resources and services are piecemeal and patchy. Since the difficulties of the children concerned are so complex, high levels of skill are called for in the practitioners concerned. Nevertheless, research increasingly

---

Table 12.3: Existing initiatives in children's emotional and behavioural difficulties

At the time of birth and in the immediate months thereafter:

1   Intensive emotional support for mothers experiencing postnatal depression in the first year of life. Such services are already in place in many parts of Britain and are being evaluated.
2   Support in the early months of the infant's life, in an effort to ensure optimum mother–infant interaction via 'talk, touch and gaze'.

In the first months and years of the child's life:

3   Intensive emotional support for mothers already expressing negative comments about their children.
4   Involvement of a range of family members to support the parents and infant.
5. 'Early Years' and 'Sure Start' initiatives.

---

identifies cognitive-behavioural theory, underpinned by skills of active and empathic listening, as of primary use in helping these children and their families. The task of training practitioners, health visitors, school nurses, educational welfare officers and school pastoral workers to add cognitive-behavioural principles to their repertoire of knowledge and skills has already begun. Among others, the Leicester, Leicestershire and Rutland Health Trust has established training for a large number of practitioners to work with parents in this preventive way, and both the training and the subsequent impact of the trained practitioners on families is being quantitatively evaluated. As this body of theory becomes better known and its principles practised, so coordinated approaches across professional groups can develop.

At the tertiary level

This concerns work with individual children and their families where serious emotional or behavioural difficulties already exist and where only specific, coordinated programmes of intervention are likely to prevent the slide into increased rejection and social isolation. As we saw earlier, there are already thousands of these troubled children, with only a handful of adequately qualified practitioners available to help them and their families. Drawing upon international research, practitioners from many disciplines must be equipped to engage parents, to make clear and collaborative assessments, to draw from a bank of community resources, to use principles of humanistic and cognitive-behavioural theory to support children, parents and teachers and evaluate their work.

The tasks confronting us are huge, but we have already made a good start. What a splendid challenge for the start of the twenty-first century!

Appendix 2.1:

SUMMARY OF RECOMMENDATIONS

From *Seen But not Heard. Co-ordinating Community Child Health and Social Services for Children in Need.* (Audit Commission, 1994).

DEVELOPING JOINT PARTNERSHIPS
JOINT ASSESSMENT OF NEEDS AND DEVELOPMENT OF A STRATEGY

Joint definition must be agreed of needs that can be met (para 109).

- Involvement of education and others such as voluntary bodies is important in developing a joint strategy published by health, social services and education authorities (para 110).
- Use should be made of OPCS and other demographic data to build up a picture of the incidence of risk indicators in a local area (para 111).
- Full commitment from the top of the organisation, and a corporate approach to developing the strategy is important (para 113).
- Parents are partners and should also be involved (para 114).

OPERATIONAL AREAS OF COMMON INTEREST
Family Support
- Good, written information for new parents should be provided and a contact point for further advice including an out-of-hours help-line (para 117).
- Contact by HV after a first visit to each family with a new baby should be based on assessed needs and agreed priorities (para 118).
- Any reduction in HV resources should take place only after a proper assessment and evaluation of current cover (para 119).
- Family centres could provide a focus for multi-agency community support for parents and children (para 120).
- Inclusion might be possible of some child development centre activities at appropriate family centres (para 121).
- HV activity in areas of high needs and their public health and group work could be organised with advantage with social services on a geographical basis (para 122).
- Distinction between roles of family centres and nurseries should be clear (para 123).
- A mixed system of open access with a quota of referred families is a preferred system for family centres where possible. Open drop-in facilities needed if centres are for referred families only (para 123).
- Voluntary organisations offering programmes of support to parents by parents can be cost-effective (para 125).
- DHAs should be prepared to allow funding for the design and evaluation of support programmes (para 126).
- After joint agreement on needs and priorities joint agreement on skill-mixes are required (para 127).
- A broader approach in social services should divert some families into universal provision but such approaches must be evaluated (para 128).
- A broader approach in social services will require a redirection of resources (para 129).
- A broader approach in social services will require an effective duty system, good training and clear procedures (para 130).

Child Protection
- Greater efforts are needed to develop good liaison with and cooperation of schools (para 132).
- Improvements needed in management information e.g. numbers of referrals, progress through investigation, services provided and outcome (para 133).

Support for Children with a Disability
- The central role of the parent must be supported with better information (para 135).
- Medical support needs to be co-ordinated (para 136).
- A focal point is needed for joint assessment. Child development centres provide this for pre-school children (para 137). Options should be explored for older children (para 138).
- A single person is required to co-ordinate care for an individual child and family (para 139).
- Agencies must act together jointly to produce strategies and operational agreements. Joint equipment budgets and shared respite care would be a good beginning (para 140).

AN AGENDA FOR HEALTH COMMISSIONERS
SURVEILLANCE AND IMMUNISATION
- Department of Health guidance on child health surveillance should be adopted by all health authorities unless there is contrary evidence. Authorities must ensure practioners are aware of the policy (para 145).
- Commissioning authorities must move from 'block' contracts to those which specify the health surveillance checks and other activity required. Resources for these should be calculated and contracts linked to coverage and outcomes (para 146).

CHILD HEALTH CLINICS
- Type of clinic provided should be based on the assessed needs of the locality; some may be appointment-only for child health surveillance checks, others open-access for anyone (para 147).
- For some needs in some areas drop-in facilities as part of a multi-agency family centre might be appropriate (para 148).
- Health commissioners should ensure that community run clinics are rationalised according to attendance and the growth of GP run clinics (para 149).
- FHSAs must ensure standards of GP clinics are maintained (para 150).

GP FUNDHOLDERS – to be revised as Primary Care Groups come on stream
- GP fundholders should be engaged with other commissioners in the development of child health strategies (para 151).

SCHOOL HEALTH
- Local reviews should be carried out of the current school health service unless this has been done. Parents, children and schools should be consulted (para 153).
- For many schools a universal school entry medical should be dropped in favour of a selective approach (para 154).
- The functions of the school health service should be clarified, with school nurses becoming the lead professional (para 155).
- Health commissioners must ensure school nurses are appropriately and effectively trained if they carry out health education or health promotion activities (para 156).

MONITORING AND EVALUATION
- Improved information systems and use of currently available information are required. The process should be dialogue between commissioners and providers (paras 157–159).

AN AGENDA FOR PROVIDERS OF COMMUNITY CHILD HEALTH
WHAT ARE THE HEALTH NEEDS OF THE POPULATION?
- Providers should not wait if commissioners are not yet working with them to assess the local needs. Demographic information can be used together with practitioner information (para 161).
- Practitioners should continue to develop caseload profiles (para 162).

WHAT PRIORITIES AND CRITERIA ARE BEING ADOPTED?
- Priorities and criteria for services must be developed with professional groups (para 163).

WHAT SKILLS ARE REQUIRED?
- Reviews and adjustments to skill mixes may be necessary. These should be done on the basis of needs assessments, not a cost-cutting exercise (paras 164–166).
- Staff should be adequately trained and updated, especially for child health surveillance tests such as sight and hearing (para 167).

WHAT INFORMATION IS REQUIRED?
- Management information is required, e.g. details of clinic usage, coverage and referral rates of child health surveillance, referrals above specific ages for some conditions. Results should be fed back to practitioners (para 168).

HOW SHOULD THE SERVICE BE ORGANISED?
- A consultant community paediatrician can bring benefits of increased status and drive for quality and evaluation (para 169).
- Organisation of health visiting should take needs of local population into account in order to be cost effective (paras 170–172).

Appendix 2.2:

AREAS FOR CONSIDERATION WHEN PLANNING MULTIDISCIPLINARY CARE FOR A CHILD (AFTER HORWATH AND CALDER, 1998)

The initial consultation discussion
Guidance for members on:
- members' role in identifying core group membership
- their contribution to designing the family support plan
- specifying when the core group should meet
- setting out boundaries of responsibility
- clarifying the type of assessment required

The core group
Guidance for members on:
- the purpose and function of the core group
- possible attendees
- circumstances for convening more than one core group
- methods to promote family and child participation
- systems for managing problems of inter-agency cooperation
- reporting back to participants
- management of process issues
  - frequency of meetings
  - chairing
  - minute taking

The plan
Guidance on:
- overall aim of plan
- when, where and by whom the plan is constructed in outline and detail
- procedures for alterations to the plan
- timescales for implementation
- procedure for managing professionals not completing tasks as identified in the plan/managing conflict
- proforma child support plan
- engaging the child and family
- evaluating and monitoring implementation of plan

The key worker
Guidance on their role in terms of:
- co-ordination of the core group
- working with the family
- managing inter-agency difficulties

The review
Guidance for members on:
- the remit of the review
- authority to delegate decision-making to the core group
- reporting to the review
- process for offering on-going support

Appendix 3.1:
GUIDELINES FOR GOOD PRACTICE OF BEHAVIOURAL AND COGNITIVE PSYCHOTHERAPY

INTRODUCTORY STATEMENT

1. All members of the BABCP are required to endeavour to adhere to these guidelines.
2. Most BABCP members will already be members of the helping professions and hold appropriate qualifications. They should, therefore, be bound by a code of practice by virtue of their belonging to a profession and so a detailed statement of general ethical/legal principles is not included in these guidelines. It is expected that all members of BABCP approach their work with the aim of resolving problems and promoting the well-being of service users and will endeavour to use their ability and skills to their best advantage without prejudice and with due recognition of the value and dignity of every human being.
3. The term "worker" and "service user" are used throughout to designate the person responsible for helping and the person being helped respectively and should be taken to subsume similar relationships, e.g. doctor/patient, therapist/client, teacher/student etc. as appropriate. Similarly "assessments/ interventions" is used to subsume training, treatment, programme etc.

1. ASSESSMENT AND BEHAVIOUR/COGNITIVE CHANGE PROCEDURES

(i) The worker will ensure that any intervention procedures adopted will be based upon evaluation and assessment of the service user and the environment. The worker will also strive to ensure than any assessments/interventions will be in the best interests of the service user, minimising any possible harm and maximising benefits over both the short and long term whilst at the same time balancing these against any possible harmful effects to others.

(ii) Assessments/interventions will always be justified by the available public evidence taking into account all possible alternatives, the degree of demonstrated efficacy, discomfort, intervention time and cost of alternatives.

(iii) Assessments/ interventions will be planned and implemented in such a way that effectiveness can be evaluated.

(iv) The aims and goals of assessments/interventions will be discussed and agreed with service users at the outset and may be renegotiated, terminated or a referral made to another worker at the request of either party if the goals are not being met after a reasonable period of time or if they later appear to be inappropriate.

(v) On both ethical and empirical grounds assessments/interventions used will be of demonstrable benefit to the service users both short and long term and will not involve any avoidable loss, deprivation, pain or other source of suffering. It is recognised, however, that circumstances might exist where long term benefits could only be achieved by interventions which involve relatively minor and transient deprivation. Workers will ensure that no such assessments/interventions are used where effective alternatives exist or where long term benefit does not clearly out-weigh the short term loss. The design of such assessments/interventions by virtue of the aims would minimise any suffering involved and ensure that dangerous or long term deprivation will not occur. Whenever there is room for doubt about jus-tifying the use of such interventions, workers will always seek advice from an appropriately qualified and experienced colleague who is in a position to give an independent and objective opinion.

2. CONSENT

(i) It is understood that consent to particular assessments/interventions is an ongoing process which places emphasis upon the service users' role in the continual evalua-tion of the assessments/interventions.

(ii) Where a worker sees a service user only for evaluative or diagnostic procedures, this will be explained clearly to them.

(iii) Upon team agreement regarding the best procedure to implement, the aims, rationale and alternatives of assessments/interventions will be explained to the service user at the start as explicitly and as fully as is consistent with therapeutic effectiveness and the person's best interests. If the assessments/interventions are experimental rather than established and proven, this will be communicated to the service user. If this has been fulfilled, the service user gives consent to the intervention and this is recorded.

(iv) For people unable to give informed voluntary consent, written consent will be obtained from a relative after informing them as described above. If no relative is available, consent will be obtained from an advocate or other responsible professional.

(v) Retroactive consent will only be considered sufficient in emergency situations such that any delay in intervention would lead to permanent and irreversible harm to the person's well being.

(vi) If a service user, when capable of informed consent, or other appropriate person when 2(iv) applies, chooses to withhold consent, the intervention does not proceed. This applies equally to involuntary service users or those referred from the courts.

(vii)Where a service user is within an institution, whether voluntary or otherwise, interventions may take the form of institutional management or specific programmes in which all members take part. In these circumstances informed consent may be difficult to achieve but the conditions of 1(iv) are taken as minimum requirement. People are informed of the extent to which they are free to withdraw from any aspect of assessments/interventions. In addition, those responsible for the procedures have the responsibility for collecting objective evidence for their continuing efficacy.

3. QUALIFICATIONS AND TRAINING

(i) No workers represent themselves as having qualifications or skills they do not possess.

(ii) Workers recognise the boundaries to their competence both from formal training and from work experience and if faced with a situation outside their competence, either refer the person to a colleague who has the required skills or, if taking on the situation themselves, ensure that they received supervision and training from a competent other.

(iii) Workers expect to continue to develop expertise after formal training has finished and take reasonable steps to keep up-to-date with current research and practice, e.g. reading current research, by attending appropriate courses and receiving regular practice supervision from an appropriately qualified and experienced person.

4. INTERPROFESSIONAL RELATIONSHIPS

(i) Workers in a multi-disciplinary setting keep their colleagues informed of their decisions, consult with them when appropriate and establish clearly the limits of their involvement with a particular service user.

(ii) Where workers have in practice overall responsibility for service users, they recognise aspects where their own professional competence ends and consult other professionals as appropriate.

5. CONFIDENTIALITY

(i) Information acquired by a worker is confidential within their understanding of the best interest of the service user and the law of the land. Written and oral reports of relevant material are made available to other persons directly involved.

(ii) The service user's consent is required where information is passed beyond the normal limits of persons concerned or made available for the purpose of research.

(iii) The service user's consent is required if they are presented to an individual or group for teaching purposes and it is made clear that refusal would have no implication for intervention.

(iv) If an intervention is being published, personal details are restricted to the minimum required for describing the intervention.

(v) If a video tape, film or other recording is made, consent in writing is required specifying whether the recording may be shown to: (a) other professionals; (b) students; (c) the lay public.

6. **RESEARCH**

(i) If a service user is asked to be tested or interviewed as part of a research project, it is made explicit when the procedures used are not of direct therapeutic benefit to that individual and formal consent is obtained.

(ii) When service users are in a research project where interventions are being compared or a control condition included, if one intervention or condition emerges as the most effective it is subsequently made available to those in the less effective control groups.

7. **EXPLOITATION OF SERVICE USERS**

(i) Workers have a clear responsibility not to exploit service users in financial, sexual or other ways. Though some interventions entail workers and service users socialising together, a clear distinction between personal and professional relationships is still made.

8. **PRIORITIES**

(i) Workers will often have to decide areas in which to specialise and this choice is made with due regard to the priorities involved taking into account the known efficacies of interventions available and the overall benefit conferred on service users in general.

9. **ADVERTISING**

(i) Membership of BABCP does not confer any professional status or qualification. Workers will not refer to their membership of BABCP in advertising or elsewhere to imply any such professional status or qualification.

(ii) Workers accredited by BABCP as Behavioural and/or Cognitive Psychotherapists to meet the criteria for registration with the Behavioural and Cognitive Psycotherapy Section of the United Kingdom Council for Psychotherapy, are free to advertise or otherwise announce that fact.

Note: BABCP = British Association for Behavioural and Cognitive Therapy

Appendix 5.1:
PARENT ASSESSMENT MANUAL: INITIAL SCREENING TOOL

NAME *of Parent*　　　　　**DATE**　　　　**ASSESSOR** [　　　　　]

　　　　　　　　　　　　　　　　　　　　Assessed　　　**Score**

[　　　　　]　[　　　]　　　M ☐　　F ☐　　**Both** ☐　　[　　]

Mother:————— Date of birth:_____

Father:_____ Date of birth:_____

Child:_____ Date of birth:_____ Child:_____Date of birth:_____

Child:_____ Date of birth:_____ Child:_____Date of birth:_____

Address:_____

_____ Tel: _____

GP:_____ Social Worker: _____

Health Visitor:_____ Other:_____

Please include details of any relevant information
(e.g. medical information, criminal convictions) relating to the family:

_____

_____

_____

Child Profile

1. Child FEEDING
SCORE [　　]

0	**Criterion Reached**	No concerns about child's feeding.
1	**Low Priority**	Occasional concerns about the quality of food/feeding
2	**Medium Priority**	Day-to-day feeding is of poor quality and/or erratic.
3	**High Priority**	Requires immediate attention. Child's weight or health is affected. Referred to health professionals e.g. dietician, paediatrician. CPR.

2. Child HEALTHCARE *General*
SCORE [　　]

0	**Criterion Reached**	No concerns about child's healthcare.
1	**Low Priority**	Occasional concerns about healthcare, symptom recognition and managing childhood illness.
2	**Medium Priority**	Concerns because parent has not reacted promptly/appropriately to a medical situation.
3	**High Priority**	GP/HV/Paediatrician/Hospital are seriously concerned about

parent's ability to manage child's health/medical condition. Parent mismanages medicines. CPR.

3. Child HEALTHCARE *Hygiene*

SCORE ☐

0 **Criterion Reached**	No concerns about child's hygiene.
1 **Low Priority**	Hygiene is an anticipated/occasional problem.
2 **Medium Priority**	Day-to-day hygiene is erratic and/or of poor quality.
3 **High Priority**	GP/HV/Paediatrician are concerned. Child is being treated for condition caused by poor hygiene. CPR.

4. Child HEALTHCARE *Warmth*

SCORE ☐

0 **Criterion Reached**	No concerns about child's body temperature.
1 **Low Priority**	Occasionally parent needs to be told that child is too hot or too cold.
2 **Medium Priority**	Concerns expressed about one/few incidents when child was exposed to extreme temperature differences.
3 **High Priority**	GP/HV/Paediatrician/Hospital are concerned about parent's ability to maintain child's normal body temperature. CPR.

5. Child PARENTAL RESPONSIVENESS

SCORE ☐

0 **Criterion Reached**	No concerns about child's emotional development.
1 **Low Priority**	Signs of poor emotional development emerging.
2 **Medium Priority**	Concerns regarding poor attachment/bonding. Referred for therapy/counselling.
3 **High Priority**	Anticipated/actual damage of child's emotional development resulting from persistent and/or severe emotional ill-treatment or rejection. Multiple family placements. CPR.

6/8. Child DEVELOPMENT

SCORE ☐

0 **Criterion Reached**	No concerns about child's general development (physical/sexual/ emotional).
1 **Low Priority**	Signs of developmental delay emerging.
2 **Medium Priority**	Child referred to paediatrician, psychiatrist, physiotherapist, etc. because of developmental delays/inappropriate development.
3 **High Priority**	Child has a Statement of Special Educational Needs. Attends Assessment/Special Unit or Special School. CPR.

9. Child GUIDANCE & CONTROL

SCORE ☐

0 **Criterion Reached**	No concerns about parental guidance and control.
1 **Low Priority**	Poor house-rules in place. Signs of parent's inability to set limits for child and/or to handle misbehaviour.
2 **Medium Priority**	Family needs professional input/support to help them establish/regain guidance and control of child. Risk of harm increasing to child (including possible physical/emotional/sexual abuse).
3 **High Priority**	Parents have partial control of child. Risk of actual or likely

harm to child or others. Alternative care needed/already provided. CPR.

---

10. Child RESPONSIBILITY & INDEPENDENCE

SCORE [   ]

0 **Criterion Reached**   No concerns about responsibilities and independence given to child.
1 **Low Priority**   Some concerns too little/too much responsibility/independence given child.
2 **Medium Priority**   Family referred for guidance regarding appropriate parent/child responsibility and independence.
3 **High Priority**   Child has been harmed by restricted/excessive levels of responsibility/independence. Alternative care needed/already provided. CPR.

11/15. Parent INDEPENDENT LIVING SKILLS

SCORE [   ]

Reading, writing, numeracy, maintaining routines, time-telling, telephone, travel and budgeting.

0 **Criterion Reached**   No concerns about living skills.
1 **Low Priority**   Minor difficulties.
2 **Medium Priority**   Concerns expressed. Poor living skills. Teaching/support programme required.
3 **High Priority**   Intensive teaching/support required. Parent is erratic and disorganised. Basic routines (mealtimes, washing, cleaning, bedtimes etc.) not well established. Poor access/use or maintenance of services outside of the home.

16/18. Parent HOMECARE *Domesticity*

SCORE [   ]

Shopping, cooking and washing skills.

0 **Criterion Reached**   No concerns about cooking, washing and/or shopping routines.
1 **Low Priority**   Minor concerns.
2 **Medium Priority**   Parent's domestic skills are poor. A teaching/support programme is required.
3 **High Priority**   Intensive teaching/assistance needed. Professional input is arranged/currently provided to improve/maintain these skills.

19/22. Parent HOMECARE *Hygiene*

SCORE [   ]

Hygiene in kitchen, living room, bedroom and bathroom.

0 **Criterion Reached**   No concerns about household cleanliness.
1 **Low Priority**   Minor concerns.
2 **Medium Priority**   Increasing concerns regarding household hygiene in general. Parent requires a teaching/support programme.
3 **High Priority**   Child at serious risk from infections and diseases. Parent requires intensive teaching programme.

23/29. Parent HOMECARE *Safety*　　　　　　　SCORE ☐

General home safety in kitchen, living areas, bedroom, outside of home. **Exposure to physical/sexual abuse.**

0 **Criterion Reached**　No concerns about child's safety in or outside of home.
1 **Low Priority**　Minor concerns. Parent could benefit from some advice/guidance/support in some areas of safety.
2 **Medium Priority**　Increasing concerns expressed regarding child's safety. Parent needs a teaching/support programme. Past incidents of accidental/non-accidental injuries/abuse.
3 **High Priority**　Child is unsafe whilst in parent's care. Parent requires intensive teaching programme. An alternative family placement is needed. Care proceedings imminent or will be instigated.

30/32. Parent HEALTHCARE　　　　　　　SCORE ☐

Mental or physical health and self-care.

0 **No Concerns**
1 **Low Priority**　Occasionally, parent reports feeling unwell or looks unwell.
2 **Medium Priority**　Parent has physical or mental health problems and the home situation is deteriorating.
3 **High Priority**　Parent's physical/mental health has/may require medical/psychiatric/statutory intervention. Standard of parenting has deteriorated rendering the child at risk from significant harm.

33/34. Parent SUPPORT AND RESOURCES　　　　SCORE ☐

Relationships and family/community support & resources.

0 **No Concerns**
1 **Low Priority**　On occasions parent requires professional/voluntary support to help them manage.
2 **Medium Priority**　Parent appears isolated with few friends/family/services and their child is vulnerable.
3 **High Priority**　Parenting has deteriorated and there is a history of crises intervention. Antagonistic/poor social/family support. Parents withdrawn or threatening to withdraw from services. Vulnerable children (CPR: history of abuse/neglect; special needs).

0 ADDITIONAL FACTORS

SCORE ☐

Other concerns which you might consider relevant.

SPECIFY:

0 **none**
_____
_____
_____

1 **Occasional**
factors affecting
parenting
_____
_____
_____

2 **Intermittent**
factors causing
concern
_____
_____
_____

3 **Recurring factors**
which negatively
affect the parenting
_____
_____
_____

Completed by: _____

Designation: _____   Date: _____

Notes:

1. CPR = Child Protection Register
2. It is important to treat each item separately. The 'scores' cannot be added up to give an overall score.

   McGaw, S., Beckley, K., Connolly, N. and Ball, N. (1999) *Parent Asssessment Manual*. Trecare NHS Trust. Reprinted with permission. For further information write to: Dr Sue McGgaw, Special Parenting Service, 5 Walsingham Place, Truro, TR1 ZRP.

Appendix 5.2:

PARENT ASSESSMENT MANUAL: I NEED HELP ... FORM

NAME *of Parent*   **DATE**   **ASSESSOR**

Assessed   **Score**

M ☐   F ☐   **Both** ☐

SCORING 0 Don't need help **1** Need some help **2** Need lots of help **3** Not coping

Child Profile

1. Child FEEDING

SCORE

To give my child healthy meals and make sure that he/she eats them.

2. Child HEALTHCARE *General*

SCORE

To learn about children's illnesses, looking after a sick child and giving medicines.

3. Child HEALTHCARE *Hygiene*

SCORE

To learn how to keep my child clean and healthy.

4. Child HEALTHCARE *Warmth*

SCORE

To make sure my child doesn't get sick because he/she gets too hot or too cold.

SCORING 0 Don't need help **1** Need some help **2** Need lots of help **3** Not coping

5. Child PARENTAL RESPONSIVENESS

SCORE [   ]

To make sure that my child feels loved and not hurt by the things that I say or do.

_____
_____
_____
_____

6/8. Child DEVELOPMENT

SCORE [   ]

To help me teach my child new skills (reading, writing, doing sums, recognising money, etc).

_____
_____
_____
_____

9. Child GUIDANCE & CONTROL

SCORE [   ]

To teach my child about right and wrong behaviour and to help me manage when he/she is being difficult.

_____
_____
_____
_____

10. Child RESPONSIBILITY & INDEPENDENCE

SCORE [   ]

To learn when to let my child do things by themselves e.g. going to the shops alone.

_____
_____
_____
_____

11/15. Parent INDEPENDENT LIVING SKILLS

SCORE [   ]

To manage routines e.g. tell the time, fill out forms, manage money.

_____
_____
_____
_____

SCORING **0** Don't need help **1** Need some help **2** Need lots of help **3** Not coping

16/18. Parent HOMECARE *Domesticity*   **SCORE** [ ]

To learn skills so that I can manage the cooking, washing or ironing.

_____

_____

_____

_____

19/22. Parent HOMECARE *Hygiene*   **SCORE** [ ]

To help me manage the cleaning in the kitchen, living room, bedrooms, bathroom etc.

_____

_____

_____

23/29. Parent HOMECARE *Safety*   **SCORE** [ ]

To learn about safety inside and outside of the home.

_____

_____

_____

_____

30/32. Parent HEALTHCARE   **SCORE** [ ]

Because I feel unwell.

_____

_____

_____

30/32. Parent SUPPORT AND RESOURCES   **SCORE** [ ]

To help me to start, manage or finish relationships with family, friends, neighbours or professionals.

_____

_____

_____

_____

0. ANYTHING ELSE   **SCORE** [ ]

_____

_____

_____

_____

Note:
1. It is important to treat each item separately. The 'scores' cannot be added up to give an overall score.

McGaw, S., Beckley, K., Coonolly, N. and Bell, N. (1999) *Parent Asssessment Manual*. Trecare NHS Trust. Reprinted with permission. For further information write to: Dr Sue McGgaw, Special Parenting Service, 5 Walsingham Place, Truro, TR1 ZRP.

Appendix 5.3:
STRENGTHS AND DIFFICULTIES QUESTIONNAIRE (GOODMAN 1997)

For each item, please mark the box for Not True, Somewhat True or Certainly True. It would help us if you answered all items as best you can even if you are not absolutely certain or the item seems daft! Please give your answers on the basis of the child's behaviour over the last six months or this school year.

Child's Name ....   Male/Female

Date of Birth ....

	Not True	Somewhat True	Certainly True
Considerate of other people's feelings	❏	❏	❏
Restless, overactive, cannot stay still for long	❏	❏	❏
Often complains of headaches, stomach-aches or sickness	❏	❏	❏
Shares readily with other children (treats, toys, etc).	❏	❏	❏
Often has temper tantrums or hot tempers	❏	❏	❏
Rather solitary, tends to play alone	❏	❏	❏
Generally obedient, usually does what adults request	❏	❏	❏
Many worries, often seems worried	❏	❏	❏
Helpful if someone is hurt, upset or feeling ill	❏	❏	❏
Constantly fidgeting or squirming	❏	❏	❏
Has at least one good friend	❏	❏	❏
Often fights with other children or bullies them	❏	❏	❏
Often unhappy, down-hearted or tearful	❏	❏	❏
Generally liked by other children	❏	❏	❏
Easily distracted, concentration wanders	❏	❏	❏
Nervous or clingy in new situations, easily loses confidence	❏	❏	❏
Kind to younger children	❏	❏	❏
Often lies or cheats	❏	❏	❏
Picked on or bullied by other children	❏	❏	❏
Often volunteers to help others (parents, teachers, other children)	❏	❏	❏
Thinks things out before acting	❏	❏	❏
Steals from home, school or elsewhere	❏	❏	❏
Gets on better with adults than with other children	❏	❏	❏
Many fears, easily scared	❏	❏	❏
Sees tasks through to the end, good attention span	❏	❏	❏

Do you have any other comments or concerns?
Readers should write for details of how to score this questionnaire and for forms of the SDQ for use with the children or young people themselves to Dr Robert Goodman, Institute of Psychiatry, De Crespigny Park, Denmark Hill, London SE5 8AP.

Appendix 5.4:
AN EXAMPLE OF A GENOGRAM (FINCH AND JACQUES, 1985)

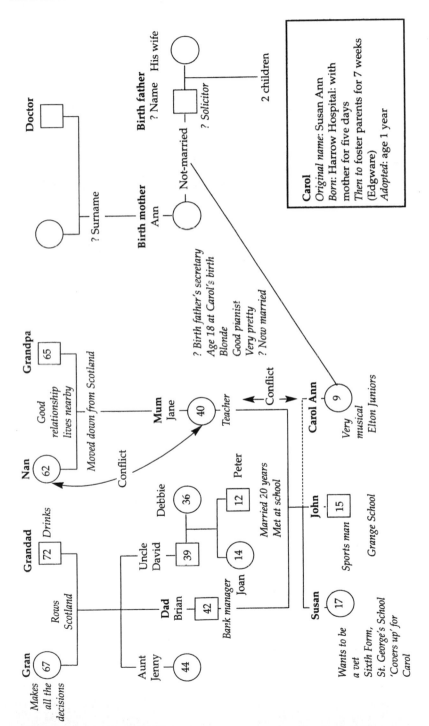

Appendix 5.5:

EDINBURGH POSTNATAL DEPRESSION SCALE*

This form to be completed by the **client**

The Edinburgh Postnatal Depression Scale (EPDS) was developed by J.D. Cox, J.M. Holden, J.M. and R. Sagovsky, to assist primary care health professionals to detect mothers suffering from postnatal depression; a distressing disorder more prolonged than the 'blues' (which occur in the first week after delivery) but less severe than puerperal psychosis.

Previous studies have shown that postnatal depression affects at least ten per cent of women and that many depressed mothers remain untreated. These mothers may cope with their baby and with household tasks, but their enjoyment of life is seriously affected and it is possible that there are long-term effects on the family.

The EPDS was developed at health centres in Livingston and Edinburgh. It consists of ten short statements. The mother underlines which of the four possible responses is closest to how she has been feeling during the past week. Most mothers complete the scale without difficulty in less than five minutes.

The validation study on 84 women showed no false negatives for mothers with major depressive illness, and mothers who score 12 or more are likely to be suffering from a depressive illness of varying severity. Nevertheless the EPDS score should not override clinical judgement. A careful clinical assessment should be carried out to confirm the diagnosis. The scale indicates how the mother has felt *during the previous week*, and in doubtful cases it may be usefully repeated after two weeks. The scale will not detect mothers with anxiety neuroses, phobias or personality disorders. For full details of the scale's development, validity and threshold scores, see Cox *et al.* (1987).*

The Edinburgh Postnatal Depression Scale has been translated satisfactorily into Swedish, French, Greek, and also modified slightly for use in North America. Difficulties were encountered when translating some items into Asian languages, and the need to consider cultural equivalence is mandatory in any such undertaking. The scale should be re-validated for use in non-Western cultures.

Reproduced with permission of Cox, J.L., Holden, J.M. and Sagovsky, R. (1987). 'Detection of postnatal depression: development of the ten item Edinburgh Postnatal Depression Scale', *British Journal of Psychiatry* 150, 782-86.

Instructions for using the EPDS

1. The mother is asked to underline the response which comes closest to how she has been feeling in the previous seven days.
2. All ten items must be completed.
3. Care should be taken to avoid the possibility of the mother discussing her answers with others.
4. The mother should complete the scale herself, unless she has limited English or has difficulty with reading.
5. The EPDS may be used routinely at 6-8 weeks to screen all postnatal women. The child health clinic, postnatal check-up or a home visit may provide suitable opportunities for its completion.

Scoring
Each of the ten items is scored from 0 to 3 according to severity (see below) and the total score is calculated by adding together the scores for each of the ten items.

Item No.		Score	Item No.		Score	Item No.		Score
1.	Laugh	0-3	5.	Panic	3-0	8.	Sadness	3-0
2.	Enjoyment	0-3	6.	Coping	3-0	9.	Crying	3-0
3.	Self-blame	3-0	7.	Sleep	3-0	10.	Self-harm	3-0
4.	Anxiety	0-3						

Interpretation

The validation study conducted by Cox *et al.* (1987) suggests that women who scored above a threshold of 12 or 13 were most likely to be suffering from a depressive illness of varying severity and should therefore be further assessed to confirm whether or not clinical depression is present. The EPDS is not a substitute for this clinical assessment, and a score just below the cut-off should not be taken to indicate the absence of depression.

Client's name: _____ **Age:** _____

Address: _____

_____

Worker's name: _____ **Date:** _____

As you have recently had a baby, we would like to know how you are feeling. Please *UNDERLINE* the answer which comes closes to how you have felt **in the past 7 days**, not just how you feel today.

Here is an example, already completed.

I have felt happy:
- Yes, all the time
- Yes, most of the time
- No, not very often
- No, not at all

This would mean: 'I have felt happy most of the time' during the past week.

Please complete the other questions in the same way.

In the past 7 days
1.   I have been able to laugh and see the funny side of things:
- as much as I always could;
- not quite so much now;
- definitely not so much now;
- not at all.

2.   I have looked forward with enjoyment to things:
- as much as I ever did;
- rather less than I used to;
- definitely less than I used to;
- hardly at all.

3.   I have blamed myself unnecessarily when things went wrong:
- yes, most of the time;
- yes, some of the time;
- not very often
- no, never.

4.   I have been anxious or worried for no good reason:
- no, not at all;
- hardly ever;
- yes, sometimes;

• yes, very often.

5.   I have felt scared or panicky for no very good reason:
       • yes, quite a lot;
       • yes, sometimes;
       • no, not much;
       • no, not at all.

6.   Things have been getting on top of me:
       • yes, most of the time I haven't been able to cope at all;
       • yes, sometimes I haven't been coping as well as usual;
       • no, most of the time I have coped quite well;
       • no, I have been coping as well as ever.

7.   I have been so unhappy that I have had difficulty sleeping:
       • yes, most of the time;
       • yes, sometimes;
       • not very often;
       • no, not at all.

8.   I have felt sad or miserable:
       • yes, most of the time;
       • yes, quite often;
       • not very often;
       • no, not at all.

9.   I have been so unhappy that I have been crying:
       • yes, most of the time;
       • yes, quite often;
       • only occasionally;
       • no, never.

10.   The thought of harming myself has occurred to me:
       • yes, quite often;
       • sometimes;
       • hardly ever;
       • never.

* Cox *et al.*, 1987

Copyright remains with the authors, but permission is hereby given to professional staff to make as many copies as they require for clinical or research use.

Appendix 5.6:
A RANGE OF SCREENING TEST USED BY PSYCHOLOGISTS (HERBERT, 1993)

Tests of mental ability/developmental status
Bayley Scales of Infant Development (2 months–2 ½ years)
British Ability Scales (2 ½–17 years)
Wechsler Preschool and Primary Scale of Intelligence (WPPSI) (4–6 ½years)
Merrill-Palmer Preschool Performance Tests (1 ½–5¼ years)
McCarthy Scales of Infant Development (2 ½–8 ½ years)
Wechsler Intelligence Scale for Children (WISC) (6½–16 years)
Stanford-Binet Intelligence Scale (2 years–adult)
Griffiths Scales (0–8 years)
Gesell Developmental Schedule (4 weeks–6 years)
Vineland Social Maturity Scale (3 months–30 years)
Stycar Developmental Sequences (1 month–5 years)
The Miller Assessment for Preschoolers (MAP) (2 years 9 months–5 years 8 months)

Specialized tests
Goldberg General Health Questionnaire (mothers at risk for mental health problems is
    one screening application)
Hiskey-Nebraska Test of Learning Aptitude (hearing defects) (3–17 years)
Snijders-Oomen Non-verbal Intelligence Scale (2 ½–7 years) (all forms of verbal com-
    munication handicap)
Leiter International Performance Scale (communication defects and multiple handicap)
    (2–16 years)
Raven's Progressive Matrices (non-verbal abilities)
Williams Intelligence Test (vision defects) (5–15 years)
Reynell-Zinkin Scales (vision defects) (0–5 years)
Columbia Mental Maturity Scale (verbal and physical handicaps) (3–10 years)
Frostig Developmental Test of Visual Perception (learning disabilities) (4–8 years)
Bender Gestalt Test (visual motor perception) (4 years and over)
Stott-Moyes-Henderson Test of Motor Impairment (motor disability, clumsiness) (5–14
    years)
Bene-Anthony Family Relations Test
Scars *et al.* Child-rearing Practice Scales

Language and vocabulary tests
Reynell Developmental Language Scale (1 ½–6 years)
British Picture Vocabulary Scale (2 ½–18 years)
Peabody Picture Vocabulary Test (2 ½–18 years)
Stycar Language Test (up to 7 years)

Behaviour problems checklists
Behaviour Screening Questionnaire (3 year olds) (Richman and Graham)
Children's Behaviour Checklist (2–4, 4–7 years) (Achenbach and Edelbrock)
Hewett Behaviour Checklist (9 months–2 years)
Rutter Scales (School-age children)
Strengths and Difficulties Questionnaire (Goodman)

Attainment tests
Neale Analysis of Reading Ability (6–12 years)
Wide Range Achievement Test (5 years–adult)
Schonell Reading Test

Appendix 5.7:

AN EXAMPLE OF A MULTI-AGENCY ASSESMENT QUESTIONNAIRE FOR CHILDREN (DEVELOPED FROM A FRAMEWORK PREPARED BY LEICESTER-SHIRE SOCIAL SERVICES DEPARTMENT)

CHILDREN WITH EMOTIONAL AND BEHAVIOURAL DIFFICULTIES

This format is intended to be used as a guideline for the production of multi-agency assessments concerning children with emotional and behavioural difficulties.

A   PURPOSE

The purpose of the format is:

2.1 To offer guidance to agencies/ professionals who may contribute to the assessment on the information which may be relevant.

2.2 To promote a consistent approach to assessment.

B   USE

All agencies involved are asked to ensure that their contributions:

i)   are ethnically sensitive and recognise and respect the importance of cultural and racial differences
ii)   take positive account of sexual differences and avoid stereotyping
iii) are sensitive to the needs of adults and children with physical and/or learning disability.

The active involvement of members of the family in the planning for and preparation of the assessment will be essential. Unless there are exceptional reasons not to do so, all information contributed will be shared with the family. The attention of contributors is drawn to the Access to Personal Files Act 1987 which gives individuals a right of access, with certain exceptions, to information held about them by the Social Services Department.

The assessment will normally be led and coordinated by a key worker, assisted by other colleagues. Other agencies/individuals will usually contribute information in writing. It is desirable that a key worker should write the final assessment report.

These guidelines should be used with discretion. It will be particularly important to avoid:

•   identifying data about the family, including family trees or genograms
•   identifying data of other kinds, either about the family or the professionals involved.

ASSESSMENT BY THE LEAD AGENCY

A   GENERAL AND MEDICAL DETAILS

1. Name of child ....

2. Date of birth .... 3. Male/Female

4. Religion: ....5. Ethnic origin ....

6. Address: ....7. First language: ....

.... 8. Other languages spoken ....

.... 9. Legal status: ....

10. Family details

Full names	Gender	DoB	Ethnicity	Relationship	Address

11. Other family members who participated in the assessment include

Full names	Gender	DoB	Ethnicity	Relationship	Address

12. Other professional workers responsible for providing information and opinion

Name	Title	Agency

13. Living circumstances of household (brief information about accommodation, etc

....

....

....

14. Emotional or behavioural difficulties being experienced with the child

1. .... 3. ....

2. .... 4. ....

15. Were there any medical difficulties at birth or during the first year of life?

....

16. Did you (mother) experience postnatal depression? ....

....

17. If so, do you recall it as being mild, moderately severe, severe or very severe?
....

18. How long do you recall it lasting? ....

19. If you received treatment for this depression, what form did this take? ....

....

20. Did the treatment help? ....

....

21. Has your child had any major illnesses/hospital admissions? ....

....

22. Is your child allergic to colourings/other substances? ....

23. Is your child having medicine/tablets for the problems? ....

If so, what?...

24. What seems to be their effect? ....

25. Have you had this difficulty with another child? ....

26. What has worried you most about your child's development? ....

....

....

....

....

....

B   FAMILY CIRCUMSTANCES

27. What age was your child when the difficulties began? ....

28. Did anything happen around that time that might be linked with the onset of the difficulties?

a) ....

b) Anything else? ....

29. Have there been any events in the family which made things worse? e.g. bereavement, loss of employment, parental separation.

a) ....

b) ....

30. What other stresses are you or other household members under?

a) ....

b) ....

c) ....

C   CHILD'S EMOTIONAL DIFFICULTIES

31. What are the emotional difficulties which your child seems to be experiencing?

a) ....

b) ....

c) ....

32. How frequently does your child become distressed? ....
....

33. Are the episodes of distress becoming more or less frequent? ....
....

34. Are the difficulties worse at some times than at others? If so, when? ....
....

35. If your child becomes distressed, how do you typically respond? ....
....

36. If you try to comfort him or her, how much time do you typically spend, for example, in trying to reassure the child? ....

37. Can you think of any other relevant information? ....
....

D   CHILD'S BEHAVIOURAL DIFFICULTIES

38. When your child is misbehaving, what exactly does he/she *do?* ....

a) ....

b) ....

c) ....

d) ....

39. Why do you think these misbehaviours happen? ....
....

40. Can you think of what seems to trigger the difficult behaviours? ....
....

41. People involved: with whom does the misbehaviour happen? ....

Is there anyone with whom it never happens? ....

42. Places involved: where does the misbehaviour happen? ....

43. Times involved: when does the misbehaviour happen? ....

44. What usually happens immediately after a misbehaviour? ....

45. In what ways have you tried to deal with the misbehaviour or difficulty?

1. .... 3. ....

2. .... 4. ....

46. What are some of your child's good behaviours or things that he or she does that you like?

1. .... 2. ....

47. Which of your child's behaviours would you like to see happen more often?

1. .... 2. ....

48. Thank you for giving me this information. Are there any questions you would like to ask me?

(At this stage it is wise to stress a multi-factorial 'explanation' for most difficulties).

The assessor should then pass these assessment sheets to the person(s) who has supplied the information and ask that it be checked for accuracy. Invite the informant to sign the assessment, if he or she is willing to do so.

Signed ....(Assessor)   Date ....

Address ....

Signed: .... (Parent/Guardian)

ASSESSMENT BY ADDITIONAL AGENCY

Health Visitor/Community Practitioner

1. General developmental progress

2. Speech development (unless Speech and language therapist is reporting separately)

3. Feeding/nutrition

4. Growth: height)   centile chart   weight)

5. Child health surveillance programme

6. Play/activities at home

7. Home circumstances: hygiene/material provision/safety/heating

8. Parents'/Carers' attitudes

i)   to child

ii) to advice from health visitor

9. Child's attitudes to parents/carers

10. Parents'/carers' relationship with health visitor

11. Significant illness/injury/disability

12. General comments

i)   highlighting particular significance attached to information given

ii) other relevant information not covered by above headings

ASSESSMENT BY ADDITIONAL AGENCY

General Practitioner

A   For children, parents/carers

1.   How long registered with practice/known to GP personally?

2.   Contacts with child or parents and any significant features relating to frequency or purpose of contact?

3.   General health

4.   Significant illnesses or accidents

5.   Parents'/carers' response to advice concerning the child

6.   Child's interactions with parents/carers

B   For children

1.   General development

2.   Emotional/behavioural presentation

C   For parents

1.   Issues of concern relating to

i)   physical health

ii)   mental health

iii)   other aspects of health

2.   Family relationship (if known)

3.   Extended family relationship (if known)

D   General comments

i)   highlighting particular significance attached to information given

ii)   other relevant information not covered by above headings

ASSESSMENT BY ADDITIONAL AGENCY

School

1.   How long at school?

2.   Attendance during previous 3 terms

3.   Educational performance in relation to potential

4.   Behaviour/attitudes in school

i)   with staff

ii) with peers

5.   Social relationships

6.   Emotional presentation

7.   Parents'/carers' attitudes to school/child

8.   Are there any special educational needs and how are these being addressed?

9.   Any relevant information under the above headings from previous school records

10. General comments

i)   highlighting particular significance attached to information given

ii) other relevant information not covered by above headings

ASSESSMENT BY ADDITIONAL AGENCY

Community Child Health Doctors

A   Community medical involvement

1.   Surveillance – relevant findings

2.   Outpatient clinic findings:

i)   physical health and growth

ii)   psychomotor and emotional development

iii)   behaviour

iv)   clothing and hygiene

3.   School health – relevant findings

4.   Concerning the parents'/carers' parenting skills

i)   interaction – warmth and understanding

ii)   provision of play opportunities

iii)   attitude to the child

B   From other medical sources

i)   Relevant medical conditions: e.g. recurring medical conditions

ii)   Any history of concern about parent's child rearing skills: e.g. failure to thrive, delayed development or behaviour problems without medical cause

iii)   Compliance with advice or treatment given

C   General comments

i)   highlighting particular significance attached to information given

ii)   other relevant information not covered by above headings

Appendix 5.8:

AN EXAMPLE OF AN ASSESSMENT QUESTIONNAIRE CONCERNING YOUNG PEOPLE

CONFIDENTIAL   TO BE COMPLETED BY PARENTS/CAREGIVERS

ASSESSMENT OF YOUNG PERSON'S BEHAVIOUR DIFFICULTY
(A VERSION OF THIS COULD BE COMPILED FOR COMPLETION
BY THE YOUNG PERSON)

A   **GENERAL AND MEDICAL DETAILS**

1.   Name of young person .... Male/Female ....

2.   Age .... Date of birth ....

3.   Address ....

         ....Telephone (if available)...............................

4.   Family composition

         Mother's name .... Date of birth ....

         Father's name .... Date of birth ....

         Other key adult's name: e.g. step parent .... Date of Birth ....

         Please list all children, including referred young person, with ages

         1 ....(age) ...... 3 .... (age) .... 5 .... (age) ....

         2 .... (age) ...... 4 .... (age) .... 6 .... (age) ....

5.   Difficulties being experienced with and by the young person

         1 .... 3 ....

         2   .... 4 ....

6.   Living circumstances of household (brief information about accommodation etc)

         ....

7.   Any other information you think is relevant: ....

         ....

         ....

8.   Were there any medical difficulties at birth or during the first year of life?

         ....

9.   Did the young person experience any major illnesses/hospital admissions?

         ....

10.   Did you (mother) experience any postnatal depression? ....

11. Are there any major difficulties in the family? e.g. frequent arguments?

     ....

B FAMILY CIRCUMSTANCES

12. What age was the young person when the difficulties began? ....

     ....

13. Did anything happen around that time that might be linked with the onset
     of the difficulties?

     a) ....

     b) Anything else? ....

14. Have there been any events in the family which made things worse? e.g.
     bereavement, loss of employment, parental separation

     a)   ....

     b)   ....

15. What other stresses is the young person or other household members under?

     a)   ....

     b)   ....

16. What has worried you most about your son/daughter as he/she has been
     growing up?

     ....

     ....

17. Why do you think the difficulties happen?

     ....

18. In what ways have you tried to deal with the difficulties?

     1 ....3 ....

     2 ....4 ....

19. Have any ways been more successful than others? ....

     ....

     ....

C SETTINGS IN WHICH THE DIFFICULTIES HAPPEN

20. People involved: with whom do the difficulties happen?
     ....

     Is there anyone with whom they never happen? ....

21. Places involved: where do the difficulties happen? ....

22. Times involved: when do the difficulties happen? ....

23. Are there any regular triggers which seem to start the difficulties off?

....

24. What usually happens after the difficult behaviour? ....

25. What are some of the young person's good behaviours or things that he or she does that you like?

1 .... 2 ....

26. Which of the young person's good behaviours would you like to see happen more often?

1 .... 2 ....

D   **EDUCATION/EMPLOYMENT**

27. What is the situation concerning school/employment?

....

28. Which parts of his/her time at school has the young person enjoyed?

....

29. What school subjects is/was your son/daughter good at?

....

30. Do the difficulties occur as often at school as at home? ....

....

31. Do we have your permission to be in touch with your son's/daughter's

school? ....

E   **HEALTH**

I'd like to ask you about your child's health. Are there aspects of his or her health that you are worried about? Let's take them one at a time:

32. What about physical health? ....

33. What about mental health? e.g. does he/she often seem anxious or

depressed?...

If so, how persistent are these feelings? ....

34   What about sexual health?

Does your son or daughter seem to worry about sexual matters? ....

Who do you think he/she might talk to if he or she were worried about sex?

....

Are you concerned about the possibility of your child being sexually active?

....

36. Do you have concerns about his or her patterns of eating? ....
....

37. Do you have concerns about his or her patterns of drinking? (alcohol) (if appropriate)

....

38. Do you have concerns about any other patterns of behaviour: for example, smoking or trying other substances? ....

39. Do you have concerns about his/her patterns of watching films/TV or using the computer? ....

40. Do you have concerns about his or her patterns of sleeping? ....
....

F   SELF ESTEEM AND IDENTITY

41. Do you think that your son/daughter feels reasonably positive about him or herself? ....

42. Would you say he or she has high, medium or low self esteem?

....

43. Do you think your son or daughter worries about any of these areas:

physical development ....

body image...

racial or national identity ....

his or her hormones (sexual feeling) ....

sexual identity...

G   RELATIONSHIPS WITHIN THE FAMILY

44. How does your son/daughter get on with other members of the household or wider family?

mother..

father:...

other adult(s) liviing in household: ....

brothers: ....

sisters: ....

grandparents: ....

45.   Do you sometimes manage to talk together enjoyably as a family?

....

46.   Do you manage to do things together at home? e.g. playing cards (according to age/culture)

mother and young person together?   ....

father/other adult together?   ....

all the family together? ....

47.   Do you have any agreed family rules or guidelines, e.g. about household

chores? ....

48.   If so, how were the rules arrived at? e.g. mum/dad make them, or were they

worked out together? ....

49.   If the rules/guidelines are not kept, what happens? e.g. are there predictable consequences, such as loss of pocket money?

....

50.   Do you manage to do things together out of the home: e.g. going swimming

....

51.   Does you son/daughter have any close friends – ones whom they see at least weekly?

with other young men of about the same age? If so, how many? ....

with other young women of about the same age? If so, how many? ....

does she or she belong to any group of friends? ....

if so, is this group of the same or other gender or mixed? ....

if he/she has few friends, do you think that he or she is lonely? ....

do friendships seem to be a source of support or anxiety to him/her? ....

H   **RELATIONSHIPS BEYOND THE FAMILY**

52.   Roughly how much time does the young person spend with friends in the

house? ....

with friends out of the house? ....

53.   Do you usually know where he or she is? ....

who he or she is with? ....

when he or she is due back? ....

54   Does he or she usually come back home at the time he/she says he/she will?

....

55.   If s/he does, what happens? e.g. Do you say, Thanks for being on time?

....

56.   If s/he doesn't, are there any sanctions that automatically take effect: e.g. having to stay in on another evening when he/she usually goes out?

....

57.   What worries you most about your son or daughter's difficulties? ....

....

58.   What has been the overall impact of the behaviour difficulties on family/household?

....

....

Thank you for giving me this information. Are there any questions you would like to ask me?

....

(It is usually wise to suggest a multi-factorial explanation at this stage).

The assessor should then pass these assessment sheets to the person(s) who has supplied the information and ask that it be checked for accuracy. Invite the informant to sign the assessment, if he or she is willing to do so.

Signed .... (Assessor)

Professional role ....

Address: ....

.... Telephone number ....

Signed: .... (Parent/Guardian)   Date ....

Note:

With acknowledgements to a group of youth and comunity work, social work and health visitor students at De Montfort University, March, 2000.

Appendix 6.1:
SOME PROFESSIONAL ROLES OF CLINICAL PSYCHOLOGISTS

Settings in which clinical child psychologists work and examples of their work.
(Source: Fielding, 1987, reproduced by permission of Oxford University Press).

Setting	Example
(a) *Health*	
(i) Community Child welfare clinics Health centres GP practices	Liaison/consultation with health visitors: Parents' groups for behavioural, sleeping, feeding problems of under-fives.
(ii) Hospital Ante-natal clinics	Counselling of mothers with suspected handicapped child. Counselling of adolescents deciding about termination of pregnancy.
Intensive care neonatal units Paediatric assessment clinics	Counselling for staff and parents. Assessment and remediation of development delays.
Paediatric hospital wards	Preparation of parents/children for hospitalization. Counselling of parents/staff dealing with terminally ill children.
Casualty wards	Crisis counselling for adolescents who have taken overdoses.
Psychiatric in-patient and out-patient units	Assessment and treatment with families of children showing emotional and behavioural problems. Consultation/training of psychiatric child care staff (in psychological procedures).
(b) *Social services*	
(i) Local authority nurseries	Advice to nursery nurses concerning problems of child abuse. Assessment of developer delays.
(ii) Community homes	Consultation with staff concerning management of difficult behaviour problems. Counselling foster parents.
(c) *Voluntary organizations*	Drop-in clinics for adolescents with drug taking or alcohol problems (e.g., Samaritans, Adoption Societies, Brook Advisory Centres, Grapevine etc)

Appendix 6.2:

SOME PROFESSIONAL ROLES OF EDUCATIONAL PSYCHOLOGISTS (with acknowledgements to Joe Dawson.)

Setting	Examples
Education	
Schools	• Advise/support staff in mainstream/special schools • In-service training to teachers, governors and other school staff on issues such as behaviour management, learning, speech, language and communication • Direct work with children: assessment, counselling, group work, social skills work
Local Education Authorities	• Training to other LEA support services • Statutory advice to LEAs on children's special educational needs • Advising on LEAs policies and procedures • Liaison and consultation with LEA Education Welfare Officers
Parents and Community	• Running parents' groups • Support for parents of pre-school children • Advice and support to pre-school providers (including voluntary sector) • Advising multi-agency initiatives • Giving talks and advice to voluntary organisations
Health	
Community child health services GPs	• Training and consultation with health visitors, school doctors school nurses. Some joint work.
Paediatrics	• Liaison and consultation with paediatricians, psychologists and
Psychiatry	clinical psychologists, supporting some joint work in assessment of children
Clinical psychology	• Work on multi-disciplinary planning forum
Social Services	
Local authority nursery schools	• Advice to nursery schools • Attendance at core-group meetings • Work on joint strategy initiatives
Other organisations	
Universities	• Research in applied psychology • Supervision of educational psychologists in training
Local authorities	• Consultation with other services: police, fire service, probation, careers service

Appendix 6.3:

SAMPLE CARE PLAN – SERVICE AGREEMENT

This agreement is drawn up between *North & West Unit of Management and Mr and Mrs Black regarding John Blank*, age *18 months*, D.O.B. *18.11.92*, who is a subject of the protection-plan.

In keeping with the requirements of the case conference decision of re-registration of *John*, we agree to work towards the goals set out below.

To improve quality of care and *John's* well-being as evidenced by:

(1)   steady weight-gain;
(2)   improvement in his general development;
(3)   improvement in parent–child interaction and relationship; and
(4)   improvement in family functioning.

All people concerned agree to keep the following arrangements:

Mr and Mrs Blank (parents) agree to:

(1)   *take John every other Monday morning to the health centre to be weighed;*
(2)   *take John every Tuesday and Thursday to the Family Centre;*
(3)   *work with the health visitor (Mrs King) and the social worker (Mrs Smith) to help them to resolve concerns regarding John's well being, physical growth, and retarded development; and*
(4)   *keep the appointments and communicate any difficulties that might occur during that time.*

Mrs King (health visitor) agrees to:

(1)   *be at the clinic every other Monday morning at an agreed time to weigh John;*
(2)   *help Mrs Blank with John's eating difficulties, and will advise the parents how to help John to catch up on his development;*
(3)   *visit the family every day at lunchtime for the first weeks (apart from Tuesday and Thursday when John is in the family centre), and then twice a week for the next two weeks; and*
(4)   *keep a weight record, and evaluate the work done jointly with the parents.*

Mrs Smith (social worker) agrees to:

(1)   *make arrangements for John to attend the family centre on Tuesdays and Thursdays;*
(2)   *provide counselling for both parents to better understand John's physical and emotional needs, and to help them to improve John's care. She will also help them to resolve their marital frictions;*
(3)   *help the parents to learn how to play with John, how to deal with his irritating behaviour, and how to deal with the mother's negative feelings towards John. She will also help to deal with John's anxiety, fear and apprehension towards his mother;*
(4)   *provide six sessions over a six week period; and*
(5)   *keep a record of work done, and evaluate progress. These tasks will be jointly conducted with the parents.*

Dr Green (the G.P.) agrees to:

(1)   *make arrangements with the paediatrician at the hospital to conduct medical investigations; and*
(2)   *see John at the surgery once a month to monitor his physical health and development (more frequently if there is a need or request by parents or professionals involved).*

The requirements and objectives are re-negotiable at any time on request by either party.

All parties agree to fulfil their obligations and to observe times of appointments. If for any reason any parties are prevented from keeping an appointment, they must communicate this to the person concerned and make an alternative arrangement.

This care plan will be reviewed in three months' time. All involved should communicate their concerns and progress to the key worker *Mrs Smith*.

1.   Case review *10 June*

Signed: _____Mr *Blank*

Signed: _____Mrs *Blank*

Signed: _____Mrs *Smith*
(social worker)

Signed: _____Mr *King*
(health visitor)

Signed: _____Dr *Green* (G.P.)

Date: _____

Signed: _____Case-Conference
Chair

The key worker draws up this agreement after the case conference and sends it for signatures. When all signatures are obtained it is sent or given to all parties concerned.

CONTRACT

This contract is drawn up between *Mrs Smith* (social worker) and *Mr and Mrs Blank* (*John's* parents) in the presence of *Mrs King* (health visitor)

Date: _____

In keeping with the requirements of the case conference decision, we agree to work towards the goals set out by both parties:

Mrs and Mrs Blank agree:

(1)   *to play with John every day after tea:*
           15 minutes for the first two weeks;
           20 minutes for the 3rd, 4th, 5th and 6th week; and
           25 minutes for the subsequent weeks.
(2)   *to talk to John (while playing with him) in an encouraging way, to praise him for*
           each good response, to talk to him in a soft, warm and reassuring voice, to show
           pleasure in his achievements, and to thank him if he participates in play;
(3)   *to read a story or to describe a picture while sitting John on his/her lap and holding*
           him close to him/her for 10 minutes every day; just before he is put to bed; and
(4)   *to have their evening meal sitting at the table (not in front of the television), to talk*
           to each other about the day's events, etc, and also to talk to John.

Mr Blank agrees to help his wife:

(1)   *to put John to bed every other night; and*
(2)   *to do the weekly shopping.*

Mrs Blank agrees:

to be more open with her husband, and to tell him what bothers her, instead of sulking or screaming at him.

Mrs Smith (social worker), on her part, agrees:

(1)   *to help Mr and Mrs Blank with the first three play sessions, to adivse them what play material or toys to use, and on how each session will be conducted;*
(2)   *to get Mrs Blank some picture books for the story reading sessions;*
(3)   *to review with the parents John's progress at the Family Centre; and*
(4)   *to see the family every Thursday for six weeks from 3.30—4.30pm to help them with their own difficulties and to help them with John's problems.*

Both parties agree:

To evaluate their work together on a weekly basis (after the counselling session) and to keep records of these evaluations.

The requirements and objectives are re-negotiable at any time on request by either party.

Bonus: *If progress is made, an early de-registration of John will be considered*

Signed: _____ Social Worker

Signed: _____ Father

Signed: _____ Mother

Signed: _____ Health Visitor

                                                        (Observer)

Date: _____

This contract will be reviewed in two weeks from the date of this agreement.

CONTRACT

This contract is drawn up between *Mrs King* (health visitor) and *Mr and Mrs Blank* *(John's* parents) in the presence of *Mrs Smith* (social worker)

Date: _____

In keeping with the requirements of the case conference decision, we agree to work towards the goals set out by both parties:

Mrs Blank agrees:

(1)   *to feed John regularly (four times a day): 8am breakfast, 12–12.30pm lunch, 3.30pm tea (snack), 5.30pm dinner;*
(2)   *to provide food appropriate for the child's age (as advised by the health visitor);*
(3)   *to encourage John to eat by talking warmly to him; and not rushing him or shouting at him when he is in difficulties;*
(4)   *to praise John when he has made an effort to eat well and is eating a reasonable amount of food; and*
(5)   *to bring John to the health centre to be weighed every other Monday morning at 10am.*

Mr Blank agrees:

(1)   to help Mrs Blank with John's eating at dinner-times and during weekends; and
(2)   to be sympathetic, warm and encouraging to John and to his wife.

Mrs King (health visitor) on her part, agrees:

(1)   to work out with Mrs Blank a range of menus which will be nutritional and within
           the family financial remit;
(2)   to show and advise Mr and Mrs Blank how to manage John during meal-times,
           three times and lunch-time during the first week, and twice a week for the following
           three weeks. Progress will be reviewed and a decision taken as to whether further
           help is needed; and
(3)   to advise Mr and Mrs Blank with John's toilet-training, play and doing things for
           himself.

Both parties agree:

(1)   to review progress on a weekly basis and to keep the record of that evaluation; and
(2)   to keep the appointments and to do the work outlined in this agreement. If for any
           unavoidable reason an appointment cannot be kept, this will be communicated to the
           parties concerned and alternative arrangements will be made.

The requirements and objectives are re-negotiable at any time on request by either
party.

Bonus: *If progress is made, an early de-registration of John will be considered.*

Signed: _____Mr Blank (father)

Signed: _____Mrs Blank (mother)

Signed: _____Mrs King (health visitor)

Signed: _____ Mrs Smith (social worker)

Date: _____

This contract will be reviewed in two weeks from the date of that agreement.

Appendix 6.4:
CHILDREN WITH EMOTIONAL AND BEHAVIOURAL DIFFICULTIES

All Purpose Commissioning Contract (Sample)

(With acknowledgements to Leicestershire Social Services Department)

1.   Commissioner:

Name of Practitioner   Tel:

Name of Team Manager   Team:

2.   Services requested for following children:

(a)   Surname   Forenames   DoB
        Ethnic Origin   Religion

(b)   Surname   Forenames   DoB
        Ethnic Origin   Religion

(c)   Surname   Forenames   DoB
        Ethnic Origin   Religion

Preferred language of communication

3.   Parents

Mother Surname   Forenames   Address   Tel.

Father Surname   Forenames   Address   Tel.

4.   Other members of the family at home:

Name   Age   Relationship

5.   Other significant person(s) to the child(ren).

6.   Location where service to be delivered to:

7.   Details of carer if child not living with parents.
        (Include status, names, address and tel. no.).

8.   Medical details:

Name of Doctor   Address   Tel no.

Name of Health Visitor   Address   Tel no.

Current medical treatment and any ongoing health problems:

9.   **Educational Details**   Educational issues

Name of School
Address
Contact Person

10.   **Other professionals working with family.**

Name   Status   Level of Visiting   Tel.

11.   **Special dietary, cultural or religious needs.**

12.   **Brief description of present family circumstances**
          (Please attach any helpful documents)

          For older children please include child/young person's perspective

13.   **Frequency of contact considered necessary to achieve objectives**

14.   **Length of Contract**

          Date of start:

          Is this a fixed term contract?   YES/NO ?

          If so give dates to start and end:

15.   **What SPECIFIC objectives do you wish the commissioned agency to work towards?**

a)

b)

c)

d)

16.   **Which of the following feedback formats do you require?**

(a)   Weekly telephone call
(b)   Mid-term assessment/review
(c)   End of contract summary/assessment.

17.   **Are parents agreeable to this commissioned work? YES/NO**
                    If 'No' clarify.

          Is the child/young person agreeable to this commissioned work? YES/NO
                    If 'No' clarify.

References

Advisory Centre for Education (1994). *Preparing for the Code of Practice: Issues for Governors.* London, ACE.

Ainsworth, M.D. (1979). Infant–mother attachment. *American Psychologist.* 34, 932–37.

Ainsworth, M.D., Blehar, M, Waters, E. and Wall, S (1978). *Patterns of Attachment.* Hillsdale, N.J., Erlbaum.

Akiskal, H.S. and McKinney, W.T. (1975). Overview of recent research in depression. *Archives of General Psychiatry,* 32, 285–305.

Alexander, J. and Parsons, B. (1973). Short–term behavioural intervention with delinquent families: impact on family process and recidivism. *Journal of Abnormal Psychology,* 81, 219–25.

Allen, D.M. and Tarnowski, K.J. (1989). Depressive characteristics of physically abused children. *Journal of Abnormal Child Psychology,* 17, 1–11.

American Psychiatric Association (1987). *Diagnostic and Statistical Manual of Mental Disorders,* (4th edn) (DSM-IV). Washington D.C., American Psychiatric Association.

Aneshensel, C.S. and Stone, J.D. (1982). Stress and depression. *Archives of General Psychiatry.* 39, 1392–96.

Armstrong, K.L., Van Haeringen, A.R., Dadds, M.R. and Cash, R. (1998). Sleep deprivation or postnatal depression in late infancy: separating the chicken from the egg. *Journal of Paediatrics and Child Health,* 34, (3), 260–62.

Askew, J., Cunnington, J. and Gregory, S. (1999). Personal communication.

Atkinson, R.L., Atkinson, R.C., Smith, E.E., Bem, D.J. and Hilgard, E. (1990). *Introduction to Psychology,* (10th edn). New York, Harcourt, Brace, Jovanovich.

Audit Commission (1994). *Seen But Not Heard. Coordinating Community Child Health and Social Services for Children in Need.* London, HMSO.

Bandura, A. (1977). *Social Learning Theory.* Englewood Cliffs, N.J., Prentice Hall.

Bandura, A. and Walters, M. (1959). *Adolescent Aggression.* New York. Ronald Press.

Barkley, R. (1995). *Taking Charge of ADHD.* New York, Guilford Press.

Barlow, J. (1997). *Systematic review of the effectiveness of parent-training programmes in improving behaviour problems in children aged 3–10 years.* Health Services Research Unit, Department of Public Health, University of Oxford.

Baumrind, D. (1971). Current patterns of parental authority. *Developmental Psychology Monographs:* 1, 1–102.

Bayley, R. (1999). *Transforming Children's Lives: the Importance of Early Intervention*. London, Family Policy Studies Centre.

Beck, A. (1967). *Depression: Clinical, Experimental and Theoretical Aspects*. New York, Harper and Row.

Beck, A. (1976). *Cognitive Therapy and the Emotional Disorders*. New York, International Universities Press.

Beck, A. (1988). *Beck Depression Inventory*. Sidcup, Kent, Harcourt Brace Jovanovich.

Beck, A., Rush, A.J, Shaw, B.F. and Emery, G. (1979). *Cognitive Therapy of Depression*. New York, Guilford Press.

Beck, A., Emery, G. and Greenberg, R. (1985). *Anxiety Disorders and Phobias. A Cognitive Perspective*. New York, Basic Books.

Belsky, J. and Rovine, M. (1988). Nonmaternal care in the first year of life and the security of infant–parent attachment. *Child Development*, 59, 157–67.

Berruetta-Clement, J.R., Schweinhart, L.J., Barnett, W.S., Epstein, A.S. and Weikart, D.P. (1984). *Changed Lives. The Effects of the Perry Pre-School Program on Youths Through Age 19*. Ypsilanti, Michigan, High/Scope Foundation.

Bexley Council with Oxleas NHS Trust (1999). *Attention Deficit Hyperactivity Disorder (ADHD)*. Bexley Council.

Blair Irvine, A., Biglan, A., Smolkowski, K. Metzler, C. and Ary, D. (1999). Effectiveness of a parenting programme for parents of middle school students. *Journal of Consulting and Clinical Psychology*, 67, 811–25.

Blanz, B., Schmidt, M.H. and Esser, G. (1991). Familial adversities and child psychiatric disorder. *Journal of Child Psychology and Psychiatry*, 32, 393–450.

Borduin, C.M., Mann, B.J., Cone, L.T., Henggeler, S.W., Fucci, B.R., Blaske, D.M. and Williams, R.A. (1995). Multi-systemic treatment of serious juvenile offenders: Long term prevention of criminality and violence. *Journal of Consulting and Clinical Psychology*, 63, 569–87.

Bowlby, J. (1953). *Child Care and the Growth of Love*. Harmondsworth, Penguin.

Bowlby, J. (1969). *Attachment and Loss. Volume 1. Attachment*. New York, Basic Books.

Bretherton, I. (1985). Attachment theory; retrospect and prospect. In I. Bretherton and E. Waters (eds), *Growing Points of Attachment Theory and Research*. Monographs of the Society for Research in Child Development, 50 (1–2, Serial No. 209), 66–104.

Brezina, T. (1998). Adolescent maltreatment and delinquency: the question of intervening processes. *Journal of Research in Crime and Delinquency*. 35, 71–99.

Brown, G. and Harris, T. (1978). *The Social Origins of Depression*. London, Tavistock.

Children Act 1989. London, HMSO.

Clarke, R.V.G. (1977). Psychology and crime. *Bulletin of the British Psychological Society*, 30, 280–83.

Cohen, S. and Wills, T.A. (1985). Stress, social support and the buffering hypothesis. *Psychological Bulletin*, 98, 310–57.

Conners, K.C. (1973). Rating scales for use in drug studies with children. *Pharmacology Bulletin*, 9, 24–29.

Cooper, C. (1985). 'Good-enough', border-line and 'Bad-enough' parenting. In M. Adcock and R. White (eds), *Good-enough Parenting: A Framework for Assessment*. London, British Agencies for Adoption and Fostering.

Cooper, P.J and Murray, L. (1997). The impact of psychological treatments of post partum depression on maternal mood and infant development. In L. Murray, and P.J. Cooper, (eds) *Postpartum Depression and Child Development*. New York, Guilford.

Cooper, P.J and Murray, L. (1998). Postnatal depression. *British Medical Journal*, 316, 1884–86.

Cooper, P.J., Murray, L., Hooper, R. and West, A. (1996). The development and validation of a predictive index for postpartum depression. *Psychological Medicine*, 26, 627–34.

Cox, A.D. (1995). Interviews with parents. In M. Rutter, E. Taylor and L. Hersov (eds), *Child and Adolescent Psychiatry*. Oxford, Blackwell Scientific Publications.

Cox, J. and Holden, J. (1994). *Perinatal Psychiatry. Uses and Misuse of the Edinburgh Postnatal Depression Scale*. London, Gaskell.

Cox, J., Holden, J. and Sagovsky, R. (1987). Detection of postnatal depression: Development of the 10-item Edinburgh postnatal depression scale. *British Journal of Psychiatry*, 150, 782–86.

Crockenberg, S.B. (1981). Infant irritability, mother responsiveness and social-support influences on the security of infant–mother attachment. *Child Development*, 52, 857–65.

Cross, M. (1997). Challenging behaviour or challenged comprehension. *Royal College of Speech and Language Therapists Bulletin*, September, 1997, 11–12.

Cunnington, J. and Askew, J. (1998). Personal communication.

Cutrona, C.E. and Troutman, B.R. (1986). Social support, infant temperament, parent self-efficacy: a mediational model of postpartum depression. *Child Development*, 57, 1507–18.

Davis, H. and Spurr, P. (1998). Parent counselling: An evaluation of a community child mental health service. *Journal of Child Psychology and Psychiatry*, 39, 365–76.

Department for Education and Employment (1999). *Social Inclusion/Pupil Support*. Circular 11/99. London, DfEE.

Department of Health (1991). *Working Together under the Children Act 1989; A Guide to Arrangements for Inter-Agency Cooperation for the Protection of Children from Abuse*. London, HMSO.

Department of Health (1995a). *Child Protection: Messages from Research*. London, HMSO.

Department of Health (1995b). Social Services Inspectorate and Department for Education. *A Handbook on Child and Adolescent Mental Health*. London, Department of Health.

Department of Health (1998). *The Quality Protects Programme: Transforming Children's Lives*. London, Department of Health.

Department of Health (1999). *Modernising Health and Social Services. National Priorities Guidance. 1999/2000–2001/02*. London, Department of Health.

Department of Health (2000). *Framework for the Assessment of Children in Need and their Families*. London, The Stationery Office.

Department of Health/Home Office/Department for Education and Employment (1999). *Working Together to Safeguard Children. A Guide to Inter-Agency Working to Safeguard and Promote the Welfare of Children*. London, HMSO.

Department of Health/Hospital Advisory Service (1995). *Child and Adolescent Mental Health Services. Together We Stand*. London, HMSO.

Dishion, T.J., Patterson, G.R. and Kavanagh, K.A. (1992). An experimental test of the coercion model. Linking theory, measurement and intervention. In J. McCord and R. Tremblay (eds), *Preventing Antisocial Behavior: Interventions from Birth through Adolescence*. New York, Guilford.

Dobash, R.E. and Dobash, R. (1978). *Violence Against Wives*. London, Open Books.

Dodge, K.A. (1980). Social cognition and children's aggressive behavior. *Child Development*, 51, 162–70.

Dodge, K.A. and Frame, C.L. (1982). Social cognitive biases and deficits in aggressive boys. *Child Development*, 53, 620–35.

Drillien, C.M. (1964). *The Growth and Development of the Prematurely Born Infant*. Baltimore, Williams and Wilkins.

Erickson, M., Sroufe, L.A. and Egeland, B. (1985). The relationship between quality of attachment and behavior problems in pre-school in a high-risk sample. In I. Bretherton and E. Waters (eds), *Growing Points of Attachment Theory and Research*. Monographs of the Society for Research in Child Development, 50 (1–2 Serial No. 209), 147–66.

Eyberg, S.M. and Johnson, S.M. (1974). Multiple assessment of behavior with families: effects on contingency contracting. *Journal of Consulting and Clinical Psychology*, 42, 594–606.

Fagot, B. and Kavanagh, K. (1990). The prediction of antisocial behavior from avoidant atachment classification. *Child Development*, 61, 864–73.

Falloon, I.R.H., Laporta, M., Fadden, G. and Graham-Hole, V. (1993). *Managing Stress in Families: Cognitive and Behavioural Strategies for Enhancing Coping Skills*. London, Routledge.

Farrington, D. (1978). The family backgrounds of aggressive youths. In L. Hersov, M. Berger and D. Shaffer (eds), *Aggression and Anti-social Behaviour in Childhood and Adolescence*. Oxford, Pergamon.

Farrington, D. (1991). Childhood aggression and adult violence: early precursors and later life outcomes. In D.J. Pepler and K.H. Rubin (eds), *The Development and Treatment of Childhood Aggression*. Hillsdale, N.J., Erlbaum.

Farrington, D. (1995a). Intensive health visiting and the prevention of juvenile crime. *Health Visitor*, 68, 3, 100–102.

Farrington, D. (1995b). The development of offending and anti-social behaviour from childhood: key findings from the Cambridge Study in Delinquent Development. *Journal of Child Psychology and Psychiatry*, 360, 924–64.

Farrington, D. (1996). *Understanding and Preventing Youth Crime*. York, Joseph Rowntree Foundation.

Farrington, D. and Welsh, B. (1999). Delinquency prevention using family–based interventions. *Children and Society*, 13, 287–303.

Feindler, E. (1991). Cognitive strategies in anger control interventions for children and adolescents. In P.C. Kendall (ed.), *Child and Adolescent Therapy: Cognitive Behavioral Procedures*. London, Guilford Press.

Feldman, R.A., Caplinger, T.E. and Wodarski, J.S. (1983). *The St. Louis Conundrum*. Englewood Cliffs, N.J., Prentice Hall.

Fielding, D. (1987) Working with children and young people. In J.S. Marziller and J. Hall (Eds.) *What is Clinical Psychology?* Oxford, OUP.

Finch, R. and Jacques, P. (1985) Use of the genogram with adoptive families. *Adoption and Fostering*, 9, 36–7.

Forehand, R. and Kotchik, B. (1996). Cultural diversity: a wake-up call for parent training. *Behavior Therapy*, 27, 187–206.

Forest, M., Pearpoint, J. and O'Brien, J. (1996). 'MAPS', educators, parents, young people and their friends planning together. *Educational Psychology in Practice*, 11, 35–40.

Forgatch, M. (1991). The clinical science vortex: a developing theory of antisocial Behavior. In D.J. Pepler and K.H. Rubin (eds), *The Development and Treatment of Childhood Aggression*. London, Lawrence Erlbaum Associates.

Freud, A. (1946/67). *The Ego and the Mechanisms of Defense*. (Revised edition). New York, International Universities Press.

Gardiner, J. (1996). Rise in primary exclusions. *Times Educational Supplement*, 1 November, 1996, 1.

Gelles, R.J. (1976). Abused wives: why do they stay? *Journal of Marriage and the Family*, 38, 659–68.

George, E., Iveson, C. and Ratner, H. (1990). *Problem to Solution. Brief Therapy with Individuals and Families*. London, BT Press.

Goldston, D.B., Turnquist, D.C.and Knutson, J.F. (1989). Presenting problems of sexually abused girls receiving psychiatric services. *Journal of Abnormal Psychology*, 98, 314–17.

Goodman, R. (1997). The Strengths and Difficulties Questionnaire. *Journal of Child Psychology and Psychiatry*, 38, 5, 581–86.

Gordon, S.B. and Davidson, N. (1981). Behavioral parent training. In A. Gurman and D. Kniskern (eds), *Handbook of Family Therapy*. Brunner, Mazel.

Greenberg, M.T., Speltz, M.L. and DeKlyen, M. (1993). The role of attachment in the early development of disruptive behavior problems. *Development and Psychopathology*, 5, 191–213.

Greeenfield, N. (1998). Parent style shapes success. *Times Educational Supplement*, 13 November, 1998.

Gunnoe, M.L. and Mariner, C.L. (1997). Towards a developmental–contextual model of the effects of parental smacking on children's aggression. *Archives of Paediatric and Adolescent Medicine*, 151, 768–75.

Hallett, C. (1995). *Inter-Agency Co-ordination in Child Protection*. London, HMSO.

Hardiker, P., Exton, K. and Barker, M. (1991). *Policies and Practices in Preventive Child Care*. Aldershot, Avebury.

Harrell, A.V., Cavanagh, S.E., Harmon, M.A., Koper, C.S. and Sridharan, S. (1997). *Impact of the Children at Risk Program: Comprehensive Final Report*, vol. 1, Washington D.C., The Urban Institute.

Harrington, R. (1994). Affective disorders. In M. Rutter, E.Taylor and L. Hersov (eds), *Child and Adolescent Psychiatry*. Oxford, Blackwell.

Harrington, R., Whittaker, J. and Shoebridge, P. (1998). Psychological treatment of depression in children and adolescents. A review of treatment research. *British Journal of Psychiatry*, 173, 291–98.

Hawkins, J.D., Doueck, J.J. and Lishner, D.M. (1988). Changing teaching practices in mainstream classrooms to improve bonding and behaviour of low achievers. *American Educational Research Journal*, 25, 31–50.

Hawkins, J.D., von Cleve, E. and Catalano, R.F. (1991). Reducing early childhood aggression. Results of a primary prevention programme. *Journal of the American Academy of Child and Adolescent Psychiatry*, 30, 208–17.

Hawkins, J.D., Catalano, R.F., Morrison, D.M., O'Donnell, J., Abbott, R.D. and Day, L.E. (1992). The Seattle social development project: Effects of the first four years on protective factors and problem behaviours. In J. McCord and R. Tremblay (eds), *Preventing Antisocial Behavior: Interventions from Birth through Adolescence*, 139–61. New York, Guilford.

Hawkins, J.D., Catalano, R.F., Kosterman, R., Abbott, R. and Hill, K. (1999). Preventing adolescent health risk behaviors by strengthening protection during childhood. *Archives of Pediatrics and Adolescent Medicine.* 153, 226–34.

Hazel, N. (1980). *Bridge to Independence.* Oxford, Blackwell.

Henggeler, S.W., Melton, G.B., Brondino, M.J. and Schere, D.G. (1997). Multisystemic therapy with violent and chronic juvenile offenders and their families; The role of treatment fidelity in successful dissemination. *Journal of Consulting and Clinical Psychology,* 65, 821–33.

Herbert, M. (1981). *Behavioural Treatment of Problem Children.* London, Academic Press.

Herbert, M. (1987). *Behavioural Treatment of Children with Problems.* London, Academic Press.

Herbert, M. (1991). *Child Care and the Family: A Client Management Resource Pack.* Windsor, NFER.

Herbert, M. (1993). *Working with Children and the Children Act.* Leicester, British Psychological Society.

Herbert, M. (1998). *Clinical Child Psychology. Social Learning, Development and Behaviour,* (2nd edn) Chichester, Wiley.

Holden, J. (1994). Using the Edinburgh Postnatal Depression Scale in clinical practice. In J. Cox and J. Holden (eds), *Perinatal Psychiatry: Uses and Abuses of the Edinburgh Postnatal Depression Scale.* London, Gaskell.

Holden, J.M., Sagovsky, R. and Cox, J. (1989). Counselling in a general practice setting: controlled study of health visitor intervention in the treatment of postnatal ddepression. *British Medical Journal,* 298, 223–6.

Holmes, T.H. and Rahe, R.H. (1967). The social readjustment rating scale. *Journal of Psychosomatic Research,* 11, 213–18.

House of Commons Health Committee. Fourth Report (1997). *Child and Adolescent Mental Health Services.* London, HMSO.

Horwath, J. and Calder, M.C. (1998). Working together to protect children on the Child Protection Register: Myth or reality. *British Journal of Social Work,* 28, 879–95.

Hudson, B. and Macdonald, G. (1986). *Behavioural Social Work. An Introduction.* Basingstoke, Macmillan.

Huesman, L.R., Eron, L.D., Ledfkowits, M.M., and Walder, L.O. (1984). Stability of aggression over time and generations. *Developmental Psychology,* 20, 1120–34.

Hunter, B. (1999). Personal communication.

Iwaniec, D. (1995). *The Emotionally Abused and Neglected Child.* Chichester, Wiley.

Jacobsen, E. (1938). *Progressive Relaxation.* Chicago, University of Chicago Press.

Johnson, D.L. and Walker, T. (1987). Primary prevention of behavior problems in Mexican-American children. *American Journal of Community Psychology,* 15, 375–85.

Katz, A. (1997). *The 'Can Do' Girls.* Littlehampton, West Sussex, Campaigns and Community Involvement, The Body Shop.

Katz, A. (1999). *Leading Lads.* Young Voice, 12 Bridge Gardens, East Molesey, Surrey.

Kazdin, A. (1987). Treatment of antisocial behavior in children: current status and future directions. *Psychological Bulletin,* 102, 187–203.

Kazdin, A. (1995). *Conduct Disorders in Childhood and Adolescence.* London, Sage.

Kazdin, A., Siegal, T.C. and Bass, D. (1992). Cognitive problem-solving skills training and parent management training in the treatment of antisocial behavior in children. *Journal of Consulting and Clinical Psychology*, 60, 733–47.

Kellmer-Pringle, M. (1974). *The Needs of Children*. London, Hutchinson.

Kendall, P.C. (ed.) (1991). *Child and Adolescent Therapy: Cognitive-Behavioral Procedures*. London, Guilford.

Kendall, P.C., Chansky, T., Friedman, M., Kim, R., Kortlander, E., Sessa, F. and Siqueland, L. (1991). Treating anxiety disorders in children and adolescents. In P.C. Kendall (ed.), *Child and Adolescent Therapy. Cognitive-Behavioural Procedures*. London, Guilford.

King, N.J., Hamilton, D.I. and Ollendick, T.J. (1988). *Children's phobias*. London. Academic Press.

Klein, R. (1994). Anxiety disorders. In M. Rutter, E. Taylor and L. Hersov.(eds) *Child and Adolescent Psychiatry*. Oxford, Blackwell.

Kitzman, H. *et al.* (1997). Effect of prenatal and infancy home visitation by nurses on pregnancy outcomes, childhood injuries and repeated childbearing: a randomized controlled trial. *Journal of the American Medical Association*, 278, 644–52.

Kohlberg, L. (1973). Implications of developmental psychology for education: Examples from moral development. *Educational Psychologist*, 10, 2–14.

Kolvin, I. *et al.* (1981). *Help Starts Here. The Maladjusted Child in the Ordinary School*. London, Tavistock.

Kolvin, I., Miller, F.J., Scott, D., Gatsnis, S.R. and Fleeting, M. (1988). *Adversity and Destiny: Explorations in the Transmission of Deprivation. Newcastle Thousand Family Study*. Aldershot, Gower.

Larson, C.P. (1980). Efficacy of prenatal and postpartum home visits on child health and development. *Pediatrics*, 66, 191–97.

Lazarus, A.A. (1971). *Behavior Therapy and Beyond*. New York, McGraw Hill.

Lally, J.R., Mangione, P.L. and Honig, A.S. (1988). Long-range impact of an early intervention with low-income children and their families. In D.R. Powell (ed.), *Parent Education as Early Childhood Intervention*. Norwood, N.J., Ablex.

Leach, P. (1998). Positively no smacking. *Community Practitioner*, 71 (11), 355–57.

Lloyd, E. (ed.) (1999). *Parenting Matters: What Works in Parenting Education?* Barkingside, Essex, Barnardos.

Lochman, J.E. and Curry, J.F. (1986). Effects of social problem-solving training and self-instruction training with aggressive boys. *Journal of Clinical Child Psychology*, 15, 467–76.

Lochman, J.E., White, K. and Wayland, K. (1991). Cognitive-behavioral assessment and treatment with aggressive children. In P. Kendall (ed.), *Child and Adolescent Therapy: Cognitive-Behavioral Procedures*. London, Guilford.

Loeber, R. (1990). Development and risk factors of juvenile antisocial behavior and delinquency. *Clinical Psychology Review*, 10, 1–41.

Loeber, R. and Stouthamer-Loeber, M. (1987). Prediction. In H.C. Quay (ed.), *Handbook of Juvenile Delinquency*. New York, Wiley.

Long, P. Forehand, R., Wierson, M. and Morgan, A. (1994). Does parent training with young noncompliant children have long-term effects? *Behaviour Research and Therapy*, 32, 1, 101–7.

Lyons-Ruth, K. (1996). Attachment relationships among children with aggressive behaviour problems: the role of disorganized early attachment patterns. *Journal of Consulting and Clinical Psychology*, 64, 64–73.

Lyons-Ruth, K., Alpern, L. and Repacholi, B. (1993). Disorganized infant attachment classification and maternal psychosocial problems as predictors of hostile-aggressive behavior in the pre-school classroom. *Child Development*, 64, 572–85.

McCarton *et al* (1997). Results at age 8 years of early intervention for low-birth-weight premature infants: The Infant Health and Development Program. *Journal of the American Medical Association*, 277, 126–32.

MacCoby, E.E. and Martin, J.A. (1983). Socialisation in the context of the family: Parent–child interaction. In P.H. Mussen (ed.), *Handbook of Child Psychology*, vol. 4. New York, Wiley.

McCord, J. (1978). A thirty-year follow-up of treatment effects. *American Psychologist*, 33, 284–89.

McGaw, S., Beckley, K. Connolly, N. and Ball, N. (1999). *Parent Assessment Manual.* Trecare NHS Trust.

Main, M. and Solomon, J. (1990). Procedures for identifying infants as disorganized/disoriented during the Ainsworth Strange Situation. In M. Greenberg, D. Cicchetti, and E.M. Cummings (eds), *Attachment in the Preschool Years: Theory, Research and Intervention*, 121–60. Chicago, University of Chicago Press.

Maines, B. and Robinson, G. (1995). *The B/G Steem. A Self-esteem Scale with Locus of Control Items.* Bristol, Lucky Duck Ltd.

Marsh, P. and Triseliotis, J. (1996). *Ready to Practise? Social Workers and Probation Officers: Their Training and First Year in Work.* Aldershot: Avebury.

Martin, G. and Pear, J. (1992). *Behavior Modification: What It Is and How to Do It.* New York, Prentice Hall.

Miller, W.R. and Rollnick, S. (1991). *Motivational Interviewing.* New York, Guilford.

Mischel, W. (1973). Towards a cognitive social learning reconceptualization of personality. *Psychological Review*, 80, 272–83.

Moore, J. (2000). Personal communication.

Mukherjee, S., Martin, J. and Mentz, G. (1999). The key to success. *Community Care*, 9–15 December, 1999, 26.

Murray, L. and Cooper, P.J. (1997). Effects of postnatal depression on infant development. *Archives of Disease in Childhood*, 77, 99–101.

Murray, L. (1992). The impact of postnatal depression on child development. *Journal of Child Psychology and Psychiatry*, 33, 543–61.

Murray, L., Fiori-Cowley, A., Hooper, R. and Cooper, P.J. (1996). The impact of postnatal depression and associated adversity on early mother–infant interactions and later infant outcome. *Child Development*, 67, 2512–26.

Mussen, P. and Eisenberg-Bern, N. (1977). *Roots of Caring, Sharing and Helping.* San Francisco, W.H. Freeman.

NACRO (1998). *Diverting People from Crime.* London, Nacro.

NHS Advisory Service (1995). *Child and Adolescent Mental Health Services.* London, HMSO.

Newton, C., Taylor, G. and Wilson, D. (1996). Circles of friends: an inclusive approach to meeting emotional and behavioural needs. *Educational Psychology in Practice*, 11, 41–8.

O'Connell, R. (1992). Healthy beginnings. *Caring*, Summer, 22–25.

Offord, D.R., Boyle, M.C. and Racine, Y.A. (1991). The epidemiology of antisocial behavior in childhood and adolescence. In D.J. Pepler and K.H. Rubin (eds), *The Development and Treatment of Childhood Aggression.* Hillsdale, N.J.,

Erlbaum.

Olds, D.L., Henderson, C.R., Chamberlain, R. and Tatelbaum, R. (1986a). Preventing child abuse and neglect: a randomized trial of nurse home visitation. *Pediatrics*, 78, 65–78.

Olds, D.L., Henderson, C.R., Chamberlain, R. and Tatelbaum, R. (1986b). Improving the delivery of pre-natal care and outcomes of pregnancy: a randomized trial of nurse home visitation. *Pediatrics*, 77, 16–28.

Olds, D.L., Henderson, C.R., Cole, R. Eckenrode, J., Kitzman, H., Luckey, D., Pettitt, L., Sidora, K., Morris, P. and Powers, J. (1998). Long-term effects of nurse home visitation on children's criminal and antisocial behaviour; 15 year follow-up of a randomized controlled trial. *Journal of the American Medical Asssociation*, 280, 1238–44.

Ollendick, T. (1979). Fear reduction techniques with children. In M. Hersen, R.M.Eisler and P.M. Miller (eds), *Progress in Behaviour Modification*. New York, Academic Press.

Ollendick, T. and King, N. (1991). Fears and phobias of childhood. In M. Herbert (ed.), *Clinical Child Psychology: Social Learning, Development and Behaviour*. Chichester, Wiley.

Olweus, D. (1979). Stability of aggressive reaction patterns in males: a review. *Psychological Bulletin*, 86, 29–34.

Open University (1980). Systems organization: the management of complexity. T243 Block 1, *Introduction to Systems: Thinking and Organization*. Milton Keynes, Open University Press.

Pagani, L., Tremblay, R.E., Vitaro, F. and Parent, S. (1998). Does preschool help prevent delinquency in boys with a history of perinatal complications? *Criminology*, 36, 245–67.

Patterson, G.R. (1974). Intervention for boys with conduct problems: multiple settings, treatment and criteria. *Journal of Consulting and Clinical Psychology*, 42, 471–81.

Patterson, G.R. (1975). *Applications of Social Learning to Family Life*. Champaign. Ill., Research Press.

Patterson, G.R. (1982). *A Social Learning Approach to Family Intervention*. III Coercive Family Process. Eugene, OR, Castalia.

Patterson, G.R., Dishion, T.J. and Chamberlain, P. (1993). Outcomes and methodological issues relating to treatment of antisocial children. In T.R. Giles (ed.), *Handbook of Effective Psychotherapy*. New York, Plenum.

Patterson, G.R. and Stoolmiller, M. (1991). Replications of a dual failure model for boys' depressed mood. *Journal of Consulting and Clinical Psychology*, 59, 481–98.

Prochaska, J.O. and DiClemente, C.C. (1982). Transtheoretical therapy; Toward a more integrative model of change. *Psychotherapy: Theory, Research and Practice*, 19, 276–88.

Reid, J.B., Eddy, J.M., Fetrow, R.A. and Stoolmiller, M. (1999). Description and immediate impacts of a preventive intervention for conduct problems. *American Journal of Community Psychology*, (in press).

Roberts, I. and Singh, C.S. (1999). *Using Mentors to Change Problem Behaviour in Primary School Children*. Research Findings, No. 95. Research, Development and Statistics Directorate. Home Office.

Robins, L.N. (1966). *Deviant Children Grown Up*. Baltimore, Williams and Wilkins.

Robins, L.N. (1981). Epidemiological approaches to natural history research:

antisocial disorders in children. *Journal of Consulting and Clinical Psychology*, 50, 226–33.

Robins, L.N. and Price, R.K. (1991). Adult disorders predicted by childhood conduct problems: results from the NIMH Epidemiologic Catchment Area project. *Psychiatry*, 54, 116–32.

Rogers, C.R. (1951). *Client-Centred Therapy*. Boston, Houghton-Mifflin.

Rutter, M. (1978). Family, area and school influences in the genesis of conduct disorders. In L.A. Hersov, M. Berger and D. Shaffer (eds), *Aggression and Anti-social Behaviour in Childhood and Adolescence*. Oxford, Pergamon Press.

Rutter, M. (1979). *Changing Youth in a Changing Society. Patterns of Adolescent Development and Disorder*. London, Nuffield Provincial Hospitals Trust.

Rutter, M., Cox, A., Tupling, C., Berger, M. and Yule, W. (1975). Attainment and adjustment in two geographical areas: I The prevalence of psychiatric disorder. *British Journal of Psychiatry*, 126, 493–509.

Rutter, M. (1986). The developmental psychopathology of depression: issues and perspectives. In M. Rutter, C. Izard, and P. Read (eds), *Depression in Young People: Developmental and Clinical Perspectives*. New York, Guilford.

Rutter, M. (1987). *Helping Troubled Children*. Harmondsworth, Penguin.

Rutter, M. and Cox, A. (1985). Other family influences. In M. Rutter and L. Hersov (eds), *Child and Adolescent Psychiatry: Modern Approaches* (2nd edn). Oxford, Blackwell Scientific Publications.

Rutter, M. and Quinton, D. (1977). Psychiatric disorder – ecological factors and resistance to psychiatric disorder. *British Journal of Psychiatry*, 147, 598–611.

Rutter, M. and Sandberg, S. (1992). Psychosocial stressors: concepts, causes and effects. *European Child and Adolescent Psychiatry*, 1, 3–13.

Rutter, M., Tizard, J. and Whitmore, K. (1970). *Education, Health and Behaviour*. London, Longman.

Schoenwald, S.K., Ward, D.M., Henggeler, S.W., Pickrel, S.G. and Patel, H. (1996). Multi-systemic therapy treatment of substance abusing or dependent adolescent offenders: Costs of reducing incarceration inpatient and residential treatment. *Journal of Child and Family Studies*, 5, 431–44.

Schweinhart, L.J., Barnes, H.V. and Weikart, D.P. (1993). *Significant Benefits. The High/Scope Perry Preschool Study Through Age 27*. Ypsilanti, Michigan, High/Scope.

Schweinhart, L.J. and Weikart, D.P. (1980). *Young Children Grown Up*. Ypsilanti, Michigan, High/Scope.

Seeley, S., Murray, L. and Cooper, P.J. (1996). Postnatal depression: the outcome for mothers and babies of health visitor intervention. *Health Visitor*, 69, 135–8.

Seligman, M.E. and Peterson, C (1986). A learned helplessness perspective on childhood depression: theory and research. In M. Rutter. C. Izard and P. Read (eds), *Depression in Young People: Developmental and Clinical Perspectives*. New York, Guilford Press.

Sheldon, B. (1980). *The Use of Contracts in Social Work*. Birmingham, British Association of Social Workers.

Spivack, G., Platt, J.J, and Shure, M. (1976). *The Problem-Solving Approach to Adjustment*. San Francisco, Jossey-Bass.

Stark, K.D., Rouse, L.W. and Livingston, R. (1991). Treatment of depression during childhood and adolescence: cognitive-behavioural procedures for the individual and family. In P.C. Kendall (ed.), *Child and Adolescent Therapy*. New York, Guilford.

Stone, W.L., Bendell, R.D. and Field, T.M. (1988). The impact of socio-economic status on teenage mothers and children who received early intervention. *Journal of Applied Developmental Psychology*, 9, 391–408.

Stoner, J. (1978). *Management*. Englewood Cliffs, N.J., Prentice Hall.

Strauss, M., Sugarman, D.B. and Giles-Sims, J. (1997). Spanking by parents and subsequent antisocial behavior of children. *Archives of Paediatric and Adolescent Medicine*, 151, 761–67.

Strayhorn, J.M. and Weidman, C.S. (1991). Follow–up one year after parent–child interaction training: Effects on behavior of preschool children. *Journal of the American Academy of Child and Adolescent Psychiatry*, 30, 138–43.

Sutton, C. (1991). Safety and threat: neglected concepts in psychology. *The Psychologist*. 4, 459–461.

Sutton, C. (1992). Training parents to manage difficult children: a comparison of methods. *Behavioural Psychotherapy*, 20, 115–39.

Sutton, C. (1994). *Social Work, Community Work and Psychology*. Leicester, British Psychological Society.

Sutton, C. (1995). Parent training by telephone: a partial replication. *Behavioural and Cognitive Psychotherapy*, 23, 1–24.

Sutton, C. and Herbert, M. (1992). *Mental Health: A Client Support Resource Pack*. Windsor, NFER/Nelson.

Sutton, C. (1999). *Helping Families with Troubled Children: A Preventive Approach*. Chichester, Wiley.

Tajfel, H. and Turner, J. (1979). An integrative theory of intergroup conflict. In W. Austin and S. Worchel (eds), *The Social Psychology of Intergroup Relations*. California, Wadsworth.

Tellegen, A., Lykken, D.T., Bouchard, T.J. (Jr.), Wilcox, K.J., Segal, N. and Rich, S. (1988). Personality similarity in twins reared apart and together. *Journal of Personality and Social Psychology*, 54, 1031–39.

Thomas, A. and Chess, S. (1977). *Temperament and Development*. New York, Brunner/Mazel.

Tizard, B., Blatchford, P., Borke, J., Farquhar, C. and Plewis, I. (1988). *Young Children at School in the Inner City*, Hillsdale, N.J., Lawrence Erlbaum Associates.

Tremblay, R.E., LeBlanc, M. and Schwarzmann, A.E. (1988). The predictive power of first grade peer and teacher ratings of behaviour: sex differences in antisocial behaviour and personality at adolescence. *Journal of Abnormal Child Psychology*, 16, 571–83.

Tremblay, R.E., McCord, J., Boileau, H., Charlebois, P, Gagnon, C., LeBlanc, M. and Larivee, S. (1991). Can disruptive boys be helped to become competent? *Psychiatry*, 54, 148–61.

Tremblay, R.E., Vitaro, F., Bertrand, L., LeBlanc, N, Beauchesne, H., Boileau, H. and David, L. (1992). Parent and child training to prevent early onset of delinquency: The Montreal longitudinal-experimental study. In J. McCord and R. Tremblay (eds), *Preventing Antisocial Behavior: Interventions from Birth through Adolescence*. 117–38. New York, Guilford.

Tremblay, R.E. and Craig, W.M. (1995). Developmental crime prevention. In M. Tonry and D.P. Farrington (eds), *Building a Safer Society: Strategic Approaches to Crime Prevention*. Chicago, University of Chicago Press.

Tremblay, R.E., Pagani-Kurtz, L., Masse, L.C., Vitaro, F. and Pihl, R.O. (1995). A bimodal preventive intervention for disruptive kindergarten boys; its impact through mid-adolescence. *Journal of Consulting and Clinical Psychol-*

ogy, 63, 560–68.

Truax, C.F. and Carkhuff, H.R. (1967). *Toward Effective Counselling and Psychotherapy*. Chicago, Aldine.

Utting, D. (1995). *Family and Parenthood. Supporting Families, Preventing Breakdown*. York, Joseph Rowntree Foundation.

Utting, D., Bright, J. and Henricson, C. (1993). *Crime and the Family. Improving Child Rearing and Preventing Delinquency*. London, Family Policy Studies Centre.

van Ijzendoorn, M.H. (1995). Adult attachment representations, parental responsiveness, and infant attachment: A meta-analysis on the predictive validity of the Adult Attachment Interview. *Psychological Bulletin*, 117, 347–403.

Warren, D. (1997). Serious failings in the 'Cinderella' service. *Children UK*. Issue 13, Summer, 1997.

Watson, J.B. (1930). *Behaviourism*. New York, Norton.

Webster-Stratton, C. (1997). From parent training to community building. *Families in Society*, 78, 156–71.

Webster-Stratton, C. (1998). Preventing conduct problems in Head Start children. Strengthening parenting competencies. *Journal of Consulting and Clinical Psychology*, 66, 715–30.

Webster-Stratton, C. (1999). *Parenting Matters. What Works in Parenting Education?* Barkingside, Essex, Barnardos.

Webster-Stratton, C. (1999). Early intervention in family life: experiences from the United States. In R. Bayley (ed.), *Transforming Children's Lives: The Importance of Early Intervention*. Occasional Paper 25. London, Family Policy Studies Centre.

Webster-Stratton, C. and Hammond, M. (1997). Treating children with early-onset conduct problems. A comparison of child and parent training interventions. *Journal of Consulting and Clinical Psychology*, 65, 93–109.

Webster-Stratton, C. and Herbert, M. (1994). *Troubled Families: Problem Children*. Chichester, Wiley.

Webster-Stratton, C., Kolpacoff, M. and Hollinsworth, T. (1988). Self-administered videotape therapy for families with conduct-problem children: comparison with two cost-effective treatments and a control group. *Journal of Consulting and Clinical Psychology*, 56, 558–66.

Wickberg, B. and Hwang, C.P. (1996). Counselling in a general practice setting: a controlled study of health visitor intervention in treatment of postnatal depression. *British Medical Journal*, 314, 932–36.

Widom, C.S. (1989). The cycle of violence. *Science*, 244, 160–66.

Wilde, E.J., Keinhorst, L.C., Dickstra, R.F. and Wolters, M. (1992). The relationship between adolescent suicidal behaviour and life events in childhood and adolescence. *American Journal of Psychiatry*, 149, 45–51.

Wilson, H. (1980). Parental supervision: a neglected aspect of delinquency. *British Journal of Criminology*, 20, 203–35.

Wilson, H. (1987). Parental supervision re-examined. *British Journal of Criminology*, 7, 275–300.

World Health Organization (1992). *The ICD–10 Classification of Mental and Behavioural Disorders: Clinical Description and Diagnostic Guidelines*. Geneva, World Health Organization.

Index